500 WAYS
TO CHANGE THE WORLD

500 WAYS TO CHANGE THE WORLD

Global Ideas Bank

Edited and compiled by
Nick Temple

Collins

An Imprint of HarperCollins*Publishers*

ISBN: 0-00-721458-8

ISBN-10: 0-06-085176-7 (in the United States)
ISBN-13: 978-0-06-085176-7

HarperCollins books may be purchased for educational, business, or sales promotional use.
For information in the United States, please write to: Special Markets Department, HarperCollins Publishers,
10 East 53rd Street, New York, NY 10022.

First US edition 2006.

Created and produced by IXOS PRESS, The Old Candlemakers, West Street, Lewes, East Sussex, BN7 2NZ, UK.

Creative Director: Peter Bridgewater
Art Director: Sarah Howerd
Commissioning Editor: Mark Truman
Illustrator: Tonwen Jones

Ixos Press wishes to thank Brian Moody for the use of the photograph on page 6, Anita Roddick for supplying the
foreword, and all those who suggested and contributed ideas, particularly Roger Knights and Yvonne Ackroyd.

Printed in China.

Note for readers: Exchange rates vary constantly. Currency conversions given in this book are approximate and
provided for rough guidance only.

05 04 06 07 08 10 9 8 7 5 4 3 2 1

contents

foreword
Anita Roddick DBE

The book you hold in your hands is like a life-mask or a snapshot—it is a representation of a moment in time, reflecting both the light cast by the best in original thinking and the shadows of the problems these ideas have been brought forth to solve. But it is just a moment, frozen; new ideas, brilliant ones, are being submitted to the Global Ideas Bank (GIB) right now, and will be again tomorrow and the day after that.

We can no more use up all the good ideas than we can breathe all the air or drink all the water; so that this is not the first book from the GIB is testament that it is also not the last, fortune willing. Social inventions are perhaps the most valuable commodity for civilization left to us, and the people at the GIB are the ones who are continuously coming up with novel ways to gather, process, and distribute them to where they are most needed, like good business leaders do.

Social inventions can be clever thinking on a modern problem—say, disposable credit-card numbers to prevent theft—or innovations thousands of years old to solve equally ancient conundrums. These latter are often the foundation of our work at The Body Shop, only we know it better as traditional wisdom—whether it is natives of Chile erecting fine mesh nets to capture the moisture in fog to provide their communities with fresh water, or Ghanian women educating me on the real restorative properties of shea butter, or Native Americans passing on to me the spectacular versatility and utility of the lowly hemp plant. In every case, the greatest idea uses the materials at hand in a way no one may have thought of before, to solve a problem no one's cracked before. And when the solutions are truly elegant, they become received wisdom, woven into the fabric of their source communities. But someone had to be the one to think of them first.

The future fathers of invention are out there thinking today. They are sketching out contraptions and mulling over mysteries. And they are, some of them, submitting the germs of their ideas at the GIB website. Tomorrow's exhaust-free engine, super-biodegradable grocery bag, non-corruptible voting system, global tax on weapons that funds conflict-resolution programs, eBay-style clearinghouse to match barterers, women's microlender in developing world communities—all of these are being mulled over, thought out, and implemented by creative thinkers worldwide.

One day, thanks to the everyday visionaries who share their ideas with the rest of us, we'll say "What did we ever do before air-powered autos?" as astonishingly as we today might say "What did we ever do before Velcro?"

This magnificent project is a monument to human creativity and generosity of both mind and spirit. I hope it inspires you to dig around in your own brain for your own unique way of looking at the world. Somewhere in those synapses may be the next thought that changes the world.

Anita Roddick

relationships

celebrate your birthday
with a car-free day

Wherever they live in the world, invite your friends and family to celebrate your birthday, not by buying a gift, but by taking part in an action that is important to you. In this way, your birthday is celebrated as an action in accordance with your principles, rather than as an exchange of finance and gifts. Arthur Orsini asked his extended family, which consists of fifteen households, to make his birthday a car-free day in collaboration with his life as a car-free dad and his work promoting sustainable transportation in high schools. Other individualized birthday "gifts" could be spending two hours in an art gallery, volunteering for a cause, giving blood, picking up a full bag of litter, or giving money to a street musician.

The social inventor Greg Wright additionally suggests that a new form of birthday card could emerge from this idea: the Day of Action card. This card would be sent to friends and family by the birthday person a few days before the big day. It would include details of what the person would like them to do in place of giving a gift. They could even say, "Please do this every year on this day."

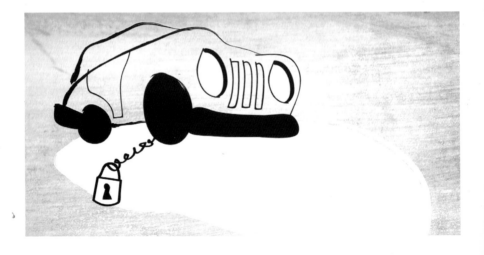

bring a touch of
tenderness to town

2

The mayor of a Belgian town set up a specific department to encourage residents of his town to act more friendly toward one another. The so-called Department of Tenderness was set up in Kruibeke by Antoine Denert, who decided to make it his personal responsibility to increase the level of niceness and sensitivity in the area under his direction.

Mayor Denert believes that fostering tenderness and even cuddling will help decrease the number of conflicts on an individual and local level. The mayor said at the launch of the new department that he "will set an example and start in my own village by caressing, cuddling, and kissing as many people as possible." This might be a little much for all politicians to take on, but the general concept of such a devoted department is perhaps one worth considering at all levels. Certainly Mayor Denert thinks so, and is encouraging national and international bodies to follow his lead: "Why not change the Ministry of Defense into the Ministry of Tenderness? The war in Iraq would never have started."

apologize worldwide
on the web

3

My proposal is an idea for an apology website, perhaps in the form of a searchable database, on which people would be able to post apologies for their past actions.

Posters could choose to identify themselves in full or more elliptically, yet in a way that their victims could identify them should they wish to do so. Apologies posted could be a prelude to forgiveness.

This site would mean that the poster would not have to contact the victim directly to apologize; this would benefit any victims who didn't want to hear from the person in question, and who didn't want to be reminded about something they might have put behind them.

Ronnie Horesh

→ **www.the-apologist.co.uk**

rent a video
without flipping a coin

A video rental shop in Bayswater in London has introduced "movie mediators" to prevent couples rowing over which film (or type of film) to take home for their evening's entertainment.

Blockbuster commissioned a relationship psychologist, Elaine Spurr, to research the issue, and she discovered that almost half of all renters could not agree on a film when part of a couple or group.

She also discovered that women, though not above using flirting techniques to get what they want, were more flexible and accom-

4

modating in the video negotiation process, while men simply tended to resort to sulking.

The mediators offered tips and advice to try to prevent the gender-based battles. Dr. Spurr stated that conflicts can arise because "men and women employ different tactics to get their choice of movie...These tactics reflect the gender divide in typical styles of communication."

A mediator scheme could help calm these conflicts a little by recommending films that both can enjoy and by outlining the benefits of flexibility and compromise.

boomerang borrowed
belongings for peace of mind

Set one day a year aside on which you search your house for things that aren't yours (that is, things that you've borrowed but have neglected to return).

This could be anything from a brother's golf clubs to a neighbor's mower. On the day in

5

question, return the items and set aside any grievances that might have surrounded the offending item.

The day would be called Boomerang Day, for obvious reasons.

Tony Paynter

respond to senior citizens' requests for foster families

A widowed eighty-year-old teacher in Italy decided to take a novel approach to tackle his loneliness: he advertised for a family who would like to adopt him as a grandfather.

The notice in the newspaper, which simply read "Elderly retired schoolteacher seeks family willing to adopt grandfather. Will pay," led to a flood of replies from all over Italy. Giorgio Angelozzi, whose wife had died fourteen years earlier, offered to pay about £300 (about $600) a month to any family willing to take him on.

The Riva family in Spirano saw Mr. Angelozzi being interviewed on television and decided to apply. They were chosen, and their new grandfather has settled in well, with his new grandchildren even calling him *Nonno* (Granddad). By all accounts, being part of a bustling household has given him a new lease on life, as well as providing the Rivas with the elder generation that their family had lacked.

Elderly relatives left on their own has become an increasing problem in Italy, due to gradual changes in family structure, despite the traditional place of family at the heart of Italian life. This fact was clear when nearly 8,000 Italians died in the heat wave of 2003; most of the fatalities were older people living on their own.

While the full-blown adoption method might not be appropriate for everyone, some local authorities in Italy have started to look at the possibility of a matching scheme in which families and elderly people are brought together to join in activities and develop friendship.

support self-esteem
with a kind word

7

When each person in a group is given a list of positive things said about them by the others, the long-term value in enhancing that person's feelings of self-esteem can be immense.

A young schoolteacher had a group of pupils who were often frustrated and frustrating, constantly carping at one another. She decided to take a lateral approach to the problem and asked each pupil to take out a piece of paper and list the names of all the other pupils in the class, leaving a space between each name.

She then asked them to write down the nicest thing they could say about every other one of their classmates.

Having done this, the teacher gathered together the papers and wrote out another sheet of paper for each pupil that listed what all the other pupils had written about them. The pupils were allowed to keep this "appreciation list" and the exercise was never mentioned again. However, the teacher noted that the pupils seemed more amicable toward one another and realized that their individual qualities had been recognized.

Many years later, when the teacher was at the funeral of a former pupil who died in Vietnam, she was approached by his parents, who told her that their son had carried his appreciation list in his wallet at all times. Other former pupils, who were also at the funeral, revealed that they too had saved their lists.

"That's when I finally sat down and cried," the teacher later wrote. "The lesson my former students taught me that day became a standard in every class I taught for the rest of my teaching career."

plant prenuptial trees
for a greener globe

8

An unusual conservation program that originated in Peru required couples who were engaged to be married to plant one or more saplings in order to qualify for a marriage certificate, with a similar green toll levied on birth certificates.

Imagine what a similar program replicated across the globe could achieve!

sign up for a spouse outside your house

Harley Cobb placed an estate-agency size notice in front of his house in Pasadena, California. It read, in large smart lettering: "Widower, 55, seeks attractive lady (40–60), friendship ... maybe more" and gave his phone number. His sign and his story appeared in newspapers and on TV and he received more than 4,000 calls from marriage-minded women around the world. He interviewed 800 and dated 81 of them before meeting his wife, Helen, who lived in his own neighborhood.

Helen, 46, recalls: "When I first saw Harley's sign, I thought to myself, 'There's a fruitcase.' But one day I happened to be walking by when he was outside, posing for a photographer. I thought to myself, 'He looks normal.'" She phoned him. They met twice. They married.

This was not a one-time occurrence, though. In 2004, a Chinese-Australian woman placed a billboard ad looking for a husband, though she was slightly more specific in what she was looking for: "A man, ideally in good health (non-smoker or drinker), aged up to 45, unencumbered and of Caucasian appearance" and preferably with "a good sense of humor, a solid financial background, and a warm and caring nature." She too attracted so much attention that she could hardly fail.

9

For those unwilling to undertake such a thing single-handedly, the online dating company Lovers2.com has used a similar technique, in which single men and women can pay to have their photos up on a billboard in their town.

calculate your love compatibility prior to proposing

Decisions about who to marry and have children with are likely to have more effect on future happiness than any other decisions in life, so they are worth considering as seriously as possible, given that you can be so easily misled in the first flush of love.

There are many complex pre-marriage questionnaires to indicate a couple's compatibility, but here is a simple version devised by the Global Ideas Bank. It can be applied to any relationship likely to involve long-term commitment and possibly caring for offspring.

10

About half the following questions derive from academic research findings about long-term success and failure in marriage and human relationships.

Simply give scores from 0 through 10 to the questions below, with 10 being "very true" and 0 being "not true at all." Answer the questions as honestly as possible since you do not have to show the results to anybody else.

→ There is generally very little conflict within our relationship.

→ When there is conflict we handle it well.

→ I find myself agreeing with my partner far more often than disagreeing.

→ If my partner ended up developing a similar character to his/her parents, I would be happy about this.

→ I believe that I can share all my feelings, good and bad, with my partner and that he/she can do the same with me.

→ My partner is very similar to me in terms of cultural, social, intellectual, as well as economic background.

→ We share similar philosophies of life or spiritual beliefs.

→ We share the same sense of humor.

→ My partner's health is good and he/she is generally happy.

→ My partner is sensitive and kind, not selfish or self-obsessed.

→ If I lived in a society where parents arranged marriages for their children, my partner is the kind of person my parents might have chosen for me.

→ I enjoy my partner's conversation and I like his/her friends.

→ Judging by their track record to date, my partner is monogamous when involved in a serious relationship.

→ Our sexual relationship is very good.

→ We have lived together: never (0/10), fewer than six months (2/10), between six months and a year (4/10), over a year (6/10), over three years (8/10), over five years (10/10).

Now add up your totals. Divide your total by the maximum possible (150) and multiply by 100 for your Marriage Compatibility Percentage. Anything over 75 percent bodes well for the future; anything below 50 percent might warn against rushing into anything just yet.

take a cultural sabbatical

11

Our world cultures should encourage us to live in a different culture for a year, three times in our lives. This different culture could be urban or rural, comprising different ethnicities and different religions.

Our first sabbatical would be just after secondary school (age eighteen), the second at mid-career, and the last just after retirement. A year is the minimum amount of time; that is how long it takes for one to go through the pangs of homesickness ("they do it all wrong here"), to fully embracing ("they do it all wrong back home"), to an understanding that we all do it right (and wrong) no matter where we are. We are all human, after all.

The age component is also important. When we're young, we have the desire but not the skills to change the world. Learning new perspectives can only help.

When we're middle aged, we have difficulty seeing from others' perspectives. Such an experience could help us truly develop a global community (in the best sense of the phrase, not the worst).

And, as elders, such visits would help us regain the respect we once had for the elder members of our communities, a recognition that they are sages, and thus have wisdom to share (and still to gain).

Shelby Clark

meet marriage mentors to dodge divorce

12

The rise in divorce rates and shorter marriages is viewed as a problem across the world. One potential remedy is found in a program called Marriage Savers, based in Potomac, Maryland, and run by Michael McManus, who developed what he calls a "community marriage policy."

The divorce rate in Modesto, California, which first adopted the policy, fell 35 percent between 1986 and 1997, while the national rate dropped by only 1.3 percent. In just two years on the program, the suburbs of Kansas City showed a decline of 1,530 divorces to 1,001, a 35 percent reduction. The policy has now been adopted in more than two hundred US cities.

The key to the program is the use of mentoring couples, usually older couples with about thirty years of marriage behind them, who spend up to four months counseling engaged couples on every aspect of marriage. The program endeavors to find mentors whose experiences match the particular needs of the engaged couple—such as second-marriage couples advising other second-marriage couples, or couples with stepchildren advising new couples in the same situation.

In this way, the project utilizes the experience of those who have lived through the highs and lows of marriage to strengthen future marriages, and helps couples avoid the pain and distress that accompanies divorce in the majority of cases.

→ **www.marriagesavers.org**

practice random kindness and senseless acts of beauty

13

When a person arrives at a toll-booth on a cold winter's day, imagine the delight at being told, "The lady up ahead has already paid for you. Have a nice day!"

Or imagine a man struggling to find change for the parking meter and then having it paid for him by a passing stranger.

Or picture a boy who, while out shoveling snow from his driveway, generously decides to do the whole street.

These are "random acts of kindness and senseless acts of beauty," a phrase that started a movement and enriched countless people's lives. It started with Anne Herbert, who jotted the phrase down in a restaurant after turning it over in her mind for several days. The simple concept she developed was to think of any good deed that should be done more often, and then to do it randomly.

Herbert's own ideas include: leaving hot meals on kitchen tables in the poor parts of town; slipping money into a proud old woman's purse.

She says, "Kindness can build on itself as much as violence can." The phrase has spread exponentially ever since, on bumper stickers, on walls, at the bottom of letters, and even on business cards. And as it spreads, so does a vision of guerrilla goodness.

They say you can't smile without cheering yourself up a little—likewise, you can't commit a random act of kindness without feeling as if your own burdens have been lightened.

The Random Acts of Kindness movement has now progressed to the point where there is a Random Acts of Kindness (RAK) Foundation and a RAK week in every year. The movement has grown massively since the mid-90s, and is now celebrated in parts of Canada, Scotland, Germany, Italy, Australia, Japan, New Zealand, and Hong Kong.

Recent years have involved schools, churches, bookstores, hospitals, youth organizations, and many assorted members of the public. The idea has also been taken up by others, most recently the Join Me organization that makes every Friday a "Good" Friday by performing a random act of kindness.

→ **www.actsofkindness.org**
→ **www.join-me.co.uk**

women welcome
women world-wide

Women Welcome Women World-Wide (5W) was started in 1984 by Frances Alexander as a way of encouraging cross-cultural friendships between women. It does so by building a membership of women from around the world who are willing to have other women come and stay with them to experience their home and work, usually for a few days.

Access to the list comes with membership, which is by voluntary donation, and 5W now has more than 3,500 members in 70 countries. Its northernmost member lives within the Arctic Circle in Norway, while the southernmost lives in Santa Cruz, Argentina. More than a hundred languages are spoken, from Arabic to Zulu.

Frances Alexander viewed the initiative as "a little contribution to bringing about more friendship in a troubled world, with something for the housebound mother as much as the feminist or company executive." It has done that and more in the years since, and continues to foster international understanding and a sense of global community through the simple act of women welcoming other women to their world.

→ **www.womenwelcomewomen.org.uk**

take the unhypocritical oath
for a sense of self-worth

15

I decided several years ago to seek out consistency in my beliefs and actions. It became important to me that, having pondered an issue, I should follow through on enacting it. In the spirit of practicing what you preach, I came up with the idea of the "Unhypocritical Oath." The commitment to avoid being hypocritical in what you do can result in a life well lived, and provide a model for others to follow. It also involves trying to limit the contradictions between various beliefs, and accepting that the answers to problems may not always be those one is comfortable with.

For example, believing in the right to choose freely might be in conflict with someone else's belief in animal rights or desire to abolish the death penalty. Reconciling such issues is not always possible, and some level of hypocrisy, or contradiction, may well be unavoidable.

Taking the Unhypocritical Oath simply states that you are adopting consistency in your beliefs and actions to the best of your ability. The benefits of such a stance could include a greater acceptance of personal idiosyncrasies, a greater openness to other people and new ideas, a more thoughtful (and less judgmental) approach to problems, and replacing the "buts" with the "ands." Rather than saying, "I know I shouldn't drive so much, but…" the oath will help change this statement to "I know I shouldn't drive so much, and I have decided to walk to work three out of five days."

In this way, taking the Unhypocritical Oath can not only give individuals more moral authenticity and perhaps a stronger sense of self-worth, but may also lead to more direct actions in their lives.

Michelle Rhodes

tax divorce to fund domestic violence charities

My idea is for a legal divorce to cost at least 30 percent of a couple's assets. This money would be donated to battered women's and men's shelters, orphanages, marriage guidance organizations, and educational programs. This would make couples reconsider whether it is worth trying

16

harder at their marriage, and provide funds for the charities which help those in violent, abusive, and failing relationships. Those divorcing because of domestic violence should not put the woman at greater risk by costing her valuable assets.

Tracy Trave

celebrate an unwedding ceremony

A ceremony called "The Ending of Marriage" was pioneered by Sheila Davis, a senior divorce courts welfare officer in Birmingham in the UK. She created the ritual herself, requesting couples to stand in her office while she takes them by the hands, and asks them to bid each other farewell along the following lines:

"Goodbye. Thank you for the good times in our marriage. I wish you luck in your new life. Our relationship will continue as mother and father of our children, but not as husband and wife."

Mrs. Davis, herself divorced and remarried, believes that the ceremony helps reduce the tears and acrimony of separation and divorce.

17

"The idea is to help people to become unstuck emotionally. It enables them to say goodbye to each other as husband and wife, and hello as mum and dad of their own children."

Since then, many couples have undertaken this ceremony of "unmarriage" both in Birmingham and around the globe, as divorce has become more common. Some have even openly announced their divorce to friends and relatives, to transform what can be a negative experience with much discussing behind doors into a positive transition to a new phase of life. This process is practical and cathartic and also offers a chance to stress that a breakup is amicable, thereby preempting any gossip.

use flash cards
to defuse rows

18

While watching a couple spend another counseling session throwing insults at each other, psychotherapist Nancy Dreyfus tried something completely new on impulse. Picking up a piece of paper and a pen, she wrote a message for the husband to hold: "Talk to me like I'm someone you love." The whole tenor of the session changed swiftly and the effects were longlasting.

Dreyfus was on to something, and she knew it. So she developed a homemade set of "Flash Cards for Real Life," and began using them with couples in her private practice. The pack of cards, which she mostly used for conflict intervention, were so successful with clients and colleagues alike that she had them professionally printed and began selling them through a local store. She found that written messages accomplish something which spoken words cannot: "I continue to be struck by the healing effect on intimate combatants when even a little decency is thrown in the face of their usual pattern of defensiveness, withdrawal, and terrible listening."

The cards have proved equally popular with parents defusing rows with teenagers, though they were not originally designed for this type of use. One mother's teenage daughter takes up the card she wants to get her point across: "Right now I don't need a lecture, I need your love." Certainly it would seem that the pen is sometimes mightier than the (spoken) word.

swap jobs with
your opposite gender

19

A husband and wife have many roles that they've played throughout history—roles that are primarily gender-based. For example, it is common for most men to do things such as take out the trash, cut the lawn, keep the yard nice, and make repairs around the house. Most women also perform the traditional tasks of cooking dinner, doing the laundry, and keeping the house clean. Sometimes men and women argue about these things, with both feeling like they do more around the house than the other. The fact of the matter is, many of them wouldn't know how much the other does unless they had to do those things themselves.

So here's an idea: let's designate one week in the year where it is the man's responsibility to complete the woman's chores and her responsibility to complete his. At the end of the week, both would appreciate everything their spouse does, and it would strengthen their marriage. This idea could go further still, with a day where the partners in a relationship swap roles entirely for 24 hours, including their work and social activities. This would give a fuller, broader understanding of what each partner accomplishes and experiences during their day.

Bill Campbell / Julie Dalyrymple

support a gender-specific curfew to cut crime

20

In Colombia's capital, Bogota, the city celebrated a "Night Without Men," after the mayor encouraged women to come out for the night to have a good time while leaving the men at home with the kids.

The gender-specific curfew had a serious side to it, with street crime and domestic abuse both prevalent in the city. Serious crime fell by a quarter on that night.

One local woman spoke for most of Bogota's women when she said, "It was great. You had a large group of people dancing and having fun in the streets."

Policemen were given the night off, as solely female officers patrolled the streets; the fire brigade was also a completely non-male institution for the evening. The police chief even resigned for the night to allow his female understudy to take over.

Mayor Antanas Mockus himself, who is renowned for his offbeat ideas, stayed in to read to his daughter. But his plans did not stop at the "Night Without Men"—following that was an "Evening of Rediscovery" designed to encourage couples to go out together, and to further improve gender relations in the city.

couple up for community care

21

With divorce rates reaching nearly 50 percent in some countries, broken homes are becoming a bigger problem. To solve this, couples should get to know each other better before marrying. What better way to do this than doing community service together? This way the couple can take the focus off themselves and focus on concern for others instead. You learn a lot about another person by seeing how they interact with others.

This plan would give couples the chance to get to know each other in real life, as opposed to in the "unreal" world of being in love, and also to help their community.

If couples used this method to evaluate whether or not their partners are actually who they want to be with for the rest of their lives, we might also be able to avoid some unnecessary marriages that end in divorce.

Ashlee Finecey

get wedding gifts
from the happy couple

22

The average American wedding costs thousands of dollars and it is a similar tale in other Western countries. However, there is a new trend led by altruistic brides and grooms who are taking their wedding funds and using them for a greater good (and a more lasting impression), rather than for honeymoons and elaborate gowns. In this way, a ceremony that has become synonymous with expense and lavishness can be less wasteful and can help improve other people's lives.

One couple from Cary, North Carolina, decided to take their wedding guests to a toy store after the reception and gave them money to choose a gift for a child at the local Toys for Tots charity. In the end, they donated three truck loads in toys to needy children. Other newlyweds have taken more simple actions, such as donating the wedding dress and accessories to a charity shop or sending leftover flowers to nursing homes.

The Centre for Alternative Technology in the UK also has a wedding list with a difference—one that will make a difference. Couples can choose from CAT's range of environmentally friendly products, and start married life in a socially responsible way. The concept is that couples need feel no guilt about extravagance on their wedding day, because every present they receive will be produced ethically and will have been designed to help people live more sustainable lives. The list includes organic bed linen, organic paints, and recycled glasses, all of which are ideal for the eco-homemaker. The Centre even suggests "a romantic weekend" away for newlyweds learning about alternative sustainable lifestyles.

Julie Blower and husband Toby used the Centre's list for their wedding and report that "in the special time around your wedding, it feels more important than ever to do business with organizations like CAT," because planning ahead should also include planning ahead for the planet. It may not be long before brides have to have something old, something new, something recycled and something green.

→ **www.thealternativeweddinglist.co.uk**
→ **www.justgive.org**
→ **www.cat.org.uk**

chapter 2

arts, leisure, lifestyle

book into
the library hotel

23

A hotel in New York now offers the perfect place to stay for those of a bookish or literary bent. The Library Hotel offers its guests over six thousand volumes organized throughout by the Dewey-Decimal Classification system. Guests can choose rooms based on particular areas of interest located on particular floors. Thus, the eighth floor is the Literature floor, and staying in room 803 will include access to volumes of poetry. Room 801, for literary couples perhaps, is Erotic Literature, unsurprisingly the most requested room. Similarly, the third floor is Social Sciences, the ninth floor is History, and so on, with each room featuring a section of specialized reading.

In addition to books in all the rooms, there is a breakfast reading room, a Writer's Den living room, and a Poetry Garden (a conservatory with countless tomes of verse). And if a guest takes a fancy to a particular book, but is unable to finish it during their stay, it can be purchased at checkout time. It hardly needs saying that it is vital to book ahead.

→ **www.libraryhotel.com**

drink to the health
of local charities

24

A new pub in Brighton has been set up with the aim of raising funds for local charities. The People's Pub hopes to take between £6,000 ($12,000) and £7,000 ($14,000) a week and give about £50,000 ($100,000) per year of net profits to charity in the UK if all goes well.

Founder and local entrepreneur, Martin Webb, sees the new venture as a neat and worthwhile fit; as he puts it, "What a great reason to buy another round!"

A notice board in the pub keeps regulars informed about which charities they have been supporting through their social activities.

If this first People's Pub proves successful, a chain of similar pubs and clubs could spring up, helping to turn Britain's drinking culture to the benefit of its own community. It might even promote a more responsible approach to drinking, in the round, as it were, and adds a new model to the burgeoning portfolio of social enterprises proliferating across the UK. As the pub will be redistributing money in this way, it is appropriately called the *Robin Hood*, named after the man who famously took from the rich and gave to the poor.

→ **www.peoplespubs.co.uk**

sign up for
section subscriptions

25

Why subscribe to a newspaper to read only a section or two regularly? Doing so wastes paper and money.

Newspaper publishers could offer custom or à la carte subscriptions, priced by section (any two sections for $X, five sections for $Y, etc.). Of course, the newspaper would still offer the regular whole paper too, but selling by section would provide the reader with more options while allowing the newspaper to print fewer sections (saving both money and paper). In this way, the environment, the reader, and the publisher could all benefit.

Entropy Rider

be the highest bidder
to land a novel role

A new way of raising money has **26** been put into practice by some of the UK's best-known authors in what was, literally, a novel auction.

Authors including Philip Pullman and Will Self put up characters in their upcoming novels for auction to the highest bidder. The successful bidders will appear by name in the novels (although they cannot choose what they will be doing, or whether they will be the hero or villain).

All proceeds from the auction went to the Medical Foundation for the Care of Victims of Torture. This simple idea could be easily replicated in other areas of the arts and in other areas of the world.

fish around for
sustainable suppers

A leading fish restaurant in London **27** has also given the lead on sustainability issues by launching a menu that contains only fish species that are not in danger.

The menu deliberately avoids those fish that have been (and are being) overfished, and focuses on less familiar varieties.

At the Aquarium, zander can be found on the menu, but rarely cod. The restaurant also rotates the menu regularly to ensure that new species of fish don't become too fashionable, which could cause overfishing of those as well. The World Wildlife Fund has endorsed the restaurant's approach as a model of best practice and hopes that other restaurants will follow suit. As well as aiding those species that are under threat, such initiatives also have an effect on raising public awareness of the problem that exists in the seas and oceans today.

→ **www.theaquarium.co.uk**

cash in by deciding what to pay for your hotel stay

In an attempt to attract guests to its hotel in the face of dwindling tourist numbers, a hotel in Jerusalem came up with a new idea: allowing the guests to set the rate they pay for a room.

In ten of the hotel's rooms, guests were allowed to stay for an undefined period and then pay as much as they considered was an appropriate price.

With this offering, the managers of the hotel filled some of the rooms that are often only half-filled, even on a good weekend.

28

That a hotel was prepared to take such a measure indicates some of the problems within the Israeli tourist industry. The number of visitors to the country has plummeted in the past few years as internal violence between Israel and Palestine has continued, and hotels and restaurants must be ever more innovative and radical to attract customers. This "pay-what-you-like" deal on hotel rooms, which lasted a month, is one such example.

→ **www.jerusalemgold.com**

firm up family bonds through book groups

29

In a new twist to the popular reading-group format, five mothers in Lexington, Kentucky, set up a mother–son book group for their preteen sons, based on a desire to share experiences with them. It was an attempt to create a new ritual, a new area of life where they could be more open and better understand one another. It is an idea that could spread as quickly as traditional reading groups.

Typically, at the ages of ten through thirteen, boys tend to grow apart from their mothers and develop either a custodial, supervisory, or achievement-oriented relationship (i.e., Have you done your chores today?), says gender researcher Cate Dooley, director of the Mother–Son Project at the Jean Baker Miller Institute at Wellesley College. She created her own ritual with her sons at dinnertime. Her goal was to teach them honesty and sincerity through a moment of silence. She too began a mom–son book group because she and other mothers want to stop the "stereotype that boys are unwilling or unable to share their emotional life." Now she says her son is teaching her about emotions, so this has benefited both mother and son.

The Lexington mothers believe the mom–son group could be the key to lasting, more intimate relationships with their sons. "They get to know us more as people and less of the 'mother' image they create as a child," says Brookline educational consultant Barney Brawer, former co-director of the Harvard Project on Boys. The side-by-side intimacy, whether in a book, cooking, film, or art group, is not as threatening to a preteen.

One of the boys in the Lexington group explained, "When we're talking books, we're not mothers and sons. We're just people. We've talked about everything, including things you aren't supposed to talk to mothers about."

The idea follows on from successful mother–daughter book clubs, perhaps a more obvious variation on the book group theme. As the self-esteem of girls drops in their early teenage years, mother–daughter reading clubs provide them with a safe, encouraging, and accepting environment in which to share thoughts and concerns. It also gives mothers a valuable chance to learn what is going on in their daughters' lives during this crucial period.

There are some key recommendations for those planning to run such a group: let the boys or girls choose the books; let the boys or girls answer first so that the mothers do not become too dominant; and keep the evenings fun.

→ **www.bcplonline.org/kidspage/dodson.html**

play piano in the park

This proposal is for outdoor pianos to be placed in various locations around the country: parks, remote areas, inner cities, and so on.

Each piano would be vandal- and weather-proof, and fixed by concrete to its chosen spot. Imagine a group of hikers coming across a piano in a remote mountain area, or young-sters learning the piano on the grounds of an inner-city estate. If need be, the pianos could be funded by a coin-operation system to unlock the keyboard (or to connect the circuit in the case of a battery-driven electric piano). Music could echo off the hillsides and enrich walks through the park, with the outdoor piano providing the means.

30

If this idea seems implausible, an expedition led by Colonel John Blashford-Snell perhaps shows its potential. In autumn 2000, he led an expedition that deliv-ered an 800-pound (360-kg) grand piano to a remote Amazonian tribe in Guyana.

The piano was pulled on a sled and carried in a canoe, and still managed to arrive almost in tune. It is now a fixture in the village church. Onlookers were said to be deeply moved by the intuitive playing of the tribe members, whose music resonated powerfully with the majestic rainforest background—a new sound introduced to a new location by an outdoor piano.

Keith Lawton

board your begonias when you go away

Crowfoot Nurseries, a garden center in Norfolk started a scheme in which people going on vacation could leave their plants there to be looked after.

31

The UK plant "hotel" charged 25p (about 50 cents) per night to care for the plants, and to keep them watered, fed, and happy.

stay on in the cinema
for post-movie discussions

32

Arthouse and repertory cinemas could host a 15-minute period at the end of each film where the audience is encouraged to remain in the auditorium and discuss the featured presentation.

The discussion would thus take place while the film was still fresh in everyone's mind. New friendships might even develop as a result of making film-going more interactive. A slightly higher ticket price could be introduced for these "discussion screenings" to cover the cinema's cost of the extra time used.

People are often fascinated by other people's comments as the audience leaves the cinema, but the conversation in a couple or small group tends to end fairly quickly. A larger audience could have a much more lively and dynamic discussion, with many and varied perspectives.

Even if the discussion period did not take place at the cinema, a brief notice could be flashed up after the film stating that those who wish to take part in such a discussion should go to a particular café or nearby location. In this way, everyone would gain: the cinema would have an extra selling point over its rivals, the audience would be able to interact and create friendships and lively debates, and the nearby cafés would gain business.

Nicholas Albery

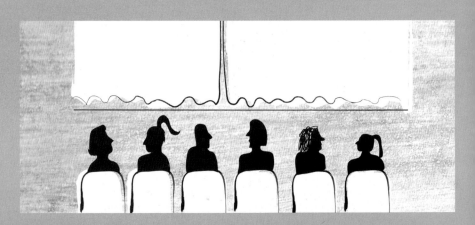

play to win
a front row seat

33

I have been to many concerts in my life and am continually frustrated by the bad seating I get. No matter what I do, for popular acts it seems impossible to sit anywhere near the stage.

Among others the majority of these seats go to: (1) ticket brokers, where patrons pay insanely high prices; (2) the owners of the venue; (3) the band/artist for their friends and family; (4) the record company; and (5) a few contest winners from local radio stations.

Instead of these people always getting the best seats, the first five to ten rows of seats at sold-out or extremely popular concerts should be given away in a lottery. To ensure only fans who support the artist are entered into the lottery, a lottery entry should be placed in every CD of that artist. Then those fans who buy the CDs can enter the lottery drawing of their choice (most likely, the venue closest to their home) and have a chance of seeing their favorite artists up close without having to pay lots of money or garner favors from someone at the record company. If fans buy more than one CD, they can enter more than once.

This idea could help fuel album sales, which have been under threat since illegal file swapping became widespread. It would also give the little guy out there, the real fan, some hope of sitting front and center at great concerts.

Allison Genco

keep club-leavers quiet
with late-night lollipops

34

Police in Blackpool have taken to issuing free lollipops to guests leaving nightclubs in an effort to reduce noise levels for surrounding residents.

The hope is that the grown-up gobstoppers will keep the decibel level of high-spirited members of the clubbing scene down; the practice may spread across the UK.

get everyone talking
with a city-wide book group

35

An idea that originated in Seattle's public library has spread throughout America and beyond since its inception. The concept is simple: help to build a sense of community in a city by getting everyone to read the same book at the same time.

In addition to encouraging reading as a pursuit to be enjoyed by all, the program allows strangers to interact by discussing the book on the bus on the way home, as well as promoting reading as an experience to be shared in families and schools. The idea came from Seattle librarian Nancy Pearl who launched the "If All of Seattle Read the Same Book" project in December 1998, with Russell Banks's book, *The Sweet Hereafter.* Her original program used author visits, study guides, and book discussion groups to bring people together with a book, but the idea has since expanded hugely to many other American cities, and even to Hong Kong, Trinidad, and Tobago.

In Chicago, the mayor appeared on national television to announce the choice of Harper Lee's *To Kill a Mockingbird* as the first book in the "One Book, One Chicago" program. Copies were distributed to public libraries, readings were funded, and an advertising campaign was undertaken, with the result that the book shot back up the bestseller lists and copies were loaned out over 7,000 times in seven weeks. Reading clubs and neighborhood groups have sprung up around the city and the next book, *Night* by Elie Wiesel, attracted a similar amount of attention. Across the US, from Kentucky (*The Bean Trees* by Barbara Kingsolver) to Milwaukee (*Snow Falling on Cedars* by David Guterson), stories emerged of parents and children reading to each other at night, waitresses sitting down to join in discussions, and strangers chatting away on the bus about plot and character.

The only problems arose in New York, where local readers could not decide on one book to represent the huge and diverse population. The literati of the city descended into bickering and infighting over whether the project was

worth getting involved in and whether this or that book was inappropriate, before finally settling on *Native Speaker* by Chang-rae Lee, a novel appealing to the near-universal New York experience of immigration and being uprooted. The initial divisive arguing may show that the idea works best in medium-sized cities or large towns, where a greater sense of unity can be achieved. Or it may show that New Yorkers rather missed the point, putting all their energy and passion into the choice of the book rather than into discussion about a book itself. Ultimately, as Nancy Pearl points out, the level of success is not measured by how many people read a book or by how many copies are sold, but by how many people are enriched by the process, have experienced a book they would never have come across otherwise, or have enjoyed speaking to someone with whom they would not otherwise have shared a word. This is not meant to be a political issue; it is a simple case of sitting down and turning the page.

step aboard the floating library

Self-appointed Floating Librarians (no qualifications necessary) select books that they have enjoyed or books that they believe others will enjoy and donate them to the Floating Library.

A short text is written in the front of the book explaining that it is property of the Floating Library and that anyone wishing to borrow it may do so, but must either pass it on to someone they know or leave it in a public place for someone to find once they have finished with it. The text should also make clear that new book donations are always welcome.

A version of the Floating Library now exists at Bookcrossing.com. Once you have decided on a book that you would like to share with the rest of the world, you should go to the site where you can register the book, print off a Bookcrossing label (with a tracking number and the website address) and release the book into the wild.

When the person who finds the book subsequently registers it online, the book can be tracked and eventually it can be seen how many people have read it.

There are presently over 1,600,000 books registered on the site, and the word "bookcrossing" was added to the *Oxford English Dictionary* in 2004.

Jane Inkle

→ **www.bookcrossing.com**

take the challenge to read for ten million minutes

37

The community of Enumclaw in Washington State, has found a novel way to encourage reading and promote literacy among its inhabitants: it challenged them to read for ten million minutes over a period of six months.

The school authorities and business leaders came up with the idea, hoping to benefit children who, as well as being encouraged to read, would also see their parents and other adults reading. Progress in the challenge was monitored by giant "thermometers" at various locations in the area and on the school district's website; people simply filled out forms with their name and the number of minutes they'd read that week, and placed them in special boxes. After three months, the residents of Enumclaw had achieved eight million minutes of reading time. They went on to smash the target by a significant margin.

The challenge originated as part of the regional schools' literacy campaign, which also included a school bus with special seat covers that hold books, a summer literacy camp, and a program in which a new book was given to every child born at the local hospital. Not surprisingly, reading standards in the area have improved substantially. Yet the challenge has had wider effects, reigniting people's love of books and leading to the formation of new book clubs and book swapping evenings. In the schools, teachers were delighted to see that children were reading even when it was not a designated reading time or class.

→ **www.enumclaw.wednet.edu**

bid on a bit part for charity

A plan could be introduced that makes one role in every movie available to the highest bidder at an auction.

The part to be auctioned off could be cast as an extra or a very small speaking part. The money that is then raised by the auction would be given to a chosen charity, according to an agreement between the bidder and the movie company.

John Tunney

picture the globe
with a postable camera

This idea consists of distributing sturdy one-time-use cameras randomly to hundreds of people around the world. Each camera should include a brief set of instructions printed with the following:

"Please take one photo of anything you like and pass the camera on to a stranger. After you have taken your photo (and before passing the camera along), please log on to this website www.xxxxx.xxx and enter the code number on this camera along with your name, city, and state. If you take the last photo, please put the camera in any mailbox to be sent back for processing."

When all the cameras have been returned and processed, a book entitled *Picture the Globe* or a website showing the various photos could be developed. For more ideas, visit the US-based project website called PhotoTag.

Adam Morgan

→ **www.PhotoTag.org**

host a whodunnit in your own home

40

Beth Shaw specializes in "Domestic Theatre," which brings plays directly into people's homes. This concept reintroduces a dormant audience to the theatrical experience, while offering people an interactive and intriguing experience to which they can contribute. It has the potential to be a more exhilarating theatrical experience than anything in London's West End. Shaw has directed more than sixty Domestic Theatre productions.

Beth's friend, Christianne Heal, wanted a play performed at a party for her new home in Cambridge, UK. Beth said she was too busy to write anything, so Christianne would have to write the script.

Beth recommended rhyming couplets as being easier than prose for beginners. Over the course of six train journeys to London, Christianne found that a one-hour script poured out of her—a Victorian melodrama which she called *Murder by Strychnine on Donkey Green*. Beth and a few others arrived the day before the performance to help prepare costumes and make hand-held props such as an owl mask, a book of murder recipes, a will, and a model of the terrace of houses.

On the day of the performance, a majority of the thirty-three adult guests had parts to read and the children had roles as "ghostettes."

"There was a feast beforehand," said Christianne, "and I could relax, with just my part as the murderess to do, and all the play directing looked after by Beth. It was wonderful with the participants constantly changing from actors to audience and back again, moving from room to room.

"There was no rehearsal or learning of lines and no expectations and therefore no fear of failure. Afterward we had a sing-song till the early hours."

let babies scream
at the cinema screen

For those film buffs who demand complete silence in the cinema, please look away now. A far worse noise than popcorn-crunching or stray phone-calls can regularly be heard at the Clapham Picture House in London: babies. The cinema offers weekly screenings specifically for mothers and babies, endeavoring to fill a niche in the market and provide a service to mothers wishing to escape the confines of home.

The idea was devised by staff at the cinema after mothers with strollers repeatedly protested being barred from adult films. Now the ushers double as stroller parking attendants, aisles are for rocking and burping, and the toilet's primary use is as a nappy-(diaper-) changing facility. And those who wish to munch popcorn and answer their phone can do so with barely an eyebrow raised.

In America, the ReelMoms project has a similar initiative, providing a chance for mothers and babies to see a Tuesday matinee movie.

→ **www.enjoytheshow.com/reelmoms/**

41

read rave reviews
of quiet nights out

While smoking has been increasingly discouraged in recent years, there is still no legislation for being seated next to a noisy table or inadvertently choosing a restaurant in which noise levels are high.

One small measure that could help prospective consumers would be for restaurant critics to include a note on the average decibel levels in a restaurant in their review. They could also add a note on the presence (or absence) and type of background music. All of which could enable the discerning diner to make a more informed choice of the most suitable eatery for them. Standards of food, service, cleanliness, and smoke are all used (correctly) to judge restaurants; perhaps it is time for noise to be added to the list.

Alison Munro

42

eat slow food to quicken your conscience

43

When McDonald's was poised to open a branch in Rome's famous Piazza di Spagna, members of the Italian gastronomical society, Arcigola, were appalled. In particular, member Carlo Petrini wondered what to do to campaign against the invasion. He came up with a simple concept to combat fast food: slow food. Petrini and his friends issued the Slow Food Manifesto, which included the remedy for the damage caused by "fast life": an "adequate portion of pure sensual pleasures, to be taken with slow and prolonged enjoyment."

McDonald's took little notice and opened the restaurant anyway, but Slow Food also prospered, transforming itself from a one-time campaigning tool into a fully fledged movement. It was formally founded as a movement in Paris in 1989 and has since become a central rallying point for the massive international backlash against homogenized, industrialized fast food. It now has over eighty thousand members in a hundred countries, organized into local convivia. At these convivia, people meet to learn about culinary history and traditions relating to the region, and to enjoy the pleasures of slow eating. They are reminded of the pleasurable social aspect of food and also encouraged to support local producers.

The Slow Food movement stages many gastronomic events worldwide each year; the largest is the annual Salone del Gusto in Turin, Italy. These events are packed with slow-food aficionados enjoying cheeses, wines, and other delights. There are workshops and seminars that give an indication of the weight the movement gives to taste education.

The movement's commitment to educating future generations is also exemplary. There are tasting sessions for children at every Slow Food festival and the movement has worked with schoolteachers to educate children on the importance of the senses as tools of knowledge. Slow Food has also been a founding partner in the formation of the first University of Gastronomic Science, which opened its doors in late 2004. There, a student can study to be a Master of Food, selecting courses from a syllabus that covers subjects ranging from wines to cooking techniques, from confectionery to cured meats.

Slow Food has also diversified, most recently with the Slow Cities project (see page 302), which extends the Slow Food objectives (respecting local culture, preserving traditional methods, enjoying life at a particular pace) into a wider context of life.

→ **www.slowfood.com**

win when you lose
your competitive streak

Brainball is a game in which those players who are most relaxed will win. Developed by the Swedish Interactive Institute, it goes against the normal competitive instincts of game players, and rewards those who are disinterested, indifferent, or more able to keep their cool.

The set-up is simplicity itself: a table with a ball on it and a goal at either end. Two people sit opposite each other and try to score a goal. The catch is that both players wear a headband with electrodes connected to a sensitive biosensor system. This system can detect and measure the signals being given out by the body of the player, and registers the brain activity going on in the frontal lobes. The brain waves that move the ball forward are alpha and theta waves, which are generated when someone is calm and relaxed. Stressed, competitive players will lose, as they will be giving off other types of brain signals.

The game may have other uses: yoga gurus wishing to extend meditative skills are interested, and there is speculation it may be useful in helping children with attention deficit disorders.

→ **http://smart.interactiveinstitute.se/ smart/index_en.php**

learn to love your locality
with the moving museum

A traveling museum that aims to tour the whole country, turning each town's interesting spots into a "museum" or fun-spot for short periods of time, could do such things as:

→ make a town's sewers accessible for public visits

→ allow access to the town's tallest building so that locals can visit

→ open up old and disused buildings of interest

→ give tours of the town's most famous landmarks.

Having done its work by reinvigorating the community's knowledge and love for its hometown, the museum would then simply move on to the next town.

John Tunney

create an emergency room for creative crises

46

For artists and artistes, there should be an emergency room (ER) specifically for instances of "creative crisis." This 24-hour "hospital" would be for people suffering from severe cases of inspiration, who have no means at the time of the "attack" with which to implement their ideas.

Immediate relief could be given to the person waking at 4:00 A.M. with a vision for a film or play; or to the person who has had weeks of sleepless nights from an idea aching to metastasize, leaving them in constant anxiety.

The facility would house studios for all art forms and a wing for inventions and patenting advice. Staffed by volunteers, unemployed artists, and struggling technicians, the center may be funded by commissions on successful projects emerging from it.

Each new "patient" admitted at the front desk would be asked about their "symptoms." Specific treatment could then begin. Once the sufferer is "cured" and the inspiration made into a viable invention or piece of art, they could arrange with the center a financial deal from whatever profits come from the process. Less successful ideas would be subsidized by the ones that took off, allowing the center to help everyone with an unfulfilled creative idea. With a center in every major city of the world, they could be joined in a network for global collaboration and cooperation.

Kathleen Willer

support sofa spuds on determination day

47

There are too many couch potatoes nowadays. Perhaps for people to realize that they can do good in this world, for others and for themselves, they need to take a day and think of a goal they want to achieve.

They can spend the day planning what they are going to do to accomplish that goal, whether it be to help themselves or others. If they do this, perhaps it will help diminish several problems in one go. To encourage them to act, a particular date could be selected to celebrate Determination Day.

Chris Hendricks

take a seat
for moving art

For four weeks a Piccadilly Line underground train in London was transformed into a moving art gallery.

Forty-two artists submitted two pieces of work each to fill six carriages of the train with art where the advertisements would usually be posted. The artists featured included Yoko Ono, Damien Hirst, and Vivienne Westwood, and the works included paintings, photographs, and fashion items. The project extends other innovative exhibitions on the Underground, including the "Platform Art" project and the famous "Poems on the Underground" scheme.

The "Art-Tube" is the brainchild of the Canadian artist Gordon McHarg, who exhibited his own drawings on Vancouver's bus system some years ago. That experience inspired him to curate the exhibition for London Underground, which reached a substantially larger audience. Each carriage travels 45 miles through London on each journey along the line and there are 52 stations on the Piccadilly Line. At peak times, there are 76 trains on the line, giving the passengers a one-and-a-third percent chance of catching an art carriage each day. Mr. McHarg pointed out the benefits of the scheme: "It will liven up people's journeys, and I'm sure thousands of people who'd never normally go anywhere near an art gallery will benefit from it."

→ www.art-tube.com

empower the homeless through musical means

49

A new professional opera company has been set up in London with the aim of empowering the homeless. Working in partnership with hostels and shelters, the company invites homeless people to get involved in all aspects of the operatic production, and that includes performing.

The company's goal is to help increase the self-esteem and confidence of those involved, as well as developing their skills in areas such as time-management, communication, and teamwork. A crucial part of the company's ethos is holding the production to a professional standard, to ensure that those taking part feel pride in their achievements and to challenge the audience's preconceptions of homelessness.

Streetwise Opera was established to help the homeless regain confidence and move forward emotionally by adding the development of internal well-being to the basic externals (food, shelter, clothing) being provided by other charitable or other sources.

The first major project was a staging of Benjamin Britten's *Canticles*, in which more than one hundred homeless people took part. Over a period of twelve weeks, people from various homeless centers in London took part in workshops, in which they learned various skills from a professional opera company. These workshops culminated in two performances of the opera in Westminster Abbey.

The impact on the lives of those who took part has already been substantial, with increased confidence and communication skills being the main outcome. As a result, some have gone into rehabilitation, some into education, some into more secure housing, and a number into employment. The feedback from these people also demonstrates the real way in which such arts can increase self-worth. One participant said, "It's the best thing that's happened to me in years," while another boldly stated that "Never has anyone got so much pleasure out of anything as I have out of this."

The project has been so successful that it now has a substantial program of performances lined up for the future. It is hoped that such work will continue to challenge those who think opera is elitist, who think homeless people are to be pitied, or who believe that involvement in the arts is an unnecessary luxury.

Most important of all, it will continue to aid and empower the homeless people involved by encouraging their creativity, increasing their confidence, or simply by providing a stable routine of work.

→ **www.streetwiseopera.org**

chapter 3

crime and law

present roses not fines
to speeding motorists

Indian traffic police in the city of Ahmedabad have taken a novel approach to the problem of speeding motorists. Instead of fining or reprimanding the drivers, the police officers remind them of the rules and offer them the gift of a rose.

The project is part of the "No sticks, only carrots" approach to policing, which aims to raise awareness and understanding, rather than being punitive.

50

As the deputy police commissioner K.K. Ojha explained, "We have decided not to treat traffic rule violators as offenders but as citizens ignorant of traffic rules. And to drive home the point, we have evolved this method: giving roses as a goodwill gesture." The sheer surprise that accompanies the action ensures the message is not forgotten, and the approach is also helping to change the attitude of local people toward the police.

give the good guys
tax breaks

At this point in time, people are fined for breaking the law. Why don't we promote good behavior by giving tax breaks to citizens who haven't been charged with any minor infractions during the past five years?

This would work in a manner similar to car insurance, in which individuals receive a "no claims" bonus for not being involved in an accident. Anyone convicted of a crime would

51

lose the tax break and would have to build their good behavior record up again. After a set number of years without again falling foul of the law, the tax break would be reinstated. There could even be "pension points" added for those who have been law-abiding throughout their life up to the point of retirement.

Chris Coolledge

plant thorny bushes to banish burglars

52

Placing particular plants in a flower garden can be a more effective security barrier than guard dogs, burglar alarms, or high walls.

Species of climber and bushes that are especially thorny and sharp can be as much of a deterrent to potential burglars as barbed wire, but are far more aesthetically pleasing. If plants are chosen wisely, they can also help keep out unwanted animals and provide a supply of fruit to the household.

Recommended species include firethorn, hawthorn, blackthorn, holly, roses, blackberry bushes, and gooseberry plants. A mix of different plants is recommended, preferably grown on a trellis that is too sturdy to be blown away in the wind yet is not able to take the weight of a burglar. Putting up a trellis with a mix of such climbers and thorny plants at the rear of the house (where most break-ins occur) can have a genuine deterrent effect.

Burglars are averse to thorny bushes not only because they are sharp and painful, but also because they make it more likely that evidence will be left behind, be that a piece of torn clothing or blood to be tested for DNA. If the hedge has berries that stain clothing as well, the evidence can begin to build up against them.

fight fires,
not the law

Inmates are being recruited to help ease the financial burden of employing and training new firefighters in the state of Colorado. In Rye, Colorado, inmates under a strict code of honor are allowed to clear tangled brush and trees from the forests and to cut and carry wood to the roadsides. When necessary, they also help fight fires. This idea has earned the state a $50,000 (about £25,000) net profit and each inmate earns $6 (about £3) a day. Their personal involvement also gives the prisoners a sense of responsibility, hope, and healthy interaction through work.

One participating inmate said that he plans to go to college and work during the summer as a firefighter. Another hopes to make parole and later become an engine boss. This program has given many others such hope for a future.

As part of a program called the State Wildland Inmate Fire Team (SWIFT), non-violent offenders at the Four Mile Correctional Facility can apply for the team and must pass physical and psychological testing before acceptance. The state spends a minimal $2,000 (about £1,000) training the inmates.

A similar scheme runs in Alte, Georgia, where the local fire department is made up of prison inmates under a non-inmate fire chief.

53

The prisoners are from the Lee Arrendale Correctional Institution, a maximum security prison, and include some sentenced for murder, drug dealing, and armed robbery. The only inmates barred from applying are those who have committed sex crimes, arson, or crimes against a law enforcement officer. Currently, the Georgia Department of Corrections operates eighteen fire stations in state facilities, with 220 inmates involved at any one time.

→ **www.cijvp.com/serviceproviders/swift/**

sport facial hair
for improved reputation

54

The Indian police force is trying to better their reputation by growing moustaches. They believe that sporting a moustache will boost an officer's social standing and morale, and will make him appear smarter. Research has shown that officers with facial hair are taken more seriously, so the idea is being put into practice.

Moustaches have long been a sign of virility and authority in India. By encouraging their growth, with a monthly financial bonus, the police hope to improve their reputation.

use music to shoo,
not soothe

55

A shopkeeper in Lancashire in the North of England has managed to drive away youths loitering outside his shop by playing opera music at high volume. As soon as the arias and cantatas started to blare out from the loudspeakers erected on the roof of the shop, the gangs began to disperse.

Boston police in the USA piped George Gershwin music into an underground (subway) station to deter teenagers from hanging around, while others in the area used the music of John Philip Sousa. Several teenagers complained about the music, which only served to convince the authorities that the approach was working. The London Underground authorities took steps to introduce the playing of opera arias and classical music at stations with particular crime problems.

promote peacemaking, not punishment

56

The Navajo Nation has begun an experiment in which peacemakers take the place of judges, prosecutors, and prisons. In January 2000, the Navajo Nation Council changed their criminal code to eliminate jail time and fines for 79 offenses, to require the use of peacemakers in all criminal cases, and to require the courts to see to the rights of victims. They also incorporated the traditional Navajo concept of *nalyeeh* into the code, a word which refers to the process of confronting those who have hurt others with a demand that they talk things out. It is in this area that the peacemakers become involved.

A Navajo peacemaking session involves the person accused of an offense and the person who suffered from it. The relatives of the accused and the person hurt by the accused are also invited. A community leader (or peacemaker) moderates the session, and the people talk about what happened and how they feel about it. Navajos believe that a harmful act is "something that gets in the way of living your life," and their method of peacemaking deals with such an act by identifying it, discussing it, and formulating a plan to deal with it. For example, the family members of the accused might be asked to watch over their relative to be sure he does not reoffend, or the accused might be asked to give a symbolic object as part of the restitution process. Horses, for instance, are prized possessions of the Navajo people and are often given as restitution for serious sexual insults. Such a symbol might mean anything from "I'm sorry" to "Let this be a symbol and something tangible to remind us that we have talked this hurt out and entered into good relations with each other."

This experiment could prove to be an invaluable one. The Navajo Nation courts see 28,000 criminal cases every year, but have enough jail space for only 220 people. By returning to a traditional method of justice that concentrates on the effects of a crime rather than punishing its perpetrator, the Navajos could be offering a lesson to the rest of America and the western world. It is simply not viable to keep locking up a major portion of the population, and peacemaking may be a way of reducing that prison population while holding the offenders accountable for the effects of their crimes. Most importantly of all, perhaps, it puts the victim (or the person harmed by the crime) at the center of the justice process.

fine judges for wrongful releases

Steven Landsburg, an economics professor, has suggested a novel idea for improving the judicial system. In order to reduce the number of crimes committed by defendants released on bail, he suggests that the judges be fined whenever this occurs.

In essence, the judge is made personally liable for any criminal damage resulting from his decision to release an accused criminal. The theory is that the judge will then focus more closely on determining the right decision for the criminal and the community, because he has a personal financial incentive to get it right.

Clearly, introducing the fining system alone would not work, because judges would simply never release anyone out on bail, thus avoiding the possibility of a fine. Landsburg therefore proposes that there be "a simultaneous countervailing incentive" in the form of a cash payment to the judge for every defendant he releases. In this way, the introduction of financial incentives could be used to make judges directly liable for their decisions: liable to benefit if they get it right, and liable to be fined if they get it wrong.

The level of cash incentives and fines could be adjusted depending on the wishes of the particular legislature.

→ **www.landsburg.com**

57

pay prisoners properly
to reduce re-offending

58

The work of criminals in jail should be adequately paid. The money, or a major portion of it, should be kept by the state and paid out over the course of several years, only under the condition that the former convict reintegrates into society and does not offend again during that period.

If he or she does reoffend, the salary earned in prison (or at least part of it) would be revoked by the state. The justice of this is easy to convey to those reconvicted; they will understand that reoffending will create further expense to society.

The longer people have been inmates, the more money they will have accumulated and the stronger their desire will be to avoid falling back into crime. During imprisonment, inmates can plan systematically (perhaps with the support of mentors) for the time after jail and they will know that, due to the salary they have accumulated during their sentence, they will have a fair chance of starting a legitimate business.

The incentive to develop an optimistic and constructive perspective on life will be very strong. Falling back into crime would mean losing the fruits of years of hard work and would become extremely unattractive.

Hans-Peter Voss

create sentences to correspond with crimes

59

Judge Howard Broadman of California's Tulare County Court believes that there is something radically wrong with the current judicial system, so he decided to test the boundaries of sentencing procedures to prove it.

For his unusual and creative efforts in devising sentences that were appropriate to the crimes committed, he was variously appealed, applauded, criticized, and shot at.

A few examples of his sentences will give an indication of why he provoked such strong reactions:

→ He gave a beer-thief probation on condition that he wear a T-shirt proclaiming his crime.

→ A man convicted of hitting a woman was told to donate his car to the local battered women's shelter.

More credible alternative sentencing programs that give judges options other than prison or parole continue to proliferate, particularly in the US.

Ten years ago there were about twenty such programs in the States; now there are more than three hundred, according to the Sentencing Project, a Washington, DC group that promotes the use of sentencing experts for most non-violent crimes.

Sentencing experts—usually lawyers or social workers—put together some sentencing packages that were appropriate to the criminal and the crime with a view toward rehabilitation of the individual.

Many judges and sentencing experts argue that creative sentences can serve both justice and the community. Here are some further examples:

→ In Portland, Maine, a Bowdoin college graduate who had been convicted of smuggling several thousand pounds of marijuana was sentenced to set up and run a hospice for people with AIDS. The logic behind this sentence was that the city needed the hospice, and the smuggler had the organizational and business savvy to make it work.

→ In Edmonton, Canada, as part of the sentence for several clients who had been picked up during prostitution busts, Judge Sharon Vandeveen informed their wives what their husbands had been caught doing.

→ In one case from a court run by teenagers (but overseen by a judge) a boy who had been involved in creating graffiti was sentenced to six months of guarding the wall that he had vandalized. If anyone marked the wall, he had to clean it.

file suit for
the future

60

The Supreme Court of the Philippines ruled that the three children of Antonio Oposa, along with forty-one other children, have standing to sue on behalf of their generation and subsequent generations. If the lessons of this decision are taken on board, the way the world views environmental issues could change dramatically.

Oposa, an attorney with the Philippines Ecological Network, was representing the children in an effort to try to cancel all existing timber license agreements between timber interests and the Philippine Department of Environment and Natural Resources. The court's decision held that minors have standing to represent their own and future generations under the doctrine of intergenerational equity.

The Court stated that: "This case...has a special and novel element. Petitioners' minors assert that they represent their generation as well as generations yet unborn. We find no difficulty in ruling that they can, for themselves, for others of their generation, and for the succeeding generations, file a class suit.

"Their personality to sue on behalf of the succeeding generations can only be based on the concept of intergenerational responsibility insofar as the right to a balanced and healthy ecology is concerned.

"Such a right, as hereinafter expounded, considers the 'rhythm and harmony of nature.' Nature means the created world in its entirety. Such rhythm and harmony include, inter alia, the judicious disposition, utilization, management, renewal, and conservation of the country's forest, mineral, land, waters, fisheries, wildlife, offshore areas, and other natural resources to the end that their exploration, development, and utilization be equitably accessible to the present as well as future generations."

Courts everywhere would do well to study the pronouncement, for there is no doubt that today's generation is stealing the ecological wealth of future generations, whether that wealth lies in the forests, the oceans, the wetlands, the prairies, or the genetic integrity of the world's species, ourselves included. Recognizing the right to sue of future generations would act as an additional spur to take action for the long-term consequences of all.

Guy Dauncey

→ **www.elaw.org**

put puppies behind bars

61

The introduction of pets into prisons has proved to be a remarkably successful venture.

One of the most noteworthy is the program set up at the Purdy Treatment Center for Women, Gig Harbor, Washington. Established with the help of Kathy Quinn (now Sister Pauline) who is promoting this idea at other correctional institutions, the object is for inmates to train dogs to aid disabled people.

Wardens and governors were wary at first, but the project has been successful. The self-esteem of prisoners has increased dramatically and they feel that they have a link with the outside world, as well as being able to do something worthwhile. Many of those involved go on to work with animals on leaving the prison, and the relationships between inmates and staff have improved greatly.

In another initiative, puppies being groomed as guide dogs spent a year in prison, where they were trained by convicted prisoners. Pilot Dogs, a company that trains guide dogs for the blind in Columbus, Ohio, placed the potential guide dogs in the care of five inmates with lifelong experience of living with animals.

→ **www.puppiesbehindbars.com**

buckle up or take a toe-tag

62

Police in Alberta, Canada, handed out morgue toe-tags to drivers not wearing seatbelts in a campaign to warn offending motorists. The officers asked offenders to fill out their own names on the tags, along with details of their next of kin. On the back of each tag was a list of various injuries that drivers (and passengers) can suffer in a car crash when seatbelts are not being used.

Giving the safety message in this way is not subtle, but the police hoped it would have the desired effect on offenders. As Sergeant Steve MacDonald put it, "We'll be telling them, 'If you don't wear a seatbelt, fill this out to make it easier for us when you're in a crash.' We'll be able to recognize them even if they're unrecognizable, and be able to tell their loved ones what has happened."

use web alert services
to catch criminals in the net

A number of Internet-based alert services that encourage communities to take a collaborative role with the police are proving effective in obtaining and distributing information on crime, and ultimately catching more criminals.

63

The idea is based on a simple exchange of facts—police direct warnings or alerts via e-mails and web pages to relevant brackets of their target community, whether citizens on a single street favored by bicycle thieves, members of an entire neighborhood, or high street businesses.

These groups, in turn, reciprocate by offering useful information via the web network or, in the case of businesses, alerting the police to the location of suspected criminals.

Mutually beneficial and technically efficient, the arrangement promises to unite local districts in tackling crime, while raising an overall sense of community and projecting the notion of "neighborhood watch" to new heights.

Minnesota firm Citizen Observer is coordinating one of the fastest-growing programs of this type, having initiated contracts with approximately 130 police agencies from Arkansas to Ohio over a period of three years. Its virtual crime notification package is divided into business, residential, and school networks

and a web bulletin board of fugitives, missing persons, and unsolved crimes.

This new police tool demonstrates the potential of a virtual concept in providing concrete solutions to social problems, signaling an intelligent and functional use of web space. Indeed, one success story saw the network (which lets law enforcers alert businesses within a 30-mile radius of fresh criminal activity) instigate the apprehension of a Wisconsin thief with remarkable speed. No sooner had the burglar presented a mountain of quarters to the cashier of a participating bank than he was arrested for stealing the cash: from a child's piggy bank. The bank's computers had received an advanced web warning to look out for an unusual volume of silver.

Furthermore, a focus on involving residential communities in police work via Internet networks could hold an even bigger potential for cracking crime, for reasons linked to the web medium itself. Bill Berger, chief of police in North Miami Beach, Florida, believes that the ability to submit information via websites and e-mail makes participation more likely, because of the anonymity this method supplies to users. "It's almost like it creates a veil, an extra level of distance and safety," explains Berger, whose police department has set up a similar independent network to employ the public more actively in helping solve and prevent crimes.

Indeed, Brent Council members, in north-west London, have set up a new affiliated website to address crime problems in the area. Features on the Brent Resource and Information Network website include, uniquely, an online directory of recently reported crimes in the area. Recent crime incidents can be viewed by local people who can then contact the police with information about any particular incident via an online form. In addition, local citizens can sign up to receive e-mail and text alerts that will be sent out after crime incidents have been reported. This will allow much greater inter-action with the public in an effort to solve crime, as well as greater transparency and cooper-ation between the authorities and the public.

In this way, the appeal for help goes out directly to the local audience, much sooner after the crime has been committed, when people's recollections are clearer and more accurate. Though the service will inevitably depend on critical mass to solve crimes (the more people who sign up, the more successful the scheme will be), the whole approach is to get the public involved in viewing information about crime incidents directly, being aware of current situations in their area, and taking an active role in solving problems that concern all residents.

If widely implemented, such web-based communication networks could transform the way the police project and gather their facts into a community-conscious information flow. This will not only widen the crime data pool, but it might also be an important step in the evolution of the police force from a distant and separate institution into a fully integrated part of the community they serve.

→ **www.citizenobserver.com**
→ **www.brentbrain.org.uk**

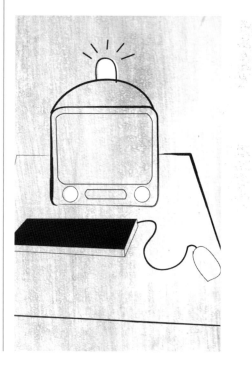

hire holistic lawyers
who like to listen

64

William Van Zyverden, a Vermont lawyer, is the founder of the International Alliance of Holistic Lawyers.

What is a holistic lawyer? Van Zyverden defines the term as someone dedicated to the use of arbitration and mediation rather than litigation. Through intense questioning of his client, the holistic lawyer seeks to identify the roots of a conflict, to foster a client's self-awareness and feelings of responsibility for a problem, and to develop the client's empathy for his opponent rather than catering to the desire for revenge. Another precept is civility to adversaries, even if they are loathsome. Van Zyverden insists his clients conduct their own investigations, take their own pictures, interview potential witnesses, and assemble documents—everything except research the law. The theory is that it helps the individual client to heal inner conflict, and shows that working things through can defuse anger.

The International Alliance of Holistic Lawyers has grown from a small beginning to hundreds of members worldwide.

→ **www.iahl.org**

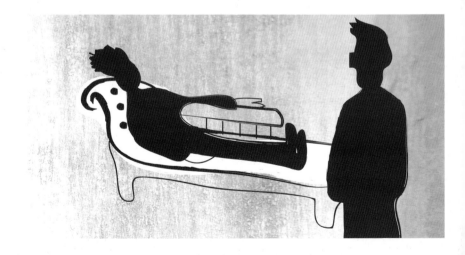

give dogs number plates so foulers can be fined

65

Officials in Frankfurt, Germany, proposed a new scheme under which dogs would have to have license plates, as do cars.

This will allow members of the public to identify dogs that foul the pavement or the street, and thus allow their owners to be traced. Under the plan put forward, offending owners could be fined. This plan would form part of the ongoing "Clean Frankfurt" campaign. The head of the campaign, Peter Postleb, said: "If they [the owners] know their dog can get them rumbled, they might just think twice about it."

bring insubordinate inmates to book with bread bricks

66

Prisons in the state of Maryland have introduced a tasteless dietary loaf for inmates who flout prison rules. The loaves are low in fat and cholesterol and contain recommended daily allowances of Vitamin C, calcium, iron, and other nutrients, but their taste is unpalatable enough to bring even hardened prisoners into line. Especially when it is served to them for breakfast, lunch, and dinner with only water to wash it down.

Michael Jackson, a Baltimore inmate who's been on the bread diet twice, described it as smelling "kind of foul" before adding, "The first few days are the worst. I can't even describe it. It's awful." Others merely describe it as bland beyond belief, but all have noticed an effect on those having to eat it. Maryland prison officials have said that adding the bread to other disciplinary measures doesn't usually last long, because it has such a noticeable impact on the prisoner's behavior. And because the loaf provides everything you need for a well-balanced diet, the prison is not harming or depriving those under its control.

This version of medieval bread includes: dehydrated potato flakes, grated imitation cheese, powdered milk, raisins, carrots, tomato paste, wheat bread, beans and a can of spinach. The mixture is molded into a loaf-shape and baked for an hour. And there you have it: the new low-tech tool for controlling prisoners—the "special management meal."

lighten up prison life with laughter

67

In an effort to reduce inmates' stress, Thailand's Corrections Department decided to introduce a laughter contest. Administrators of the project, called "A Little Laugh A Day Brightens Your Day," determined the winner of the contest and awarded a trophy to the inmate contestant with the most contagious laugh. Prison authorities further supplemented the contest with a joke-telling competition.

There are 132 prisons in Thailand, intended to hold 100,000 prisoners; they presently contain a quarter of a million. This severe overcrowding has resulted in a great deal of stress and poor health among inmates. The laughter contest is one of several innovative projects brought in by the prison authorities to try to help counter this trend; other activities have included choral singing, cooking lessons, meditation, and a football tournament.

In the first contest to be held, 383 contestants were chosen to compete, having been identified by psychologists as suffering from severe stress and distress.

Fifteen finalists made it through, and each performed (or rather laughed) for a minute before Amporn Petchana was declared the winner.

Sorasit Chongchaeron, the director of the Pathum Thani Special Correction Facility where the contest was held, said that they had "organized the event to boost the inmates' mental health" and that the event had been a "success," although they would further evaluate those who had taken part.

Based on the success of this first competition, the contests could become a more regular feature at the prison.

→ **www.correct.go.th**

forgo parking fines
to banish bribery

In an effort to stop the corruption of city police, a Mexican mayor recently made a drastic and radical change: all traffic and parking fines were abolished.

68

Mayor Eruviel Avila Villegas, the newly appointed mayor in Ecatepec, Mexico, introduced the initiative to cut out the opportunity for police bribery. His decision was based on the belief that reducing corruption is more important than fining people for minor traffic offenses.

Demanding bribes instead of issuing tickets is a big problem in Ecatepec and other Mexican towns. A recent survey showed that there were at least 200 million bribes in the country each year, two for each member of the population.

Mayor Avila also plans to abolish some policies in other city departments to curb corruption. Residents have said that they feel liberated by the changes, which give them a temporary respite from bribe-seeking officers, and places the emphasis on the current priority. Avila simply said, "The police don't have the trust of the people. I want to give them the means to be honest."

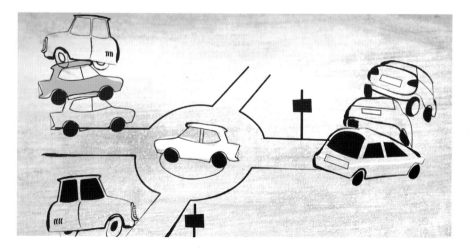

paint your tools pink
to put off petty criminals

69

Police in Burton-on-Trent, Staffordshire, recommended that residents paint their garden tools garish colors to make them less attractive to thieves.

The "Paint It Pink" project suggests that painting gardening equipment, such as lawn mowers and trimmers, will deter crooks because they will find the tools difficult to sell later on.

PC Nigel Fermor said that "Criminals will not want the bother of having to re-paint the items and I doubt they will able to resell them whilst they are pink."

If the implements are stolen, the colors will also make identifying the stolen goods significantly easier. PC Fermor was keen to point out that the recommended technique was not intended to replace more obvious security measures, such as locks on sheds, but he said that it could prove a useful additional method of crime prevention in the UK.

peruse paradise in a pacific island prison

A Mexican prison takes the principle of rehabilitation to the extremes— the prison itself is a beautiful Pacific island on which inmates live with their families.

There are no bars, no cells, no uniforms, and only 36 unarmed prison guards for the 3,000 inmates. The concept behind the Isla Maria experiment is that if prisoners are going to have to return to everyday life at some point, why not let them live in a community that simulates that everyday life? Only inmates who have shown the willingness to reform are allowed on the island, with the warden weeding out those who he thinks are less suited to the unique circumstances of the prison. The island also has its own bakery, church, and dance hall, while the inmates live in ordinary houses and work on farms.

The island prison is all the more remarkable because it started out as a kind of Mexican Alcatraz for the most hard-bitten criminals in the country, a place renowned for its harsh treatment of inmates. Although Mexico has quite a liberal judicial system (neither the death penalty nor life imprisonment are allowed by law), some prisons have become infamous for bribery and illegal punishments. Therefore, on Isla Maria, much of the power has been taken out of the hands of the guards to avoid similar occurrences.

70

Some criticize the expense of the prison (three times more per prisoner than a normal prison) and apparent laxness of its regime. The island's inmates are mostly drug traffickers, but a few have committed assault and murder. In its first nine months, 93 prisoners had to be transferred to the mainland, with others being punished by banishment to the other side of the island (away from music, TV, and family). There are also concerns over children being raised in a community of criminals, although this is common in other Mexican prisons and helps to keep families intact, another key factor in rehabilitation. Furthermore, the neighborhoods and housing are often safer and of a better standard than those that the families left behind on the Mexican mainland.

One woman, Lorena Avila Suarez, came to the island with her father (a convicted murderer) when she was eight, but still lives there, having fallen in love with a cocaine trafficker who has another 18 years left to serve. Her father has long since left, but she could remain until she is 43. Her mother, Mrs. Suarez llago, praises the island's rehabilitative effect, pointing out that her husband received schooling on the island, worked diligently on a farm, and has been in no trouble since his release.

promote spiritual purpose for prisoners

71

In 1969 Bo Lozoff and his wife Sita were living a Utopian lifestyle on a trimaran sailboat in the Caribbean, when their boat became involved in a drug smuggling saga that ended with a close relative being sent to jail for forty years.

Bo Lozoff's eventual response was to seek a job as a prison guard. He was turned down, and instead set up the Prison Ashram Project, which now encourages meditation in American jails throughout the world and sends free, to any prisoner anywhere in the world, a compendium of wisdom entitled *We're All Doing Time—A Guide to Getting Free*. In this book, Lozoff outlines the philosophies of karma and reincarnation and suggests a simple set of meditation, yoga, and breathing exercises.

Lozoff is not just proselytizing a philosophy but sharing personal insights with individual prisoners, and he includes in the book a series of moving letters from prisoners, along with his replies. One chapter, for instance, is devoted to the inner development of Maury Logue at the Oklahoma State Penitentiary. Logue had stabbed a number of other inmates and was locked up for almost 24 hours a day. In an early letter to Lozoff, Logue wrote how eight guards had beaten him with clubs while he was handcuffed, scarring him for life, and how he intended one day to exterminate society's leaders: "No mercy offered and none shall be given. My record speaks for itself." The breakthrough in their correspondence began when Lozoff sent Logue an illustrated fable about a mean, tough convict befriended against his will by a prison cat. Ironically, Logue was writing: "I'm making an honest attempt to readjust my conduct; I'm trying to clean up my act," shortly before being stabbed to death by two other inmates as he stood handcuffed in the showers.

Lozoff's project continues to this day, aiming to turn the negative situation of a prisoner into something more positive by enabling him or her to use their cell as a retreat and to find a spiritual purpose to their life, rather than merely serving time.

This is achieved via correspondence (between inmates and "outmates"), publications, and workshops, all educating on the need for positivity, self-awareness, and relaxation. Spiritual and social rehabilitation, as well as housing and financial rehabilitation, is necessary for full integration back into life on the outside, and the Prison Ashram project continues to strive to achieve that.

→ **www.humankindness.org**

guide girl scouts
to crime-free life

An unusual group of Girl Guides has been set up in Maryland for the daughters of women who have been incarcerated in state prisons.

72

The initiative comes in response to alarming statistics, showing that children of jailed parents are six times more likely to go to prison themselves. Melanie C. Pereira, former warden of the women's prison, recalls having had "the grandmother, the mother, and the daughter in prison all at the same time."

To make matters worse, crime among girls has increased by 22 percent during the last decade.

"Girl Scouts Beyond Bars" meets every Saturday. Twice a month, they go to a Baltimore church, where outings and activities have been arranged for them.

On the other Saturdays, a minibus takes the girls to visit their mothers in jail. Here, as well as getting to spend quality time with their mothers, the girls are given talks about careers and sex education and go in for such traditional guide activities as cookie baking.

The program has been a great success and has since been copied in many other states. As Pereira puts it, the scheme makes it clear to these girls that "there is a better way." Mothers and children involved are all enthusiastic about the program—and the fringe benefits are enhanced mother–daughter relationships and greater self-confidence (among the prisoners as well as their children, the former taking a sense of pride in their daughters' achievements). A senior staff member is pleased to recall a Christmas party where one six-year-old was asked by her mother what she wished for the coming year. "Well," she said in a very maternal fashion, "My wish is that you will have learned your lesson and will never be back here again."

In recent years, Girl Scout groups have also been set up in juvenile detention centers, in an effort to give incarcerated girls the opportunity to develop life skills, self-esteem, and a stronger social conscience.

→ **www.girlscouts.org**

make mini-neighborhoods
to clean up the streets

73

In the 1990s, Five Oaks in Dayton, Ohio, was in decline. Poverty, prostitution, and drug dealing had become rife.

The city of Ohio hired Oscar Newman, author of *Defensible Space*, to put together a plan that ultimately cost nearly $700,000 (£350,000) to implement. City workers put in speed bumps and barriers, closed streets, and put up gates tastefully decorated with plaques bearing the neighborhood logo.

The residents decided to divide one big neighborhood into many mini-neighborhoods.

Smaller neighborhoods would enhance the sense of community while making anonymous crimes harder to commit. Street closures make getting about more difficult, but also discourage outsiders.

Two years after the measures were introduced, residents noticed a remarkable change. It was wonderful, one local man observed, to sit on the porch and not hear gunfire. City officials were no less pleased. In a one-year period, community traffic decreased by 67 percent and violent crimes fell by half.

create cardboard crime-fighters
to cut down crime

74

The introduction of cardboard cut-out policemen placed beside sections of road notorious for speeding has reduced speeding offenses by 33 percent around Copenhagen, Denmark, and the experiment may be extended to other policework.

Cut-outs were also erected at crossings where drivers often drive through red lights. The cut-outs are from time to time replaced by real officers, to ensure motorists do not become complacent.

Likewise, in Japan, as a warning to motorists, concrete policemen stand at sections of road where accidents are frequent.

In Bradford, UK, shops and garages erected plywood police officers in an attempt to reduce shoplifting, despite protests from local police, who thought these plywood representatives would be mocked and reduce public confidence in the police. In Tyne and Wear, UK, shoplifting fell 70 percent in a trial, when retailers installed cardboard cut-out policemen.

"cancel" concerts
to put off illegal posters

Sticking concert posters in unautho-rised places (known as "fly-posting" in the UK) can have a high cost in cash and cleaning time, but may have met its match in a creative solution from Oadby and Wigston Borough Council in Leicestershire.

The cheap and effective solution entailed spending about £240 ($480) to produce a series of "Cancelled" stickers to be placed over offending posters advertising sales, raves, or concerts.

The fear such tactics induce in the offend-ers is enough to make them take down the offending posters themselves, thus saving the council a great deal of time and money that would normally go for cleaning them up and taking them down.

At a time when Camden council in London has taken Sony and BMG to court over the problem in their borough, the idea proposed by Oadby and Wigston Council is a cheap and easy alternative to a potentially risky and high-powered court case.

"One of the main reasons for the success of the scheme is that it has the potential to hit the profit margins of the companies putting them up," says Graham Norman, head of client serv-ices and contracts at the council. The simplicity and cost-effectiveness of the idea has seen it

75

taken up in Northampton, Welling-borough, Leicester, and Rotherham. It may also be implemented in Bedford, Birmingham, and Liverpool city councils, as they take up the battle cry, "If you can't beat them, join them."

→ **www.oadby-wigston.gov.uk**

pit prisoners against students in chess challenges

76

An initiative that pits prisoners against university students in chess matches is proving useful to both parties.

The inmates get a break from their routine and improve their concentration and strategic thinking. The students, who are from Princeton, are introduced to people whom they might not otherwise meet: people from different backgrounds with vastly different life experience.

The state Corrections Commissioner, Devon Brown, believes that this practice helps the inmates improve their life skills, as lessons learned in chess can prove useful when applied to other areas of life. As Commissioner Brown puts it, chess "teaches its players to think ahead, to recognize traps, and to avoid costly mistakes, all of which are useful skills to have when emerging from prison to be rehabilitated into society." In that sense, the chess project is about more than just bringing two different groups of people into contact in a break from routine; it is about introducing structured thinking patterns and processes that can help inmates in the future.

→ **www.state.nj.us/corrections**

recycle phones to serve as safety alarms

77

As the inexorable rise of mobile phones continues, there is also a proportionate rise in energy used in producing them and in waste when they are discarded for the newest piece of technology.

Many methods for recycling phones exist, but an initiative in south London puts a new spin on reusing phones. Coordinated by the Community Recycling in Southwark Project and backed by government, local police, and mobile phone companies, this project recycles phones into personal safety alarms, addressing both global environmental concerns and local concerns on crime and disorder.

The alarms, which give one-touch connection to emergency services, are distributed to those most affected by crime, violence, and antisocial behavior: namely, the elderly, sick, and disabled. The safety alarms can be used only for phoning emergency services, but they can accept incoming calls from selected welfare and support agencies. Not all phones can be reconfigured in this way, so the remaining phones are recycled.

→ **www.communityfonebak.com**
→ **www.wirelessfundraiser.com**
→ **www.collectivegood.com**

apply for adulthood in advance

78

Most nations confer the status of adulthood on its citizens only when they reach a legally defined age, such as eighteen. This fails to consider different rates of mental development and unnecessarily holds mature but young people back from entrepreneurial and other "grown-up" activities.

An alternative system would be to give the child the freedom to declare his or her independence. After proving their independence to a panel of selected judges, they could then undergo an attachment to someone mature, or take a month to "test drive" their freedom.

Once they successfully complete this probation period, they would legally gain adult status, regardless of age.

Eric Chen Yixiong

hand over prisons to communities to break criminal cycle

79

A project in Brazil that puts the community in charge of its local prison is hoping to transform the way criminals are treated in the country by radically altering the prison system. The idea is based on communities taking responsibility for each prisoner's rehabilitation and care. In this way, the current state prison system, which is rife with maltreatment and corruption, can be circumvented.

The project consists of a plan for 30 prisons, or "centers of resocialization," each of which can house 210 prisoners. An association consisting of people from the local community is then assembled to administer the prison in their particular town or city. The government signs an agreement with the local association, under which it is made clear that the community organization is responsible for the prison's administration, while the government provides a budget for each inmate. Administering the prison includes providing healthcare, food, work, security, and education.

A trial of this model in Sao Paulo prisons was a success, and has led to the scheme being expanded as detailed above. Roberto da Silva, the man behind the idea, is an advisory expert to the United Nations on the prevention of crime and the treatment of the criminal. He grew up in foster care, and also spent six years in jail,

where he met many others from backgrounds and experiences similar to his. This led him to believe that placing children in the draconian Brazilian care system leads to criminal behavior; this led in turn to his involvement with the jail-citizenship project.

Da Silva went on to study a sample of 370 children who were his contemporaries in the care system, and found that over a third of them had become criminals of some sort and had committed over 400 crimes between them (including 40 murders). The root causes of this pattern are found in the lack of education for children in care, the lack of familial support, and the sometimes arbitrary sending away of the child for minor behavioral problems. The government also failed to inform many children of the whereabouts of their siblings in other parts of the country; da Silva himself found two of his brothers in the course of his own research.

Having pursued legal proceedings against the government and published a thesis that argued that the treatment of teenagers and children needs to be a priority if crime levels in Brazil are to fall, da Silva continued to look for solutions. His beliefs engendered the prison project, which places an emphasis on education and human rights for prisoners rather than just distrust and punishment.

chapter 4

housing

turn a tower block into a flower block

A plan involving an environmental charity, an enterprising journalist, and a Midlands housing association in the UK has shown how tower blocks (high-rises) can be effectively "greened" to create a better living environment.

By offering tenants of a tower block in Coventry two free window boxes filled with plants and compost, the project has transformed an imposing grey block of flats into a brighter, more colorful place to live. As well as changing the look of the tower for the better, the initiative helped create a community feeling among the residents.

The "flower block" project was based on the initiative of local journalist Barbara Goulden, who spotted a balcony of color and greenery in the tower block.

Having met with the responsible high-rise gardener, she got to thinking of the possibilities if 5 or 10 percent of the tenants were to follow his lead.

80

In collaboration with the environmental charity Groundwork (as part of its sustainable tower blocks initiative) and the local housing association, each tenant was offered window boxes. Nearly half of the 120 flats in the block took up the offer, with any spares being quickly snapped up by nearby tower blocks. The resultant green, bright, and colorful environment has changed the way the residents view their home and the possibilities of making it more sustainable.

Indeed, the project has been such a success that it is now hoped that it will spread to other areas of the country, wherever the urban landscape is blighted by plain grey slabs. Greening urban architecture on a grand scale has massive potential and would encourage greater community feeling, create brighter and nicer places to live, and get people actively involved in sustainable living.

→ **www.groundwork.org.uk**

push open doors
to welcome the homeless

Push Open Doors is a not-for-profit organization, the primary purpose of which is to enable the housing industry to help the homeless.

81

Redirecting a percentage of the capital generated by the real estate industry will help alleviate homelessness and the toll that it takes on people's lives. Projections indicate that, with the exception of an initial investment, Push Open Doors can function as a financially self-sustaining entity, capable of donating all but its relatively minimal operating costs to its target beneficiaries.

The organization's goal is to establish and maintain an extensive network of donors (funding partners) consisting of real estate companies and banks that finance home purchasing, as well as private buyers and sellers, and to facilitate their opportunity to make a tax-deductible gift of one hundredth of one percent of the selling price of the property to the cause of homelessness. For example, a house sold for $300,000 (£150,000) would generate a donation of $30 (£15). With an average of 5.6 million homes bought and sold in America each year, the potential exists for hundreds of millions of otherwise inaccessible dollars to be willingly pledged to fight a widely acknowledged modern social plague.

The role of Push Open Doors will be to generate and encourage these donations by designing and executing a series of homelessness awareness campaigns targeting both real estate industry professionals and the public at large. It will also act as a liaison between the donation sources and the recipients of the funds.

It will be the responsibility of Push Open Doors to allocate the money pledged to highly respected, already existing homelessness assistance organizations, as well as to provide documentation to donors and potential donors regarding the projects funded by their contributions.

This project has the potential to circumvent common logistical barriers to the public financing of otherwise well-designed efforts to combat homelessness. It will act on the principle that many, if not most, people are willing and eager to contribute to such a cause, but usually lack an opportunity to do so that is both simple and convenient. By connecting the role of homeownership with acknowledgment of the reality of homelessness, Push Open Doors will provide that opportunity.

Jerice Bergstrom

→ **www.pushopendoors.org**

save lives with smart bricks

82

Combining sensory and communication technology in a simple household brick could be the key to making buildings safer and, ultimately, saving lives.

The so-called "smart brick," developed at the University of Illinois is fitted with sensory equipment, a transmitter, an antenna, and a battery, all of which work wirelessly. The brick is consequently able to monitor a building's vibrations, temperature, and overall movement.

This resulting information could be vital to firefighters trying to put out a fire, rescue workers checking the soundness of a structure, or scientists analyzing the results of earthquakes. The researchers also point out that the technology could, theoretically, be embedded in any number of different building materials, including concrete blocks and structural steel girders.

Chang Liu, one of the scientists behind the idea, hopes that it will transform the construction industry in the future: "We are living with more and more smart electronics all around us, but we still live and work in fairly dumb buildings. By making our buildings smarter, we can improve both our comfort and safety." To extend its battery life, the brick could be programmed to transmit building information intermittently, and could then be recharged as needed via a wall-mounted system.

Furthermore, as the technology develops further, the "smart" part of the brick could be constructed on a smaller scale, thus allowing its use in any number of other materials. Liu foresees a day when smart bricks are not only used to monitor nurseries, hospices, and daycare centers, but also fitted in toys and video games to provide greater interaction. The combination of advanced sensory capability and wireless communication technology has the potential to be used in a myriad of ways; the smart brick is just one of them.

→ **www.ece.uiuc.edu**

rent private homes
to help housing shortage

83

Amajor problem of council housing (state-funded housing) in the UK is providing temporary accommodation to those who need it. A shortage of available housing often means that tenants are housed in expensive bed-and-breakfasts. This situation often leads to unsuitable housing for tenants and unsustainable costs for the council.

Several councils in Cornwall have hit upon a simple solution: they rent flats or houses from private landlords, pay a prearranged rent, and house their tenants there. The council saves money, the tenant has a nicer home, and the private landlord has guaranteed income from a reliable source.

In addition to paying a prearranged rent, the council also guarantees that the flat or house will be returned in excellent condition at the end of the rental period and pays the rent even if there are no tenants in the property. Many private landlords are happy to receive rent at or below the market rate if it is assured in this way, especially as the council automatically repairs any damage to a property leased to one of its tenants. The agency at the forefront of the scheme, IPM in Truro, has more than half of their approximately 300 landlords presently utilizing the council option.

→ **www.ipm.uk.com**

erect an earthship
from recycled rubber

84

The Earthship, originally devised by Michael Reynolds and others in New Mexico, provides what could be a truly sustainable housing system for the future.

It is built primarily from discarded car tires filled and then "bermed" with earth, with non-load-bearing walls being built from a combination of tin cans, glass bottles, and cement. The main tire walls are not only strong enough to take the weight of the structure, but also create the thermal mass needed to keep the interior at a comfortable temperature in all seasons with no need for external heating or cooling. This is achieved through a cleverly angled south-facing window that receives, converts, and stores the maximum heat from the sun in winter, but minimizes the sunlight that is let through in the summer.

As well as solar heating, Earthships are also solar-powered (or with additional wind turbines where needed), use catchment systems to store rainwater for household use, and recycle their own gray water (from sinks, baths, and washing machines) for further use. They truly provide a model for sustainable housing and have been proven to work in various environments in the USA, Bolivia, Australia, Mexico, Japan, Canada, Honduras, and even Scotland.

The innovative aspect of the idea is its combination of existing renewable energy, recycling, and eco-building systems. The use of tires as a building material alone could have a huge impact; in the UK, there is a tire mountain growing at the rate of 40 million tires per year. Building 20,000 Earthships would use up the entire mountain. If those 20,000 homes—using no power from traditional sources—heat themselves, reuse and recycle much of the household water, and allow for growing plants and food inside, the potential for financial and environmental savings is obvious and substantial.

It is also worth noting that the method for building an Earthship has been deliberately developed and designed to make it possible for those with little or no construction experience to take on the task. Again, the emphasis is on reducing costs to society and to the individual: not contracting builders, using materials that are waste products, using the earth to keep temperature constant.

The Earthship is also about empowering homeowners. If they are involved in building it from the start, they will better understand how it functions and, in the future, better understand how to maintain and repair it. In this way, individual owners are made part of the sustainable lifestyle; they too are self-sufficient, just as the Earthship is.

The whole package is an inspiring one, and one that provides a model for truly sustainable living in this modern age. Combining ingenious design, common sense, and a return to nature, Earthships are also adaptable in size and shape, making them suitable for transference to many areas and climates of the world.

→ **www.earthship.org**

simulate slums
to spread awareness

A village designed to show the poverty-stricken housing and lifestyle of people in South America, Asia, India, and South Africa is on display for visitors to Americus, Georgia. The replicated "slums" are designed to show people how bad conditions of poverty are around the world and to inspire them to donate either time or money to this global problem.

Habitat for Humanity, with its new Discovery Center and Global Village, has built thirteen homes that span 6.5 acres to mirror the poor housing conditions of other countries. "If we can get people to think of the needs of those who live in poverty housing, then we are accomplishing one of our goals, which is to raise awareness," said Habitat spokeswoman

85

Barbara Webber. People who may never see the places in the world that need aid will get a chance to walk through the simulated land.

Since 1976, Habitat for Humanity International and its affiliates in more than 3,000 communities in 100 nations have built and sold more than 175,000 homes to partner families with no-profit, zero-interest mortgages. The houses are built by the prospective homeowners and volunteers under trained supervision, thus contributing "sweat equity." Financial support comes from individuals, companies, and other groups, and recycles money from mortgage payments to build more housing.

→ **www.habitat.org/gvdc/**

recycle trash
to build new homes

A project by an American designer and architect aims to prove that recycled materials can be used to build homes. Dan Phillips hopes to show that affordable housing for the poorer elements of society is achievable, and that costs can be kept to a minimum through salvage and reuse.

Phillips and his wife, Marsha, who run the Phoenix Commotion project in Texas have already built two homes from recycled building materials. Sources of material are various, including garage sale leftovers, individual donations, and even dumpsters. He estimates that

86

10 percent of landfill is building materials that could be reused, but salvageable waste is nearly impossible to recover once it reaches the landfill sites. By approaching building contractors, salvage contractors and others, material can be obtained to build houses. Phillips also uses an unskilled labor force on minimum wage, which he trains as they build. So, the project helps solve environmental, housing, and employment problems in a potent and unique combination.

→ **www.phoenixcommotion.com**

exchange your house
to cut your commute

87

In the current model of sprawling subur-bia and metroplexes, the daily commute becomes a wasteful and tiresome process for millions. This situation could be improved if people could trade houses in situ-ations where doing so would reduce the commute for both parties.

How about creating a city-funded website where this trade could be assisted? The data entered would include place of employment and home address, plus home value. The website could alert people for whom a comparable home is available that would improve their commute by at least 50 percent (or a figure of their choosing).

If both parties agree to the trade, they could apply for a tax-assisted home trade transac-tion where the closing costs and other fees would be minimized and a tax credit granted for the resulting reduction of strain on civil infra-structure and pollution.

Fred Becker

trade homes
for vacation swaps

88

More and more people are buying second homes in the country or pied-à-terres in cities, leaving others home-less and requiring the building of thousands more homes.

People who have moved to the country miss the culture of the city and people who live in the city yearn for fresh air now and then. Neither should have to buy a second home if they can join up to swap homes for the odd weekend.

A website could be created and managed in a similar way to vacation home exchange sites, but dedicated to this specific issue. If you always exchange with the same household, you build up trust and friendship and it is less stressful to prepare your home for the exchange. The website may not be as commercially viable as a vacation exchange site as once you have a partnership you no longer need to advertise, but if this was offered on a global scale it could be workable.

Bridget McKenzie

→ **www.homelink.org**

add art clause to builders' contracts to aid regeneration

89

An inner city regeneration project in Glasgow, Scotland, was revolutionized by a simple clause in the builders' contracts: 1 percent of the total construction costs must be set aside for art.

An idea that started in the US and has spread to Europe, the "percent for art" scheme has become an integral feature of the regeneration of the Gorbals estate in Glasgow. As well as raising the whole tone of the development, the artwork, which includes a four-storeyed photograph and a bronze sculpture weighing over a ton and a half, resulted in the development becoming more attractive to prospective purchasers.

There are problems with such an idea, including developers being put off by the cost or viewing it as something to consider when they have finished the rest of the building: the art is then added later as an afterthought. The key to the Gorbals project, though, was the involvement of the artists from the planning stage on. This meant that they worked alongside the architects, which allowed them to make the art more integral to the design of the whole development.

Already, further installations are planned for the next phase of development, including a conversation-producing computer, an inner-city orchard, and vast sculptures of birds. While it might not be appropriate for every new development to incorporate art, the cash for art clause could help to revitalize areas in need of imaginative regeneration.

blow up your home
for movie-makers' money

The wealthy owners of a Florida mansion have come up with a novel idea for having their unwanted house demolished: they are offering it to any film company that might want to have a house explode in one of their films.

The 38,000-square-foot (12,700-square-meter) property was being built by an heir to the Coca-Cola fortune, but was never finished. To save on demolition costs, Eric Cherry hopes to persuade a film company to do the work

90

for him. Some neighbors expressed concern about the effect such a blast might have on their own homes, but others showed little worry, saying, "It won't be atomic. There are people around here."

It seems unlikely that the trend will catch on, but there could be an unusual market emerging here: as well as house demolitions, cars going to scrap could be used by TV producers in need of cars to wreck in a chase scene. This is a no-lose situation for all concerned.

learn pattern language to create your community

91

A Pattern Language for community architecture was devised by Christopher Alexander in the late 1970s, in his book of the same name.

The book contains 253 patterns, each of which relates to a particular area of architecture and the solutions devised for it. For example, a house needs a method for people to go from the outside to the inside; different ways of doing this (or accumulated knowledge) are written up in the form of a pattern about entrance transitions. Through choosing from and linking these patterns, they can be combined to form a network or language for a particular building or project.

The simplicity of the procedure empowers communities to play an informed role in the design of their neighborhood. A community can put together a language including patterns about cars, parking, shared areas, and roof gardens in a way that fits their objectives and wishes. Rather than having a solution imposed on them by an architect, the vision comes from those who will use it in an organic way.

→ **www.patternlanguage.com**

help the homeless with a hotel-restaurant

92

This would be, quite simply, a restaurant with a hotel attached. People could live in the hotel rooms if they were willing to work in the restaurant or hotel, a willingness that would gain them approval. They could stay for up to six months, along with any dependents, and use the support of secure work and shelter to build for their future. Within the hotel, Alcoholics Anonymous meetings and other support networks could be made available to aid rehabilitation. The restaurant could earn its own money, and rent for the hotel room could come out of the residents' pay. Childcare and rehabilitation could be provided by trusted residents and also be paid for from the hotel rent. The restaurant–hotel model could thus provide a sustainable all-in-one-place solution for the homeless and jobless to start their reintegration into society.

Marvalee Vanderplas

support straw-bale building for greener future

Straw-bale housing has existed for more than a century in North America and was used by early settlers without conventional building materials to improvise shelter for themselves. After the 1930s such houses were rarely built, but the durable buildings provided inspiration in the 1970s for a worldwide resurgence of interest in the approach.

One of those who caught the bug was Briton Barbara Jones, founder of the women's building collective, Amazon Nails. For Jones, the appeal of straw-bale housing is not only that it is cheap, environmentally friendly, and flexible. The simplicity of the technique (there's no need for advanced construction expertise) is also, she says, a means of restoring people's creative connection with the place they dwell.

"Over the past decades people have become divorced from their own houses because someone else designs and builds them. Women in particular are at a disadvantage because the construction and

93

building trades are dominated by men. Straw-bale building changes all this," she says, explaining its popularity with women in particular.

Straw is a popular building material for several reasons, including its exceptional insulation quality (which reduces heating and cooling costs), the ease of its construction (which places building back in the hands of the owner/community), its structural stability, its natural soundproofing qualities, and, of course, its eco-friendly nature.

Indeed, not only is straw an annually renewable product, but using it in construction reduces the air pollution from farmers burning it, reduces the amount of wood needed for building, reduces the hazardous materials used in the building, and provides the farmer with additional income. It may be an old technique, but it is one that meets modern needs.

→ **http://mha-net.org/html/sblinks.htm**
→ **www.ironstraw.org**

settle down in a city in the sky

94

UK architect Lord Foster has put forth a vision for city housing in the future: whole towns of 55,000 people in tower blocks (high-rises) three times the size of Canary Wharf in London.

The massive skyscrapers would reach up to 2,600 feet (792 meters) and would be designed to be completely self-contained and self-sufficient. Thus, they would include schools, hospitals, cinemas, shops, and parks, while being powered by a combination of solar and wind power.

The "tower town" or "city in the sky" is proposed in response to the ever-growing challenge of housing an increasing population on decreasing amounts of land, particularly in urban areas. As well as including all the aforementioned amenities, Foster envisions the tower as having various different types of housing within it to cater to different incomes and needs.

The idea would aim to reproduce a normal community spread over land, incorporating small apartments for younger workers on low incomes right through to large, expansive properties for the super-rich. Architects and urban planners have been looking at a number of housing alternatives, with many holding the view that people will either have to live in smaller properties on the ground or, as this idea suggests, in the sky.

There are clear issues with such a town in a tower block, not the least of which is that evidence of the experiences of many residents in high-rise blocks from the 1960s and 1970s shows they often feel isolated and unhappy with their lot. In the post-9/11 world, huge new skyscrapers will inevitably also become a target for copycat terrorist attacks.

Nevertheless, there will have to be a radical change in urban housing in the future, and these giant tower cities could be one alternative worth pursuing.

Lord Foster certainly thinks so. He says: "The first city that puts up a really interesting and successful tall community is going to set a precedent. I predict that once it happens it will quickly spread to all the major cities throughout the world."

→ **www.greatbuildings.com**

protect tenants' deposits to dispel disputes

A government-funded initiative in the UK helps protect the deposits of tenants renting properties and helps resolve tenant–landlord disputes.

95

Under the Tenancy Deposit Scheme (TDS), landlords can either bank the deposit in a building society account or take out insurance guaranteeing repayment of the deposit should the the courts find against them in a dispute. The initiative was introduced because so many students and low-income tenants were losing out on their deposits unfairly: very few have the means to even argue the case, let alone pursue the matter through the courts. The TDS sets out to counter that trend.

The initiative gives landlords two options. First, the custodial option ensures the deposit is put into a special Nationwide Building Society account, overseen by the Independent Housing Ombudsman. If there is no dispute at the end of the tenancy, both the landlord (or the agent for the landlord) and the tenant sign the withdrawal form to release the money. The form instructs how it should be paid. Landlords can only order the money to be withdrawn under their own signature alone if they instruct that the tenant should receive the whole sum. If there is a dispute, there will be no payment until the court has made his decision. The Nationwide will then pay out the deposit in accordance with instructions. The interest gained by the deposits is then used toward the costs of the scheme.

The second choice for the landlord, the insured option, is to hold the money in a personal bank account. The landlord pays for insurance from the CGU Guarantee Society to ensure that the deposit will be repaid if there is a dispute and the Ombudsman finds in favor of the tenant. If there is no dispute, the landlord will keep or repay the deposit according to their agreement with the tenant. If there is a dispute and the Ombudsman decides partly or wholly in favor of the tenant, he will instruct the CGU Guarantee Society to make the repayment. The insurance company will then recover the money from the landlord.

Essentially, the scheme assures a fair and just system for both parties, and avoids the incessant and interminable squabbling over deposits that often occurs at the end of an antagonistic tenancy. This system is completely free for tenants and free for landlords choosing the custodial option. It is an idea that could prove useful in many areas of the world where deposit-based renting occurs.

→ **www.ihos.org.uk**

give tenants vacuum cleaners and vocational classes

96

John Lantz took over the 103-unit Shallowford Gardens Apartments, in Doraville, Georgia, in 1991. A lot of back rent was owed and a heroin dealer was using one unit as a base.

There were 77 vacancies at the end of 1992, and the turnover of tenants was high. Lantz told tenant Alice Markley, a certified teacher of English as a second language, that he believed people were behind on rent and moving out because "their emotional needs weren't being met." Most tenants were immigrants with little formal education or knowledge of English; half were Hispanic. After working long hours at factory, restaurant, and day labor jobs, they had little time for learning. They didn't speak with the owner about problems, lost jobs, late rent, broken faucets, or drug dealers.

Lantz asked Markley to teach English classes to residents four nights per week in exchange for a reduction in rent. Markley thought that Lantz "was nuts, or had some ulterior motive." And Lantz offered to build a community center, complete with classroom, if enough people signed up for classes. Markley says:

"This was not normal. No one who owns buildings in this neighborhood of poor whites and blacks and immigrants cares if their tenants are happy. They just want their rent on time."

Within two years of Lantz taking over, the building was waiting-list only. Tenants were happier, nobody moved out (unless they had to for jobs) and he got his rents on time.

Other simple actions, including installing a basketball net in the car park and purchasing a communal vacuum cleaner, only served to increase the change.

On Lantz's bookcase a sign reads, "Perform random acts of kindness." He has covered the word "random" and replaced it with "planned."

enjoy an eco-village experience

At Torup in the north of Zealand in Denmark, some 150 people inhabit an eco-village displaying some of the most striking and varied architecture anywhere in Scandinavia.

97

The founders' vision was to create "wholeness out of the split lifestyle of our time, by integrating dwellings, organic food production for self-sufficiency, and local business activity."

The eco-village group started planning in 1982. In 1988, they were able to buy Dyssekilde Farm on 32 acres (13 hectares) of land. Construction began in 1990.

The eco-village now consists of five groups of houses: the Dome group (of dome-shaped houses); Dysager (three hexagonal, individually designed houses, largely made of second-hand materials); Solpletten (three Folkesol houses, with six flats and two double houses, all designed to trap a maximum of solar heat); Yggdrasil (individually designed houses made of ecological building materials such as straw, timber, clay, and sea shells); and Höjager (a group of terraced houses).

Some houses are wholly owned by the occupants, while others belong to a cooperative association and still others are rented out. The old farm buildings are now used for communal activities as well as offices and guest rooms.

The village has its own biological wastewater cleaning system, which filters wastewater through a large earth mound before reuse on the land. Some 12 acres (5 hectares) of land are used for organic gardening and grazing sheep. There is also a 450kW wind turbine, which provides a substantial source of energy. All the houses also have active solar heating.

The eco-village is governed by meetings of all members, held four times a year. All members over eighteen must contribute 3,000 DKK (£240/$480) a year toward general expenses, and must do three to four hours' free work per week. For this, they receive vegetables for free, as well as the use of such facilities as the communal car and tandem bike.

→ **www.torup-by.dk**

gain control of your community through cooperative land banks

Cooperative Land Banks are a way to make all users of residential property the owners and controllers of their neighborhoods, whether in an industrialized society or in squatter settlements of an underdeveloped economy.

Each resident, besides a perpetual lease on a dwelling, acquires shares in the neighborhood. Both dwelling and shares can be freely sold, but the price of the shares (reflecting improvements in the neighborhood) are determined by the bank, thus enabling it to become self-financing and a provider of cheap or free land to low-income earners. This system is a form of social capitalism.

The Cooperative Land Bank structure has been incorporated in a pilot program initiated by the Land Commission of New South Wales in Australia to establish new self-help intentional communities to house people without assets or income. Supporters of the system believe that it provides a means for upgrading the extensive run-down areas in North American cities without the use of public funds. In countries with extensive public housing estates, the bank's structure enables self-management and privatization of housing estates.

The ability of a Cooperative Land Bank to make housing sites and services self-financing allows traditional banks to help upgrade squatter settlements. Because such a bank creates a grassroots self-governing precinct, it offers both political and financial advantages to sponsoring governments.

Over 80 percent of all housing in the world is constructed by the occupants and their families. The greatest problem in obtaining affordable housing, whether or not it is self-built, is obtaining suitable land. The more suitable the land in terms of access to income-producing activities, water, and other services, the more expensive it becomes. The effectiveness of a Cooperative Land Bank in making land self-financing increases as the value of land increases with its development.

As the value of land is typically around 30 percent of the cost of housing, this bank structure would provide a means for eliminating the deposit gap for housing everywhere. This benefit indicates how much more efficient it is compared with traditional land tenure systems; and more equitable too, as it eliminates the capture of "unearned" windfall gains in land values, a feature which substantially increases its economic efficiency.

Shann Turnbull

→ **www.iceclt.org/clt/index.html**

build green and benefit from a break

New York State has started offering a "green building credit" to developers to encourage them to build environmentally sound buildings.

The aim of the tax credit is to lay the foundation for a shift to environmentally progressive building materials and practices. By rewarding those developers who make commercial and residential buildings with better indoor air quality, and who use recycled and recyclable materials, the state hopes to start a movement in the industry itself.

To receive the tax credit, developers must meet certain criteria. In new buildings, for example, energy use cannot exceed 65 percent of use as permitted under the state's energy code; for rehabilitated buildings, the figure is 75 percent.

Having met these criteria, the developers can then claim back money per square foot for using environmentally preferable materials. They can also recoup 10 percent of the cost of ozone-friendly air conditioning, 30 percent of the cost of hydrogen fuel cells, and 100 percent of the cost of built-in solar photovoltaic (PV) panels. This encouragement of green behavior in the building world could be a keystone of a truly green economy.

The state of Maryland has since followed suit with similar legislation, while California's Emerging Renewables Rebate program offers incentives to consumers to install wind and solar power.

Similar initiatives are sweeping across Europe as well, as energy-efficient building becomes of primary concern. One of the most ambitious of these is the Spanish government's legislation that all new homes must include solar panels, a bold approach that could reap dividends in an oil-scarce world in the years ahead.

→ **www.dec.state.ny.us/website/ppu/grnbldg/**

turn lousy landlords into tenants

The idea is itself a cliché: a punishment to fit the crime. Yet innovative sentences are few and far-between in today's justice systems.

A landlord in Des Moines, Iowa, was on the receiving end of such a judgment when he was given the stark choice between going to jail and living in the apartment building that he had allowed to fall into disrepair.

The tenants had to live in apartments with mold, rats, and fire damage due to the landlord's neglect. So the judge offered him the choice, if he was unable to pay for the necessary repairs, of living in one of the units. He had to live there under home detention and

100

was electronically monitored until all the safety problems were fixed.

The judge took this unusual step because there had been no progress in correcting more than thirty serious health and safety violations. In the first six months of 2001, there were four fires at the complex, one of which completely destroyed the building's phone system. The situation had deteriorated to the point where many residents stopped paying rent as a protest. The residents, though they would prefer it hadn't reached this stage, feel the judge's decision is a fair one. As Tony Correia, a resident of the building, put it, "It'll give him a taste of what's going on."

choose a co-housing concept for communal living

Situated in the town of Birkerod, just north of Copenhagen, Denmark, Trudeslund's 33 residences and a large common house were completed in 1981.

The residences line two pedestrian streets, with the common house located at the highest point where the streets meet. With cars kept at the edge of the site and houses clustered

101

together, much of the lower end is left wooded, making it a favorite place for the children to play.

A cooperative store in the common house is stocked with household goods, from toothpaste to cornflakes. Each household has a key so that residents can pick up goods at any hour. They write down what they take in the account book and receive a bill at the end of the month. The store is run by one of nine "interest groups." Every adult is a member of one such group. Other interest groups are responsible for the outdoor areas, special children's activities, the monthly newsletter and minutes of meetings, the heating system, the laundry room, general maintenance, social events, and overall coordination of community activities.

When residents take the laundry out of one of the two communal washing machines, they put the next load in, so no one has to wait for an empty machine. Detergents are bought in bulk. Also located in the common house are a workshop, a darkroom for photography, a television room, a walk-in freezer, a guest room, a music room for teenagers, and a central computer connected to the personal computer in each home.

Many residents eat in the common house dining room three or four times a week, and have more intimate family dinners at home the other evenings. On any given evening, 50 percent of the residents, and often more, eat together. Two adults, assisted by one child, plan, shop, prepare, serve, and wash up after dinner. Each resident has to cook only once a month. Residents sign up for dinners at least two days in advance and pay for the meal after dinner, when the cooks have divided the cost by the number eating.

Two families share a car, five others own a sailboat together. There is only one lawn mower. Older kids keep an eye on the younger ones. Babysitters are never lacking. Afternoon tea after school provides a meeting place for both children and adults. As one Trudeslund resident put it: "I know I live in a community because on a Friday night it takes me 45 minutes and two beers to get from the parking lot to my front door."

At the outset, the group invited four firms to submit design proposals. Completion of construction came two and a half years after the first planning meeting. Half of the original members had dropped out. Now each resident owns a house and a portion of the common areas. Prices worked out as comparable to those for single-family residences in the surrounding area that have no common facilities. Resale value of Trudeslund houses has steadily climbed.

The co-housing concept continues to spread beyond Denmark's borders. In the UK, there are twelve or so groups in existence, while one of the first American communities was established in Davis, California, in 1991. San Francisco has since become something of a spiritual center for the co-housing movement in the United States, with some projects now on their second group of residents. Others in the area have waiting lists due to the movement's popularity.

→ **www.cohousingco.com**
→ **www.cohousing.org**

design a dollhouse
to encourage green goals

The Green Dollhouse Project is a competition to promote eco-friendly house building via an old childhood favorite—the doll's house.

The project invites submissions from design professionals and design students that inspire children and adults alike to make their homes greener and healthier. The project's objective is to elicit inventive doll-size buildings that can demystify the field of eco-building and encourage people to take simple steps themselves. The winning entries go on a tour of the US in various museums and venues.

The panel judges the entries based on two simple criteria: first, the doll's house must be

102

fun, functional, and creative (i.e., a real doll's house); second, the "completed dollhouse and design statement should teach children and adults about one or more aspects of green home building, and inspire them to do something now to make their own home a little greener."

These mini-projects could include, for example, energy efficiency, non-toxic building materials, water conservation, solar heating, and roof gardens. In future, submissions may be invited from members of the public. A grant might even be awarded to the winning entry.

→ **www.greendollhouse.org**

home in on a house that floats on floodwater

As countries become more and more densely populated and as climate change continues to raise sea levels and increase the likelihood of floods, housing has become a major problem. This is particularly true of a case in Holland, the most densely populated country in Europe, and also the most low-lying and at most risk of flooding.

A new project in the town of Maasbommel offers a solution to both these problems: houses that float up and down with the water levels. The new houses are midway between a normal house and a houseboat or floating home, as they are built on solid ground but designed to rise up and float on floodwater.

The homes, made by the Dura Vermeer Company, are made of a lightweight timber superstructure and a hollow concrete base to give it buoyancy.

The structure is fastened to 15-foot (4.5-meter) concrete piles that guide the concrete base when it moves up with flood water; all electrical wiring, water, and sewage is contained in flexible piping inside the mooring piles. In this way, the whole house can rise by up to 12 feet (3.5 meters) when floodwaters come, before returning to its original position when the flood has lessened. The houses are, essentially, a hi-tech version of the floating villages of Asia with added solidity and know-how; for example, they are also capable of storing floodwater for reuse.

Such housing could provide a real solution to the problems faced not only in Holland but also in other low-lying or sea-surrounded countries. Over a quarter of the UK is now thought to be prone to flooding, and more and more houses are being built near rivers or in coastal areas. Amphibious houses provide an innovative housing option that can respond to changes in climate and local environment, and that may be a much more common sight in years to come. The Dutch are already planning a floating town of 12,000 such homes near Amsterdam's Schiphol Airport, complete with floating schools, shops, hospitals, and libraries. Other towns and nations may soon follow suit, by choice or by necessity.

→ **www.duravermeer.nl**

103

restore properties and pride
with contemporary homesteading

104

A "homesteading" initiative spreading across the north of England may make it easier for people to purchase property and, simultaneously, to rejuvenate struggling urban communities.

In some urban areas, the council sells unwanted empty properties for half price with the condition that the buyers must spend half of that total on repairs over a two-year period. In other areas, homes have been sold for as little as 50p ($1) in return for commitments to renovating and converting the empty properties.

As well as allowing people on low incomes to buy their first property, the initiative also ensures that empty properties are filled, which tends to reduce criminal activity and vandalism.

Furthermore, the clauses in the contracts ensure that the houses are not only filled but also improved both aesthetically and structurally, lifting the whole atmosphere of the neighborhood.

In Sheffield, a young couple was able to buy a £24,000 ($48,000) house for £12,000 ($24,000), on the condition that they spent £6,000 ($12,000) over the following two years on new double-glazing, roof tiling, and other repairs. If that happens with five empty properties along a street, the growing problem of empty houses in that urban community will be reversed and the downward spiral of the area can be halted.

There has been a trend for homes in inner city areas to be standing vacant, particularly ones owned by local authorities. Up to 760,000 may be in this state in England alone. Vacant, boarded-up homes attract crime and vandalism, which drag the community's status downward, making the properties even more undesirable. This kind of project helps buck that trend and empowers young and low-income homebuyers, rather than leaving them at the mercy of landlords or property developers.

➜ **www.sheffield.gov.uk**

chapter 5

politics

transfer power to teens for political experiment

105

In a world in which apathy and disillusion rule, it is to future generations that we should turn. A direct and radical way to do so would be to hold a weeklong experiment in which politicians were replaced by their youth equivalents. For example, in the UK, the Chair of the UK Youth Parliament would hold the position of Prime Minister, while other representatives would take up their seats on the front bench. The same could apply for their Scottish and Welsh counterparts.

The intention is not for this to be an extended shadowing program, but a genuine transfer of power for a week, allowing the youths involved to make decisions, conduct debates, and so on (with the understanding, of course, that they could not take the country to war). This experiment could have two effects: a genuine feel for democratic politics and its workings for the youths, and a demonstration that young people are interested and involved if given power to change things.

post proposed bills for public perusal

106

Prospective (or existing) laws, constitutions, bills of rights, and charters should be publicly posted for discussion. The general public could then list reasons for believing they are good or not so good in columns provided alongside the documents. These reasons could then be reviewed to gauge whether the public thinks such measures are valid, feasible, and worth introducing, and what percentage of respondents supports their implementation. This concept could provide a simple, cost-effective exercise for all political parties to conduct research, and for the public to communicate their views and wishes outside of the traditional political system.

Michael Laub

pay politicians in proportion
to voters and votes

The public is regularly told that politi- **107** cians deserve high salaries because this encourages quality: you get the standard of people you are willing to pay for.

Given the laws of supply and demand, and given that we often seem to have more aspirant politicians then we want, perhaps we could use income as a performance incentive as it is in other walks of life?

Instead of being guaranteed a substantial starting wage, each elected representative would be guaranteed the average wage. This would then be added to in proportion to the number of votes they gained.

This could be calculated as a percentage related to, say, the average turnout or votes cast at the last four or five elections. This would effectively mean that their salary would be determined by how many votes they can get above that average. In countries where voting is voluntary, this would be a significant incentive to improve the voter turnout, and to work hard for their constituents.

The system could continue throughout the life of the government, with the salary going up or down based on a range of measures, which could include current approval rating, tasks performed, voting record, level of expenses, and so on. All of which would help shift the balance of power to the electorate, rather than the elected.

John Töns

use the drive-thru booth
for fast vote

To encourage more voter participa- **108** tion during elections, for which turnout is often very poor, local governments could institute drive-through voting. In this way, instead of fast food, you will be casting a fast vote.

give children the vote

109

The idea of giving the vote to people at birth has been considered for some years, most recently in Germany. Politicians are excited about the idea of sparking political interests among the young, as well as having some 14 million extra voters (people under the age of 18 account for 20 percent of the population). Under this particular proposal, parents would vote on behalf of their children up to the age of 18, with a further law ensuring that parents have to explain the various options to their children in order to give them an informed choice.

Antje Vollmer, a Green parliamentarian in Berlin, said, "This is no joke, because there are millions of little people living in our society today who often have more informed political views than adults, but who are currently being discriminated against simply on account of their age."

Many think that voting rights should include children, as it is they who will inherit the planet in the future. The argument goes that giving them the vote now would allow long-term perspectives to have more prevalence. At the very least, it would mean issues that interest and affect that part of the population would have greater prominence on the political agenda, be that greater investment in education, manifesto pledges on sustainability, or childcare improvements.

It should also be noted that children could bring a freshness and energy to political discussions, cutting through the jaded and cynical views of the current voting population, and therefore potentially reenergizing the whole process. Lest we forget, similar reasons were given in the past as to why women should not have the vote, and those reasons now seem archaic and ill advised.

combat voter apathy
with protest possibility

To help combat voter apathy, we should be able to vote for and against a party or candidate to provide a more representative and democratic result. Individual voters would still have only one vote but, for those to whom none of the parties appeal, the

110

vote against would allow them to express themselves in a way that would impact the result. The present system allows people only to abstain or to fill their ballot paper in incorrectly, which is, ultimately, a waste of a vote, rather than a true protest vote.

charge candidates for
mediocre motivation

The poor turnout at local and national elections in many countries is a scandal. Here is a way to encourage greater participation, especially among the young:

Whenever a local or general election is held, if the turnout is less than 75 percent of the electorate, the election must be rerun at the expense of those candidates who took part in the first place, and who clearly failed miserably to moti-

111

vate the voters. The costs of the rerun will be assigned in proportion to the votes cast. The procedure could be repeated at the discretion of the authorities as often as deemed necessary.

As a further test of the communication skills and veracity of the candidates, the votes of people under the age of 23 could count double.

Ben Nash

select sociocracy for governance by consent

112

Sociocracy was developed by a Quaker in the Netherlands and has since evolved into a full-fledged form of governance. Sociocracy is a theoretical system of government in which the interests of all members of society are served equally. It uses consent-based decision-making and minimal levels of hierarchy to achieve cohesiveness.

The four main principles used to form a sociocratic organization are:

1 Governance by Consent: The consent principle states that a decision can be made only when none of the circle members present has a reasoned, substantial objection to making the decision.

The consent principle is different from both "consensus" and "veto." With consensus the particpants must be in favor of the decision. With consent decision-making they must be not against it. With consensus a veto blocks the decision without an argument. With consent decision-making, opposition must always be supported by an argument. Not every decision requires consent, but consent must exist concerning an agreement to make decisions regularly through another method.

2 Circle Organization: The organization arranges for a decision-making structure, built from mutually double-linked circles, in which consent governs. This decision-making structure includes all members of the organization.

Each circle has its own aim, performs the three functions of directing, operating, and measuring (feedback), and also maintains its own memory system by means of integral education.

3 Double Linking: Coupling a circle with the next higher circle is handled through a double link. That is, at least two persons, the supervisor of the circle and at least one representative of the circle, belong to the next higher circle.

4 Elections by Consent: Choosing people for functions and/or responsibilities is done by consent after an open discussion. The discussion is important because it uncovers pertinent information about the members of the circle.

Ted Millich

→ **www.sociocracy.biz**

organize organizers
to serve, not govern

The central organizing institutions of every society are usually called its government. Is government the best name to have for central organizing institutions? I would argue not.

To govern means to control and limit. Do we really want our central organizing institutions to operate with a mentality that seeks to control, limit, and subjugate us? Again, I would say no.

There is an alternative to government, which we could call *servicement*. If people insisted on having their central organizing institutions called servicement, our representatives, senators, president, judges, and servicers (as opposed to governors) would be constantly reminded that voters want to be served and not governed.

Politicians would see that we do not want them bugging our homes and computers. It would also be made clear that we do not want to be dictated to in regards to our personal and private behaviors. In a servicement, too, officials would be better able to focus on deterring and punishing people who violate our persons or our property. This focus is achieved by eliminating attempts to control or govern non-malicious personal behaviors.

Scott Pleune

113

join the government of the moon republic

114

A potentially important and far-reaching idea is the concept of a free and sovereign government for the moon. This concept is being built into a working model by the Lunar Republic, which was formed by several groups involved in the commercial space industry who want to make sure that no individual earthly government takes control of the moon and its resources.

The project began with a distinctively American flavor, but has become more of an international issue. Elections for a democratic government are being held and local groups of Lunar Republic citizen partners have been formed in England, Germany, India, Japan, and Australia.

The Lunar Republic raises funds by selling properties on the moon, then investing the proceeds into private and public organizations that are working with them to make the goal of lunar colonization a reality.

John Hart Rodger

→ **www.lunarrepublic.com**

launch a lottery
for political power

115

Due to the way political systems work, the people who rise to positions of power as political representatives are often far from representative of their country's demographic profile.

There are far fewer women than is proportional, and a far from representative number of politicians from minorities. A simple way to overcome the many barriers that prevent these groups from rising to these positions would be to use a lottery to select representatives. Just as is the case for a jury, the body of people therefore elected would be both impartial and representative. There could be some additional clauses: people should have the right to turn down the job if they do not want it. There should also be some basic testing to ascertain that people are fit to do the job.

This approach has been suggested in the past for both US Congress and the UK House of Lords. Indeed, with reference to the latter, the Lords have been selected somewhat by lottery for many years, in the sense that they inherited their title or were awarded their position. This has been seen as a strong point, as few Lords are what could be called professional politicians. The lottery idea would simply take this idea to its natural conclusion. It could even be tied in to the particular country's lottery system, with a second draw each week resulting in a seat in the second chamber for the winner (and a limit of one ticket per person to prevent people bulk-buying).

Rule by lottery has worked in the past. In ancient Athens, the cradle of democracy, the day-to-day business of government was entrusted to the Council of Five Hundred, which was chosen annually out of the whole citizen body by lot. The only qualifications were that each winner had to be more than thirty years old and a citizen of good standing.

Similarly, the Talmud records that Moses used lots to choose the seventy elders of the Children of Israel and the 22,000 designated first-born. The ancients knew, observed the renowned classical scholar Jowett, that election by lot was the most democratic of all modes of appointment.

Daniel Lightman / Nicholas Albery / Brian Eno

allow citizens to make their own laws

116

Mike Gravel, a former US senator, has put forth a proposal that would allow American citizens to make laws directly, independent of their elected and appointed representatives.

Under the title National Initiative for Direct Democracy, the proposal includes a Direct Democracy Constitutional Amendment and a Direct Democracy Act. The former asserts the right of the American people to make laws using ballot initiatives, while the latter proposes a federal law to establish legislative procedures and an Electoral Trust to administer such law-creating initiatives. Collectively, these tenets would be known as the Legislature of the People, a supplement to the present representative government. In essence, this legislature would allow American citizens to put direct democracy into action and to introduce legislation in a deliberate and clear manner.

The process would be as follows:

→ An initiative is proposed for election either by referral from the legislature, citizen petition, or public opinion poll.

→ All corporations, unions, political action committees, and organizations are banned from contributing to campaign funding for or against an initiative; all campaign contributions will be fully disclosed and available as public records.

→ The initiative cannot be modified or blocked before being voted on, either by the legislature, the judiciary, or the executive, although they can advise on a law's constitutionality and suitability.

→ There will be a deliberative process of public hearings, public information, and findings from a randomly selected Deliberative Committee, to allow a full debate of the new initiative.

→ The proposed law is then voted on in a national election; if the majority votes for the new law, it is enacted.

This direct democracy is particularly sophisticated because of the safeguards it includes against exploitation by wealthy corporate interests, against undue influence from lobbyists, and against citizen ignorance and lack of understanding. All possible options are considered and there is a clear process along which each new initiative must pass. It is a system that others might want to consider, as flaws continue to be exposed in current democratic systems around the world.

→ **www.vote.org**

beat voter apathy
with beer and tax breaks

In the US and the UK there is a large problem of voter apathy and disillusionment with the electoral system. While there has been a myriad of suggestions to combat this, it is now clear that there is no cure-all solution. Rather, it may be wiser to introduce a number of measures designed to increase levels of voting. The six below are offered by Jay Walljasper, longtime editor of *Utne Reader*.

117

1 Free beer. Making it a social occasion for the community would encourage people to come out, meet up, and vote.

2 Election Day on the weekend. In the US, Election Day is always on Tuesday; in the UK, Thursday. If it was held instead on the weekend, or established as a national holiday, more people would be able to vote, especially if this measure was combined with Number 1 above.

3 Voter discounts. Another voting carrot could be discounts coupons from selected stores for those who have voted. Walljasper suggests that this be done with redeemable "I Voted" stickers, thus reinforcing the notion that voting is a positive action to be rewarded.

4 Free lottery tickets. An easily implemented incentive for voters: everyone who votes receives free entry into that week's national or state lottery.

5 Tax break for voters. A radical measure that may inspire those for whom money talks.

6 Fines for non-voters. A preferential approach to the oft-suggested legislation to make voting compulsory. It would instill the belief that voting is rewarding (financially, morally, and democratically) and that it is the right thing to do.

→ **www.utne.com**

improve your well-being
with direct democracy

118

Direct democracy and local autonomy could be important factors in people's happiness, according to economic research. Professors Bruno Frey and Alois Stutzer asked 6,000 Swiss citizens how satisfied they were with their lives. They discovered that those who lived in towns that were governed by direct democracy via budget voting and referenda felt generally happier. It appears as though individual well-being depends not only on personal circumstances and state of employment, but also on the type of democracy people live under.

Frey and Stutzer believe that the positive effect of local autonomy and direct democracy can be attributed to political outcomes being closer to voter preferences and to the perceived utility of participating politically. People value voting power, and anything that changes that power also changes their level of satisfaction to some extent. In the case of the Swiss people surveyed, for example, they were more content with a referendum system even if the result went against them.

→ **www.res.org.uk**

attach lie detectors
to public-speaking politicians

119

Politicians ought to wear lie detectors whenever they engage in political debates or speak in public. Since we have the technology, why not use it? Even if it does not stop all dishonesty, it will act like a speed camera on the road: people drive slowly knowing that they might get caught.

Michael Laub

meet the mayor
in a town center square

Ringerike, a municipality northwest of Oslo, is a quiet, unassuming area in Norway. But visit its regional capital, Hönefoss, on a Wednesday at lunchtime, and you will see radical politics in action.

At that time, the mayor of Ringerike sits down on a red bench in a central square for an hour and invites community members to talk to him. Mayor Kolbjörn Kvaerum believes so passionately about the importance of open dialogue with his people that he started up the novel scheme in August 1993, and it has continued ever since (come rain or shine). The mayor is rarely alone for long, and there have been times when people have had to queue in the square for their turn on the bench.

The open hour was originally held in an office, but the mayor soon decided that the square was a much better place to meet people, particularly as most people in the area cross the square fairly often. Ulla Nevestad, a

120

colleague in the neighboring municipality of Lier, followed Kvaerum's basic example, with the exception that she moves around, doing her bench sitting in different places each week. In 1999, as part of their attempt to radically decentralize, councilors in Oslo's Uranienborg–Majorstuen district began a similar project. In their scheme, inhabitants could meet politicians from their area on three days each week, and have a discussion on the bench. In the colder wintertime, these meetings simply switched indoors to the local library.

Such initiatives are simple but effective measures to open up local government to the people. Meeting their representatives in an open and informal setting can make such meetings more enjoyable and relaxed, and the bench can be a place where people can express both their problems and their ideas for improvement.

→ **www.ringerike.kommune.no**

volunteer your district
for social experimentation

121

Particular counties, townships and districts, college towns, small cities, and other identifiable jurisdictions within nations might, in the course of daily living, perform a distinct service to their own and other nations—and to themselves—by volunteering to explore the effects of various social, economic, and political arrangements, to be decided by consensus in local elections.

The national government would first hold a referendum or election to decide whether a two-thirds majority would like their area declared, for a set length of time (perhaps five to ten years) a Social and Political Experiment District (SPED). An adventurous and well-educated populace, such as a college town or a rural enclave of counter-culture types, might vote in favor of such an experiment.

Proposals for programs and experimental laws to explore in a SPED would be voted on three times: first, should a given idea be considered further? second, does the proposal need to present alternative versions? and third, should the final version of the proposal be accepted?

The benefits for SPED participants could include:

→ Tax relief from the central government in recognition of the risks residents would be taking;

→ Government start-up money for some of the innovative experiments;

→ Rotating heads of local government;

→ Prestige and a sense of increased group and personal meaningfulness, helping determine future trends in the larger society;

→ Benefits from particular experimental projects that work as intended.

Examples of projects that could be tried abound in the Institute's publications. Further possible examples include:

→ Car-free and car-limited regions;

→ Self-planned independent study programs in schools;

→ Basic income initiatives;

→ Weekly TV-free days;

→ Total redesign of street and other exteriors through massive public arts programs.

Gregory Wright

do your duty in a citizens' jury

122

Citizens' juries are an alternative way for considering policy ideas and options using a representative sample of voters from a particular area. Participants are briefed on the research and current thinking relating to a particular issue (such as transport) and then asked to discuss various solutions and ideas, a process that is sometimes televised.

The effectiveness of the system is that it involves citizens in real decision-making with access to all available information. The opinions expressed by such a jury can attract the attention of the legislative body and may carry greater weight, since they tend to be more representative than other groups.

The juries work as follows: between twelve and sixteen jurors are recruited randomly from various sectors of the community. They are fully briefed and meet key witnesses or experts. The jury then splits into smaller groups to study the information, cross-examine witnesses, and discuss different aspects of the issue. The smaller groups' findings are presented to the main jury and these conclusions are presented to the body that commissioned the jury in the first place. A unanimous verdict is not needed, nor must the proposals be binding. However, the commissioning body should publicize the jury's findings and respond to them within a given time, either by implementing the recommendations or by stating publicly the reasons for not following that course of action.

The jury model can be a powerful tool for consensus building and creating a better understanding between members of the public and decision makers. Citizen juries can be used not only by local or national government but also on a smaller scale by organizations. Studies show that the jury format appears to help participants take a broad, objective perspective, while many who take part continue to have an interest beyond the end of the session.

vote for victors' term time

The number of votes that are cast during an election should be represented by the length of time that the victorious party is in office.

123

The closer the vote between winner and first loser, the shorter the time before the next election. For example, if one party won 60 percent of the vote, it might receive three years in power, while the other main party, which received 40 percent, might serve one year in power.

The obvious downside to the system is that it might limit what the government could achieve, but there may be ways around this. Perhaps there were elements of each manifesto that were similar, ensuring continuity on these issues. Or, instead of time in power, the losing party could have the opportunity to pass one piece of legislation that has proven popular. The system might only come into play in the case of very close elections.

Kerry Brown

change capital city
to deter domination

The domination of the UK by London and its environs has long been considered something of a problem. Having one city completely dominating the economic, political, and cultural landscape is viewed as unhealthy by many commentators, with others observing that people now live in either London or the UK, as if the two were mutually exclusive. An old solution to this problem has been reconfigured for the 21st century by Paul Barker, who suggests moving the capital to a more central or northern location.

Originally suggested by *The Economist* in the 1960s, the idea aims to reduce the London-centric focus of the media, politicians, and businesses, thus spreading the benefits of those areas more equally across the country. The UK government has already given some measure of devolved power to Scotland and Wales, and is following that with possible elected mayors and regional authorities, but all this is centered around London, and its utter domination of the scene cannot be challenged unless government moves to another location.

The original proposal in the 1960s was for a city in Yorkshire called Elizabetha with a palace of Northminster and civil servants living in flats powered by wind turbines on the moors. The new capital, the place of government,

124

would not only cure any problems of over-centralization in London, but also boost the north of the country through its very existence. In his article, Paul Barker at first proposes an updated version of Elizabetha called Williamsburg, but eventually concludes that the best alternative to London is Manchester, with a media tradition, a successful airport, a regenerated city center and a definite independence from the southeast. He further suggests that the House of Lords could be relocated to Liverpool, with the House of Commons in Leeds. It is only another step on from here for the royal family to be housed in Lancaster or Skipton Castle.

Much of this is clearly tongue-in-cheek, but there is an important basis underlying these suggestions.

The fractured economy (the north–south divide) has also been the cause of much debate, with no amount of local initiatives making a real impact on the problem.

The American capital is not in New York; the Canadian capital is not Montreal or Toronto; the Australian government is not in Sydney; perhaps it will take something as radical as moving the UK government to address the regional splits that threaten its overall livelihood.

establish time limits
for political careers

125

Western democracies are staffed by career politicians. Since politicians enjoy a good income and often thrive on the power the job gives them, they are quite naturally fearful of making mistakes that could cost them their jobs. So often the main focus is on doing what it takes to stay in the job, rather than spending time thinking of ways to make a contribution.

If all politicians were limited to a maximum of ten years in a political career, perhaps it would change their mindset. At the end of that decade, they would not be eligible for re-election to any paid political office. To ease the transition, they would continue to be paid their salary for a brief period while they looked for alternative employment.

Ten years should be plenty of time for any politician to contribute to good governance, and this proposal might have the effect of making politicians more sensitive to the real purpose of government, beyond providing employment security.

John Töns

sponsor a ceremonial suit
to reveal political payments

126

An interesting and revelatory idea for politicians is the ceremonial sponsor suit. Patches and corporate logos of all his or her contributors would be affixed to the suit. The politicians would, as a result, resemble racing car drivers sporting chevrons of all their sponsors. This suit will be a visual representation of what truly lies behind the machinations of the political system.

The patches would be sized according to the percentage of each individual or corporate contribution. For example, if a corporation contributed 10 percent of the overall campaign fund, their logo would cover 10 percent of the politician's suit.

This might be viewed as a wild idea, but there is a serious side: imagine if the media had the chance to photograph each politician in their campaign finance suit each year. At one glance, the public could see who is really paying for political influence.

Patrick J. Therien

encourage e-government
with the e-vote

Every day our political representatives **127** pass new laws that directly affect lives. The public does not have any say on whether or not some of these new laws, or amendments to old laws, should be passed, although we have voted the representatives into place. Do we have a fully democratic system of governance in place when the only decisions we have a hand in are at times of election?

My proposal is to bring power back to people, so they can make a difference to the town they live in. There are too many laws going through each week for every one to be voted on by the general public. It would, however, be possible to prioritize certain papers into a category called Relevant Public Interest (RPI) and publish those entries for a local vote. For example, a paper encouraging new low-speed zones in all high-risk accident areas would be deemed high in RPI. Eligible voters would be able to vote electronically (with security in place) for or against the paper within seven days of it being published. People would enjoy seeing the outcome of the vote and knowing that they are making a difference to the world they live in.

Marlon Savin

review political decisions to improve future process

128

Central and local governments often reach decisions that in due course of time may appear to have been ill advised and therefore to vindicate opponents who had presented counter arguments. Insofar as there is any subsequent analysis of such an outcome, the politicians involved are usually treated as if they had simply been misguided or mistaken in their judgment rather than having deliberately ignored the public interest for baser reasons such as short-term electoral advantage. It is commonplace to view a regrettable decision as the consequence of an inevitably imperfect process. In effect, it is written off as a lost cause with nothing to learn about how to make such errors less likely to occur in future.

Could adopting a process of reappraising past decisions lead to making better current ones? One method might be to choose by public consultation or vote a limited number of key decisions on contentious issues reached in the past. An independent scrutiny panel would review the outcome of the original decision two, three, or four years later, as appropriate. Its aim would be to determine whether the outcome was as originally envisaged and whether the evidence previously presented had been fair, reliable, and objective. Resembling a small House Committee inquiry with all-party representation, it would also include some co-opted independent members with expertise in any critical aspects of its examination.

Such a procedure could represent an invaluable learning process for politicians, civil servants or council officers, and professional advisers as well as for the general public, especially those who represented opposing evidence and views on the issue under review. More optimistically, over time the experience should result in an improvement of both the process employed and the quality of decision-making.

There can be little doubt that possible reappraisal of contentious decisions at some time in the future could encourage those involved to take their responsibilities more seriously, especially with the prospect of critical media coverage. It could also promote presentation of more carefully prepared evidence from all the parties involved.

Mayer Hillman

appoint a government ethicist
to ensure laws are fair

129

People often find themselves confronted with situations that, though perfectly legal, are ethically suspect. People do not have redress if an action is legal: no democracy in the world has an independent person in place whose role it is to alert society to processes that may result in unjust outcomes.

Ethicists are most common in hospitals, where unpalatable choices have to be made. The role of the ethicist is to guide people through that process to arrive at a decision consistent with the goals of the hospital. Governments and bureaucracies have to make choices in accordance with the law and under that law the people have no redress.

The ethicist's role would be to help bureaucracies and governments to determine whether the processes they have put in place are fair. The ethicist can also comment on cases where the individual has been treated unjustly but where there are no remedies under existing laws.

John Töns

fax your MP
for free

130

People who have direct contact with their constituency Member of Parliament (MP) tend to be lobbyists, pressure groups, and those who can get time off work, but a new online innovation in the UK could change all that. The website WriteToThem.com uses a customized web-to-fax gateway to enable you to fax your questions or concerns direct to your own MP. The process is simple: type in your postcode (Zip code) to discover the name of your MP, enter your own details, write your letter, and then click to send the fax.

The website is run by a not-for-profit group of individuals who belong to no lobbying groups, no political parties. and will happily declare any interests if asked. Their aim is to allow constituents to make direct contact with the MP who is duty bound to represent them. This is in keeping with the Internet's rationale of broadening access and making contact easier, and the site itself is an example of technological democracy in action.

→ **www.WriteToThem.com**

be clever and work with a wisdom council

131

To establish a Wisdom Council, the citizens of a city, county, or state would pass the following resolution.

We, the People of [*fill blank*] resolve that:

→ Section 1: Every six months a group of sixteen registered voters shall be randomly selected and assembled to meet for one and a half days. Those who attend both days shall form a Citizens' Wisdom Council whose unanimous views are termed Statements of the People.

→ Section 2: The Citizens' Wisdom Council will present these Statements and how they were developed back to the people in a new ceremony. If possible, the ceremony and perhaps the meetings will be televised.

→ Section 3: Meeting facilitators shall assure that the conversation in the Citizens' Wisdom Council is collaborative, open-minded, and creative. In addition, they will assure that the views of each member are respected and help the group reach consensus. Facilitators shall not determine topics nor shall their personal views influence decisions.

→ Section 4: After the presentation, the [city, county, state] will support and encourage informal dialogues so that all citizens have an opportunity to meet with others and to consider and respond to the Statements. The Statements will be widely disseminated until the next Wisdom Council.

→ Section 5: A Wisdom Council Oversight Committee will assure the integrity of the process, hire facilitators, and provide expert information when requested.

→ Section 6: For deciding procedural issues within the Citizens' Wisdom Council, such as meeting times and agendas, a majority vote may be used.

Without challenging the existing structure of an organization, the Wisdom Council establishes a framework for creating a wise and responsible We the People.

It involves all people in a high-quality dialogue about the most important issues and, over a few cycles of the process, helps them reach consensus decisions on those issues. It does this through a briefly existing small-group process that resonates with the whole system. The small group selects the issues, addresses them in a thoughtful, heartfelt way, articulates consensus Statements, and presents the Statements to all the people. The resulting whole-system dialogue builds community and a powerful political will in the public interest.

Jim Rough

→ **www.wisedemocracy.org**

gear up for government gender balance

It is still rare in modern governments to achieve anything close to a gender balance. My suggestion is for a serious push to mentor and support the election of women in all levels of government, at a balance of 50 percent. It is my conviction that this would completely change the character of our culture and possibly result in an unprecedented era of peace and prosperity.

132

It can be argued that politicians are not inherently corrupt nor that the system is fatally flawed—it is simply grossly out of balance hormonally. This may not be the only cause, but a balance in attitude, expertise, and experience would be helpful. There is no more powerful unit than a marriage. Why not bring its good aspects to our government?

David Spensley

boost sustainability with world council broadcasts

The World Future Council is a body that aims to challenge the world community to inject long-term, ethically motivated thinking into today's actions. The Council, an independent body, aims to express our values as world citizens, rather than just as global consumers. The Council has been formed by the belief that, in today's world, there is no values vacuum, but rather that widely agreed values are not being acted upon.

We, the people, have the power to damage the planet and profoundly affect future generations, yet have thus far seemed incapable of dealing with the global and long-term impacts of our actions. The world's greatest problem is not poverty, environmental collapse, or terrorism, but the collective failure to respond to the great challenges of our time despite having the knowledge and power to do so.

The Council will be made up of a hundred globally recognized wise elders, pioneers, and youth leaders, who will work with decision-makers to provide direction for a sustainable future. In this way, the Council will address the important issues of the age by encouraging the implementation and enforcement of treaties and laws. It will do this primarily by considering and publicizing its proposals for action at annual meetings to be broadcast

133

throughout the world. These pronouncements alone will not be enough, so the Council will endeavor to influence policymakers and legislators in individual countries (and at global institutions).

In essence, the Council will attempt to represent the shared ethical values of citizens across the globe. In the future, it could be a new global network that can enhance the implementation of bold future concepts and its legitimacy and authority will grow as the years pass.

→ **www.worldfuturecouncil.org**

vote on values
but bet on beliefs

Robin Hanson proposes a form of government in which betting markets become our primary source on matters of fact. Such a futarchy would mean that democracy would decide what we want, while speculators would say how to get it. Or, more precisely, elected representatives would define and manage a measurement of national welfare, while market speculators would say which policies they expect would raise national welfare.

This idea rests on the evidence that shows betting markets as superior to academic-style institutions in aggregating and distributing knowledge on many important issues. In this way, betting markets could work in an advisory capacity for government policies. We could, for example, ask betting markets to estimate murder rates both conditional on passing gun control laws, and conditional on not passing gun control laws. If the markets estimate of murder rates was clearly higher given gun control than not, then that would argue against passing gun control laws. Similarly, markets could estimate student test scores given school vouchers, life spans given universal healthcare, or the chance of a war given a treaty. Betting markets can produce such conditional estimates

134

in several ways, including via called-off bets (bets that are called off if a condition is not met).

By way of substantiating these ideas, Hanson points to examples of betting markets doing better at predicting election results than opinion polls, and to betting markets beating official company forecasts of their own sales.

Ordinary people and governments alike could turn to betting markets to learn about political institutions and economic interventions and policies. To take this idea a step further would be to award betting markets a formal role in the democratic process. A betting market could estimate whether a proposed policy would increase national welfare by comparing two conditional estimates: national welfare conditional on the adoption of the proposed policy and national welfare conditional on non-adoption of the proposed policy. The basic rule of such a government would be that when a betting market estimates that a proposed policy would increase the national welfare (be it financial or otherwise), then that proposal becomes law. As Hanson puts it, "In futarchy, the public would vote on values, but bet on beliefs."

Robin Hanson

participate in a protest march
without moving a muscle

135

A protest march of those who could not demonstrate in the traditional manner took place online and via phone lines in the US.

The virtual march registered 400,000 people to participate in calling in their opposition to the authorities about the war in Iraq. The intention was to swamp telephone switchboards, fax machines, and e-mail boxes at the White House and the Senate, as a demonstration of the opposition to the war. This protest, conducted from homes and workplaces, allowed those who might be either unwilling or unable to physically demonstrate to play their part in getting the message across. Targeting the communications of Senators and officials also varies the line and tactic of the protests.

One Senator, Dianne Feinstein, said her office had received about 40,000 calls on the day of the protest, meaning she had to assign six people solely to answer calls. She added that "this was probably the highest number of phone calls we've gotten for anything."

Another estimate put the total number of calls and faxes at one million. Whether one agrees with the reason behind the protest or not, the method is extremely effective, forcing those in authority to register the disapproval of thousands of people, all on the same day. It shows the power of the Internet to draw people together for a cause and to organize them in coordinated action.

One of the organizing websites, MoveOn.org, is fast emerging as a powerful political force and continues to be at the forefront of demonstrations and protests outside the mainstream of political life. The virtual march can also be considered as an example of the smart mobs that Howard Rheingold has written about: a collective made up of people who have never met, brought together by new technology.

→ **www.MoveOn.org**

chapter 6

science and energy

publish negative results to pursue positive science

136

It is a well-known adage that people learn from their mistakes and, like all such phrases, it has a kernel of truth at its center. Scientists and researchers have been slow to take it on board, though, as negative results are rarely published in scientific journals.

Negative results at the end of a study may be disappointing, but they can add to the scientific world's knowledge of a particular subject. If such results remain unpublished, then future academics and researchers may waste time and money heading down the same path. Also, if journals do not publish research that has disproved commonly held hypotheses, then people will continue to believe them and even continue to base further research on them.

To counteract the problem, several journals have developed specifically to publish studies with negative results. Ideally, these publications will save individual researchers time and money in particular areas, and also foster a more generous attitude of collectivism among scientists: to acknowledge that successes and failures both contribute to a wider bank of knowledge.

The reasons behind not publishing negative studies vary, but often come down to pride and competitiveness. Scientists are unwilling to admit they have spent months (or even years) pursuing a hypothesis that turned out to be incorrect and they are also unwilling to share that information with other people in their field: their competitors.

Sharing their negative studies in a journal would thus be seen as giving away the advantage they have in knowing a particular idea doesn't work. In areas such as cancer research, however, there is something unpalatable about scientists not cooperating or allowing each other to waste valuable time. One journal, *Negative Observations in Genetic Oncology* (NOGO), simply asked cancer researchers to post gene mutations proven to have no association with cancer (i.e., negative results from cancer researchers) on its website, but few sent in their results.

The flipside of the argument for greater dissemination of negative results is that people may be deterred from pursuing a line that someone else has already proven to be unsuccessful. If a study found no link between cancer and mobile phone use, should that prevent others from continuing to pursue the hypothesis? Possibly not. But it will be easier to make that decision with all the results from the field of research at scientists' fingertips.

→ **www.path.jhu.edu/NOGO**
→ **www.jnrbm.com**

forecast fine times with aboriginal weather wisdom

137

Australia's Bureau of Meteorology decided to map Aboriginal knowledge and experience of the weather, in order to add to its own scientific understanding of the climate. The bureau set up a website on which it will post indigenous weather knowledge, such as the different Aboriginal seasons and traditional predictive signs. The intention is to widen the knowledge bank from which data is taken, to include not only the data from measurements, satellite readings, and experiments, but also data from the experience and observation of the indigenous people in the area. Rather than taking a purely scientific viewpoint, the bureau is acknowledging the validity of traditional knowledge passed on from generation to generation.

Different Aboriginal cultures divide the year from between two to six seasons, all founded on small signs perceived in the surrounding natural habitat. In addition to the six-season calendar, the Aborigines have a longer-term cycle view of the weather based on both 12-year and 10,000-year units. Weather is not viewed as a separate entity, but as being interconnected with people, animals, plants, the supernatural, and previous Aboriginal generations. This understanding is based heavily on watching for signs from plants around them.

The occurence of bushfires in Sydney was no surprise to them, because the queen wattle tree had bloomed heavily, which is a sign that bushfires are coming. Similarly, they do not blame global warming or El Niño for the weather extremes in Australia; rather, they see it as the result of the convergence of several climate cycles. Where this knowledge was previously passed down orally between generations, the new collaboration with the meteorology bureau will help to record their insights both for posterity and for current forecasting.

→ **www.bom.gov.au/iwk**

generate gym energy
for charity

People expend a lot of energy using the aerobic and weight machines in fitness clubs and health centers. These machines could be adapted to harness the energy generated, store it, and then use it later where necessary. Once the initial cost of upgrading the machines has been recouped, the gym will then be able to save money by providing some of its own electricity. A well-intentioned establishment could even decide to donate this saving to charity, perhaps with a system whereby gym members nominate the charities to which their exercise will contribute. This system would motivate the individual, provide great publicity for the gym, and help charitable causes.

138

A gym could be set up with this purpose specifically in mind, in which all the machines (exercise bikes, treadmills, and so on) are adapted in this way. The gym could then be offered at a low cost to the public or made available for schools to use, depending on how much electricity the outlet produced.

Hendrik / Dan Perkins / Julian

pedal to power up
your PC

139

As energy problems continue to occupy the world's greatest minds, there is an idea that could do the legwork for them. A bicycle-powered computer could be a hugely important invention.

As more and more people worldwide are seated in front of computers, so fewer and fewer receive any exercise through their profession. A simple pedal-dynamo system beneath the desk could enable employees to power their computers, desk lamps, and even printers and photocopiers. In bigger offices, there could be a central hub where all power generated is collated, before being distributed around the office where needed. The benefits would be threefold: exercise for sedentary workers, a reduction in pollution (through a reduction in power use from fossil fuels), and a cut in costs for the company.

And it need not stop there: why not have pedal-powered televisions and computers at home as well? As the amount of power needed to run these machines continues to lessen, it may be possible for an individual to power his own viewing time by pedaling. An added side benefit would be refuting accusations of being a couch potato. Any excess energy generated could be stored for future use or diverted to another part of the house.

Christopher Harris

welcome the win–win
wind farms

140

A win–win solution of two ecological problems is available to those countries surrounded by sea. The idea is to site wind farms out at sea, in areas that threatened fish species use for spawning. Siting wind farms away in the North Sea, for example, will prevent the common "not-in-my-backyard" complaints. The turbine supports can then provide a habitat and shelter for the fish, allowing them to aggregate. The wind farms would also define an area as out-of-bounds to any traveling vessels. Eventually, the adult fish will migrate and can be fished sustainably, while the electricity from the turbines can be transferred ashore via underwater cables.

Tom Pickerell

post scientific results on free-for-all website

141

In 2001, 17,000 scientists, including Nobel Laureates, vowed to boycott scientific journals unless they made old research papers available for inclusion in an Internet-based Public Library of Science (PLoS).

Michael Ashburner, a geneticist at Cambridge University, UK, said the online PLoS was essential for scientists to keep up with developments (the amount of scientific literature in genetics alone doubles every ten years). The PLoS would be like the GenBank, which makes DNA sequence information freely available.

The PLoS group asked scientific journals to make published papers freely available in the library six months after printing. The Proceedings of the National Academy of Sciences and the *British Medical Journal* plus five other journals signed up. In 2003, the organization set up an Internet-based peer-reviewed journal (*PLoS Biology*). It posts scientific research online for all. A second journal, *PloS Medicine*, followed in 2004.

→ **www.plos.org**

stand up to make science fun

142

Two Australian scientists have been doing stand-up comedy, believing that entertainment is an effective means of education. Karl Kruszelnicki and Adam Spencer, together known as the Sleek Geeks, say that comedy can increase people's knowledge on the subject, but is considerably more fun than a lecture.

They target people who have a sense of curiosity about the world, a curiosity that they can tap into by using humor. Sneaking in knowledge, and giving people facts to take with them after the show, is all part of the performance. As Karl says of their Mike the Headless Chicken sketch, in which they describe how a chicken lived for 18 months after decapitation (a true story), "What we are saying is 'Hey, it's about time you learned some neuroanatomy and neurophysiology.' But we don't put it that way."

→ **www.abc.net.au/sleekgeek**

hype up hydrogen
as energy and currency

It is becoming increasingly obvious that we need to become more far-sighted with respect to energy sourcing and distribution.

Many people are starting to recognize the pressing need for a transition to hydrogen as a primary energy source.

This suggestion takes that idea one stage further, proposing that the world economy be based on hydrogen and that all countries in the world should adopt a hydrogen-based monetary system.

This would free us from monetary systems that are bound up with oil and its distribution network, and ensure that the world moves more swiftly to renewable energy sources. Hydrogen could provide a way to organize human economic activity more justly than ever before.

A renewable energy unit could be created in the form of currency backed by stored hydrogen. Any individual, corporation, or government that generates hydrogen from renewable energy sources would, in that act, create backing for this new currency or credit.

The primary energy producers would become the creators of credit in a new, decentralized banking structure. Banking would essentially be the process of accounting for the production and use of hydrogen in the economy, which would define energy as the fundamental wealth in society. Such a system would also remove the government's ability to create money out of thin air by simply printing more of it.

Hydrogen currency, backed by stored, renewably produced hydrogen, would be circulated in the same way as currency is now. The value of these hydrogen units would rise and fall naturally with the amount of hydrogen that the primary producers in a society create, and the value of these units would ultimately be proportional to the production and service that results from the actual use of hydrogen by the society as an energy source.

At some point in the normal circulation of currency, some entity must actually purchase hydrogen for use as a fuel, and at that time the currency would be automatically consumed. That amount of the currency would be extinguished from the books, in the same way that credit issued by a federal bank is written off whenever a principal is paid off.

Dennis Spain

do try this
at home

144

Conducting scientific research at home has the ring of a past era, but Rupert Sheldrake has shown how the public can be involved in serious research; in fact, non-scientists doing experiments at home can make breakthroughs where science has failed.

Sheldrake has described experiments that could change our worldview. Each experiment covers an area conventional science considers taboo, such as telepathy and pets, and morphic resonance (a form of learning field that links all living things).

One experiment tests the belief that pets know when owners are about to return home. An observer remains at the home and notes when the pet behaves as if expecting its owner. The owner returns at unusual times. If the pet can still predict the arrival, the owner eliminates clues: using different transport, taking different routes and so on. Ordinary people can do this; positive results would upset assumptions basic to scientific research.

→ **www.sheldrake.org**

share inexplicable experiences
with scientists

145

Scientists often have unusual and transcendent experiences in the course of their work. But little is said in public about these experiences, for fear of being ridiculed by colleagues or damaging their career. The solution? A website has been set up to allow scientists to share their personal experiences safely and anonymously: a space that both scientists and the public can access.

The site, The Archives of Scientists' Transcendent Experiences, aims to change the culture of caution among scientists who have experiences they find difficult to explain. It is the work of Professor Charles Tart of the Institute of Transpersonal Psychology and the University of California, Davis. He believes that suppressing knowledge of encounters and experiences inhibits the development of a scientific understanding of such phenomena and the full spectrum of consciousness.

→ **www.issc-taste.org**

recycle space waste as protection

Through many space explorations, satellite launches, and orbiting modules, a huge amount of space waste has been left in the atmosphere.

One idea for processing the junk floating in space is to recycle it as a protective barrier for the International Space Station. Gathering up all the debris and directing it into orbit around the station could help provide an additional layer of protection against collisions with meteors and other debris and from cosmic rays and dust that could affect its internal workings. The accumulated junk could also be scavenged for useful spare parts, which might otherwise be difficult to obtain in space.

Whether recycling all of the debris into such a cosmic junkyard would appeal to the space organizations, which often spend billions on new equipment, is debatable. However, the thought of a cleaner, less cluttered flying environment may appeal, particularly in light of space shuttle crashes in the past, some of which were caused by small pieces of debris. Furthermore, as space travel becomes more accessible and more frequent, the need for a solution will continue to increase.

146

light up
the world

147

In a logical application of LED (light emitting diode) technology, the innovative Light Up The World foundation is introducing a sustainable, environmentally benign, and inexpensive way of delivering lighting to the developing world.

Canadian electrical engineer Dave Irvine-Halliday, founder of Light Up The World, designed clusters of diodes that represent a non fuel-based and extremely long-lasting light source (each device has the potential to last for 100,000 hours). This lifespan means that they are ideally suited to conditions in isolated rural villages for which a sustained electricity supply would be arduous to maintain. According to Light Up The World, the technology has the potential to illuminate an entire rural village with less energy than a single conventional 100-watt light bulb. And it is argued that just a single watt of energy is enough to produce a useful level of light via the technology. This single watt would yield enough brightness to allow a child to study at nighttime. The clean light source also promises to alleviate the ill-effects of burning fuels like kerosene, which is commonly used as a light substitute in electricity-poor regions, but which is also expensive and known to cause severe respiratory and eye problems when burned.

Nepal was a leading candidate for the illuminating enterprise, because only 200,000 of the 3.4 million households there possess the means to light up their properties in hours of darkness.

Dependent on two other components, the solid-state LED devices are run off rechargeable, maintenance-free batteries made energy-rich by renewable power sources set up by Light Up The World, using solar, wind, water, or pedal energy (depending on which is most abundant and suitable at the individual site). Once the means to create energy are installed the cost of maintenance is tiny, although there is a substantial initial cost involved.

Seven hundred homes, schools, and other community buildings in Nepal, India, and Sri Lanka were supplied with lighting through the program in 2001 alone, and the figure continues to grow with the help of monetary awards of recognition. The technology has a particularly resonant application in developing regions of the world, but Light Up The World has bigger plans for its clusters of high-brilliance white light. The organization's website states that solid-state diode technology has the potential to displace traditional lighting industries everywhere.

→ **www.lutw.org**

seek poetic responses
to scientific reports

148

On each occasion that the National Academy of Sciences (the institution created to advise Congress on scientific and technological matters) issues a report, a response should be solicited from the Academy of American Poets.

This check-and-balance process would help lawmakers and citizens examine the complex moral issues that science continually presents.

It would also introduce a non-partisan wisdom into political discourse, which could engage both the public and media on a different level than usual. A by-product of this idea would be a general elevation of the status of poetry in everyday life, giving it a more public role. The same idea could obviously be applied to equivalent organizations in other countries around the world.

offer old-timers an office
to give science a boost

149

Most scientists and intellectuals retire while they are still more than capable and willing to contribute to the development of knowledge for humanity. There are many more who become inactive through no choice of their own, and their accumulated knowledge and experience is also lost to the world. This situation led Farhang Sefidvash to propose a World Institute for Retired Scientists, a place where intellectuals could come to do whatever they wished, be that discussion of wild ideas, research on individual projects, writing articles, or teaching students. They would be provided with simple housing, office space,

and infrastructure for research, and they could stay as long as they wished.

The Institute was formally established by Dr. Sefidvash in 2001 with its headquarters in Rio Grande de Sul in Brazil. It is his hope that the institution will grow organically, and prove to be a world-changing place to visit and learn in the future. It will also allow those scientists who feel they have more to contribute, or who felt constrained by their previous research situations, to develop ideas and theories that could benefit us all.

→ **www.rcgg.ufrgs.br/wirs.htm**

turn the UN building into a source of solar power

150

Perhaps solar photovoltaic tiles could be applied to one of the flat and windowless sides of the United Nations building in New York. As well as supplying solar power for the landmark building, such an undertaking would also serve as a highly visible model for solar energy and its diverse usefulness. If one of the sides of the building faces south along New York's East River, it will be particularly suitable for solar power.

In addition, companies, organizations, nations, groups, and individual UN or solar-energy supporters across the world could contribute the tiles, singly or in blocks. Each contributor could then be given credit on a map of the wall displayed in the building's lobby, and an interactive map on a website with links to supporters' sites.

Another suggestion is to arrange the tiles in a suitable mural or pattern, such as a dove against a New York sky, the United Nations flag, or something similar. A competition could be held to come up with a suitable design. As an international landmark regularly shown on global news broadcasts and visited by international leaders and politicians, the UN building would be a wonderful place to signal the world community's commitment to sustainable technology and environmental issues.

Greg Wright

buy biodiesel to combat carbon emissions

151

Biodiesel fuel, made from recycled cooking oils, has gone on sale in some stations across the US.

It reduces emissions, recycles unwanted restaurant waste, and requires no alterations to any diesel vehicles built after 1986. Diesel fuel is known to be particularly smelly and polluting, so the introduction of this alternative is very welcome. The new yellow fuel gives off less noxious fumes with a slight smell of french fries, and although it doesn't reduce nitrogen oxides, it does substantially reduce carbon emissions.

One gas station in San Francisco is selling 100 percent biodiesel fuel made from soybean oil, a by-product of food processing. Already, recycling trucks, school buses, and the Department of Energy's own vehicle fleet are using the fuel, and many other environmentally minded people are expected to join them.

Biodiesel is more expensive, and it does reduce fuel economy slightly, but the costs are coming down year after year and the mileage can be improved by adding a small amount of petroleum diesel to the mix.

One station in Nevada has preempted this problem by selling a fuel that is 20 percent biodiesel and 80 percent petroleum diesel. This reduces the price and the economy problems, although the environmental benefits are obviously reduced to some extent as well.

Nevertheless, biodiesel does point a way forward for the future. As Jim Brandmueller, administrator of the Nevada State Energy Office, says, "By taking our waste cooking oil and turning it into biodiesel, we are not only cleaning up the air at a reasonable price, but also creating jobs."

Sales of the fuel are expected to grow massively in the next few years; the Department of Energy aims to replace 10 to 20 percent of petroleum diesel with biodiesel in the next twenty years.

As Teri Shore of environmental campaigners Bluewater Network puts it, "We've got to break our nation's dependence on foreign oil. We can use the vast source of soybeans and other fuel crops grown right here in the United States, and instead of mining in the Arctic National Wildlife Refuge, we can mine the nation's supplies of restaurant grease." Perhaps politicians will be funded by the biodiesel companies in the future.

→ **www.biodiesel.org**

go nuts for
renewable energy

152

Thousands of tons of macadamia nut shells are being used to fuel the world's first nut-run power station in Queensland, Australia, heralding the emergence of a new renewable energy resource.

In an inspired venture between Queensland state-owned Ergon Energy and macadamia nut producer Suncoast Gold Macadamia, it is hoped the 1.5 megawatt generator run purely on nut-power will reduce greenhouse gases by around 9,500 tonnes a year—the equivalent of relinquishing the emissions of 2,000 cars—while providing 1,200 homes with electricity.

Quantities of energy produced by the eco-conscious power plant are restricted only by how many macadamia nuts are eaten, and Suncoast Gold estimates current shell wastage at approximately 10,000 tons per year. Macadamia nuts are an extremely popular snack in Australia and New Zealand. Further collaborations with additional nut enterprises could perhaps boost sales. Possibilities for further production of renewable energy from various other unexpected sources are endless. This project could be replicated across a range of other industries, including peanut, timber, meat, wheat, and grain processing, where waste streams generate heat, electricity, and revenue, claims Kate Skilleter, Ergon Energy's retail general manager. Similar collaborations between energy and retail industries around the planet have the potential to reduce overall greenhouse emissions significantly, as well as lessen the current reliance on energy sources that will eventually run out. It seems that the macadamia is a small nut with a big future.

→ **www.goldmacs.com.au**

monitor your movements with a black box

153

A device has been developed for humans that is much like the flight recorder or black box used on planes; its purpose is to record information about physical health problems. Swapping mechanical data for biological data, this black box tracks a person's physiological functioning throughout his or her daily routine, providing valuable data to researchers monitoring how human bodies cope in extreme conditions.

The portable device, known as the C-POD, is simply strapped to the body and then monitors data on the person's heart performance, blood pressure, respiration, temperature, and the amount of oxygen in the blood stream. Professor Kovacs, who has been developing the C-POD at Stanford University, says that it is unique because it allows monitoring of the body without invasion of the body. Without tethering the person down, letting them go about their normal business, [it can] store data for eight hour periods for later downloading; alternatively, it can send it wirelessly, in real time, to some other device.

Initially intended to monitor astronauts in space, the C-POD also offers numerous benefits here on earth. Medical teams could benefit from this technology at the scene of an accident, gaining valuable information about a patient's condition. Firefighters' physical responses could be monitored when inside burning buildings. Physicians could use the C-POD to track a patient's reactions to a new procedure or drug. Athletes could track their physical exertion. Since the C-POD can be reconfigured, sensors could even be plugged in to track air pollution.

Kovacs and colleagues plan to further improve this device by adding software that can diagnose problems and analyze the massive amount of data the C-POD collects. The ultimate aim is to link the condition of the physical body to what a person was doing at a given time, information that could be of great use to medical professionals and researchers alike.

→ **http://science.nasa.gov**

vow to take science ethics seriously

Individual responsibility is a concept much bandied around, but not often adhered to. This is particularly the case in a world that makes hundreds of thousands of life-threatening weapons every year. One idea to change this is an oath for scientists, inventors, and engineers, in which the individual can commit to an ethical statement for life, similar to the Hippocratic Oath for doctors.

Scientists could follow Leonardo da Vinci's example: he stopped his work on submarines on the grounds that men had an evil nature and would practice assassination under the sea. Submarine warfare was thus postponed for 300 years by the actions of one man. Science is often viewed as a dispassionate search for knowledge, but an ethical component would be included in such an oath. The Global Ideas Bank's draft Hippocratic Oath for Scientists, Engineers, and Technologists is:

I vow to practice my profession with conscience and dignity;

I will strive to apply my skills only with the utmost respect for the well being of humanity, the Earth, and all its species;

I will not permit considerations of nationality, politics, prejudice, or material advancement to intervene between my work and this duty to present and future generations;

154

I make this Oath solemnly, freely, and upon my honor.

When the idea was launched, over a hundred eminent signatories were gathered, including 18 Nobel Laureates—the launch signatories were Professor Maurice Wilkins CBE FRS, Abdus Salam FRS, and Sir John Kendrew, the then President of the International Council of Scientific Unions. The wording of the Oath is, of course, very general and is applicable to thoughtful professionals of all sorts; it could simply provide a framework for more detailed codes of practice within particular disciplines.

What happens to those who obey the Oath, take a stand, and lose their jobs would have to be addressed, presumably with some kind of conscience insurance payment from a fund built up by contributors. Or alternative scientific institutes could be set up to provide jobs for those who find themselves in such situations. Eventually, such an Oath may help reduce the social standing of technologists working in armaments and similar areas—and, once aroused, social pressure is a powerful force. The long-term aim was for the Oath to become part of the graduation ceremony for students, with the reasoning that there is not much hope of converting the 50 percent of scientists already working for defense industries and who have

SCIENCE AND ENERGY **139**

families and mortgages to worry about, but it may be more possible to influence students in their choice of work at the outset of their careers.

Such an oath has emerged at some colleges—a simple pledge of social and environmental responsibility, which simply states:

I pledge to explore and take into account the social and environmental consequences of any job I consider and will try to improve these aspects of any organizations for which I work

The pledge idea, based at Manchester College in Indiana, involves the college seniors wearing a green ribbon on their graduation gowns as a public symbol of their support for the idea. Around half the graduates at Manchester wear the green ribbon at their graduation each year, and over a hundred other colleges have now taken up the idea.

→ **www.graduationpledge.org**

treat yourself (and the environment) to heat with wheat

In these times of global warming, environmental pollution, and the need to find fuel alternatives, the US and Canada are increasingly looking to grain-burning stoves and heaters for a solution. These biomass fuels (anything from cereal grains to fruit pips to wood pellets) are not only often cheaper, but also non-polluting, renewable, and non-explosive.

As oil prices continue to rise, such grain-burning could prove a swifter and more effective solution than any amount of drilling for oil in Alaska. The experience of those who already have the hardware in place is very positive. Dating back to 1994, families in Manitoba were reporting that their wheat-burning stoves offered the same heat efficiency as electricity, but at a fraction of the cost.

155

One New Hampshire couple, Dan and Barbara Burbank, changed from normal winter expenses of well over $1,000 (£500) of wood and oil to just $400 (£200) worth of wheat. The stoves also burn corn, rye, and wood pellets made from compacted sawdust. Most customers tend to be rural folk or farmers themselves, who may have stocks of wheat, corn, or wood waiting to be used.

Alternatives must be found, be they wheat-burning, corn-based ethanol, or some other mixture of wood or straw pellets. Although these renewable fuels may require a little more maintenance and storage capability, the pros appear to far outweigh the cons.

→ **www.cornburner.com**

uncover discoveries from every quarter

156

In an effort to combat public disillusionment with scientific research driven by business and government, Rupert Sheldrake proposed the creation of a National Discovery Center. The Center would receive 1 percent of the government's science budget to undertake research suggested by individuals and organizations outside the scientific establishment, in areas not currently being researched. He believes such a venture would increase public involvement in science, make it more interesting and relevant to the public, reduce the notion that science is only driven by money and business, and enable scientists to think more freely. These benefits would counteract the current situation in which research is often determined by science funding committees in the control of older scientists, government officials, and representatives of big business.

Sheldrake contends that the current system constrains scientists from undertaking radical research, or research outside the boundaries of what is considered useful or relevant. Much scientific research is led by what may get funding rather than by human imagination or innovation. In addition, the public's trust in science has been undermined greatly by health issues like mad cow disease and the triple vaccine for children, and by the involvement of big business private benefit, rather than the benefit of the public. Science is often perceived as aloof and divorced from people's concerns, interests, and curiosities.

A National Discovery Center would solicit submissions from individuals, schools, societies, and local groups on potential subjects for research, based on a list of broad areas in which grants were available. Proposals would be evaluated by experts, but the Center could be governed by a board with a wide range of interests (non-profits, amateur groups) to ensure a more open outlook. Such an organization, with its openness to public involvement and participation, would make scientific research more democratic, more accessible, and more closely aligned with public interests.

→ **www.sheldrake.org**

sponsor space tourism
and other goal-based research

157

Some people perceive fundamental flaws in the way governments fund research and development, in that some grant structures actually reward inaction (or continuation of research) rather than attaining a goal. Obviously, subjects need to be studied, conferences need to be held, research needs to be done, and theories need to be assessed. But achievements also need to be made. Giving prizes for finishing research and development, whether by developing a vaccine or a new product, might accelerate the process.

Indeed, if the prize were big enough, industry would put up money to get involved, as they would benefit from the successful technology. This change to the system could inspire performance, rather than process, as strong incentives would drive researchers to succeed.

One example of this inspiration is the independently funded X-prize, which offered $10 (£5) million to the first privately funded team to build and launch a spaceship able to carry three people to 100 kilometers (62 miles) in altitude, return safely to Earth, and repeat the feat within two weeks. The prize was founded in an effort to accelerate progress in the field of space tourism. In 2004, the prize was won, and at least one airline has since announced plans for a regular space jet in the future.

Perhaps other areas, such as medicine and renewable energy, would benefit from a similar approach.

→ **www.xprize.org**

join up with generalists to enhance expertise

158

The question of what contribution experts (specialists) and generalists in any profession (or discipline or knowledge domain) can make is a common one. Should our education system emphasize one or the other and at what point? Does a corporation or government rely on the opinions of only experts, or generalists as well?

Experts are the ones able to exclusively do the best possible job in any social setting, whether in science, technology, medicine, engineering, industry, business, administration, finance, investment, public/civil service, politics, and so on. No argument here: admittedly, there is no progress without experts in any field of endeavor where research, innovation, and development are undertaken.

However, there are unequivocal situations where advancement, or the discovery of alternatives, is only possible or likely through the involvement of generalists, in particular where a holistic or integrative approach is used. It is the generalist who can offer broad or even global viewpoints, perspectives, and contexts.

To help define whether an individual is an expert or generalist in a particular field, and to enable organizations to choose whom they want for a particular task, a simple idea could be implemented. Simply divide a person's abilities into various fields along a continuum or spectrum, and then use ratings in these areas to find a semi-quantitative measure of one person's expert-generalist makeup. Thus, a generalist's experience and abilities could be expressed as

→ science (4); writing and editing (3); philosophy (3); technology (2)

while a more narrowly trained expert's might be:

→ science (9); economics (2); writing and editing (1).

Through these simple tools, people could choose an individual in accordance with their needs. If they needed someone who combined a good knowledge of science with the ability to write articles, and the experience to base them on a solid philosophical and technological grounding, then the generalist would be best. For a pure research job, the expert would be best. Without the classifications above, however, an employer or organization might simply be looking at two individuals with the same science qualification.

Dr. Karl H. Wolf

chapter 7

war and peace

join the civilian peace service to control conflict

159

A group of UK organizations is proposing the creation of a UK civilian peace service. There is a constant call for trained civilian peace personnel, but no way of recruiting and training individuals, or of putting them in touch with the UN or the non-governmental organizations requiring help.

Military personnel are increasingly assigned to humanitarian functions that could be better handled by specialist civilian workers. Civilians can also provide training and advice on the ground to help overcome conflict, engaging with local communities and authorities in dialogue about peace and reconciliation.

The UN, the EU, and the Organization for Cooperation and Security in Europe (OSCE) have called on countries to provide civilian specialists in civil protection and conflict resolution. Other European countries, including Norway, Austria, the Netherlands, France, and Germany, have all established a civilian peace force. As independent intermediaries, separate from any government, civilian peace forces can be more easily accepted and, as a result, have more of an impact on situations on the ground.

→ **www.Peaceworkers.org.uk**

set up a peace party for political change

160

The wide-scale protests around the world against the war on Iraq demonstrated two things: first, the sheer scale of opposition, and second, the ineffectiveness of demonstrations in this context. Ultimately, despite the numbers involved, protesters achieved little: the war went ahead. What is needed is something to transform this negative demonstration (in that it was *against*

something) into a positive transformation (one that could change things). One idea might be to set up a political party, one that could exist in many different countries, and which goes under the banner of the Peace Party. If the Peace Party started to have an impact on national elections, the movement's effectiveness could become far greater.

Mohd Shamshul Othman

participate in
peace one day

161

September 21 marks the United Nations' Peace One Day event: 24 successive hours dedicated to the promotion of non-violence, advocated by political, cultural, and spiritual leaders all over the world. The day raises awareness of the unnecessary horrors of war and offers an opportunity for the people of the world to create a moment of global unity.

While influential world figures, including UN Secretary General Kofi Annan and the Dalai Lama, made Peace One Day possible, the original idea came from documentary filmmaker Jeremy Gilley, who used his filmic talent, along with three years of unflagging determination, to promote the mass support required to organize a worldwide commitment to 24 hours per year of unbroken peace.

Peace One Day started as a mission to lobby key individuals to build the case for a global ceasefire day, states Gilley, who traveled the world documenting troubled areas from Northern Ireland to Somalia. He recorded the journey with his video camera and used film footage, combined with his own passion and persistence, as leverage to convince those with power and influence to turn his vision of a global ceasefire day into reality. Finally, the filmmaker could claim to have the support of world leaders from every continent, and on September 7, 2001, a resolution for a day of non-violence was passed unanimously by the United Nations.

Peace One Day 2002 featured live music, multimedia, and speeches from key figures in the entertainment industry to spread the anti-violence message, and the annual event continues to raise awareness of the possibility of a peaceful planet, even if its brainchild himself admits that world peace may not happen in his generation.

While the idea of committing a day to a universally relevant cause is no new thing, the way Peace One Day came about makes the idea even more significant. When Gilley embarked on his journey, he was neither influential nor rich. As well as a brick in the house of world peace (to use Gilley's metaphor), the day's very existence serves to demonstrate what a focused mind and the simple tool of communication are capable of achieving on a global stage.

→ **www.peaceoneday.org**

call a halt to hostilities
by using the phone

Neighbors separated by a chasm of fear, Israeli and Palestinian citizens exasperated by chronic violence have been brought together in conversation: over the phone.

A telephone hotline linking the two sides of the Middle Eastern conflict is emerging as both a new front against the fighting and a route to simple human contact and conversation in distressed times. The idea comes from Natalia Wieseltier, an Israeli woman residing in Jerusalem, and is the result of a fortuitous accident—she dialed a wrong number and was connected to a Palestinian man who shared her aspirations for peace. Struck by the simplicity of the telephone interaction, she realized that there is nothing like a conversation between two people. Her image of uniting the minds of two cultures through fiber-optic cables came to fruition in September 2002 when the hotline was launched.

Wieseltier originally took the idea to the Forum for Bereaved Families for Peace, which brings together families from both sides, who have lost children to the conflict, but encourages an end to violence rather than revenge. With the help of Shmulik Cohen, a political campaign organizer, the Hello Peace hotline was established. It cost $125,000 (£62,500)

162

to set up and requires $1,000 (£500) a day to run. Callers can select the gender and age of a person with whom they would like to communicate and can either record a message and wait for a response or browse through submissions from other members.

Even the most casual visual contact between Israelis and Palestinians is treated with suspicion, which highlights the strengths of telecommunication in these circumstances. Those using the hotline can opt to remain anonymous, but the sheer numbers using the service—many thousands of conversations have occurred to date—point to a basic human need for communication across the divide, regardless of political pressures. "I just wanted to get to know my neighbors," was the poignant appeal of one young Palestinian man from Ramallah.

While the hotline encourages individuals to bond on a micro level, proponents understand that constitutional binding of Palestine and Israel on a macro scale is not something the innovation can easily achieve. Cohen, however, thinks the hotline would make an instant difference if the political leaders on both sides could listen in on their respective citizens and hear the voices of those who want peace.

→ **www.hellopeace.net**

create art
from arms

163

A project run by Christian Aid allows the citizens of Mozambique to hand in weapons in exchange for productive tools. No questions are asked about the origins of the weapons or even who owns them. What is received in return depends on the number, type, and functionality of the weapons, and on whether the person lives in an urban or rural area, but bicycles, hoes, sewing machines, construction tools, and school equipment have all been given in exchange. The majority of the arms are destroyed immediately after their collection, under strict safety conditions, but another innovative aspect has been added to the project in the last year or so: transforming some of the weapons into art.

The idea behind transforming some of the weapons into art is twofold: to publicize the project and Mozambiquan art throughout the world via exhibitions, and to promote a culture of peace. To see sculptured chairs, birds, and jazz instruments made from AK47s and ammunition has powerful symbolic significance: instruments of war have been rendered harmless by man's creativity and weapons have been permanently taken out of use by being changed into symbols of peace and unity.

→ **www.africaserver.nl**
→ **www.iansa.org**
→ **www.christian-aid.org.uk**

go to the top of the class
for peace promotion

164

My proposal is for a national and international league table of schools, where points are awarded to a school for its active participation in areas such as conflict resolution, reduction of violence and prejudice, uncovering the sources of harmful thought and behavior, teaching self-knowledge

through meditation and philosophical discourse, community projects involving pupils' families and wider social circle, and so on. This would be a school award initiative for excellence in the promotion of peaceful values among young people and their peers.

Matt Rhys-Roberts

address terrorist causes
with ten percent of G8 defense funds

For too long it has been assumed that opposition to the war on terror has been an unfounded voice in the dark. It has been seen more as a resistance to violence than a constructive solution. This idea puts forward not only an objection to the ongoing war on terror, but a credible alternative, which is firmly rooted in fact and tried and tested methods.

It would simply require a 10 percent diversion of G8 defense expenditure into a UN development program. This program would act impartially and independently to address the underlying causes of terror. Such a move constitutes a major shift in spending from reaction to prevention. Terrorism is a human affliction and the economic, religious, political, and social reasons behind terrorism must be addressed, rather than simply the end result. Micro-social issues that affect us all can lead to terrorism on a macro level. Simply treating terrorism with a heavy dose of bombing does not address its underlying causes or its capacity to regenerate. Prevention is better than retrospective treatment.

Dan Vockins

165

role-play conflicts for global solutions

166

All conflicts, whether on a small or a global scale, have similar characteristics and roles. One could say that they are classic plays—tragedies with comic elements—that are repeated throughout history, in families, tribes, communities, and nations.

My idea is to use a theatrical approach to the major conflicts affecting the world, by stimulating and encouraging everyone, including children (especially children) to put on plays and enact the roles of the adversaries and the role of observers.

Suppose that in classrooms and living rooms worldwide groups got together to enact a conflict, divided into three groups—the Blues, the Yellows, and the Observers (or representatives of real conflicts)—and improvised actions and dialogue. Observations and results would be collected and sent to a central database. This would yield a wealth of information and new approaches to solving the real conflict. The hope is this idea would spread around the globe and become a tradition.

Natalie d'Arbeloff

sow seeds for land mine detection

167

A private company in Copenhagen, Denmark, has created a genetically modified plant to detect land mines. Aresa Biodetection believes the detection plant may be ready in a few years.

The plant, a variation of thale cress, has been coded to change the color of its leaves to red when its roots touch the evaporating nitrogen dioxide (NO_2) from deteriorating mines underground, a process which takes three to five weeks. The plants could make land mines visible, and should reduce the dangers of both detection and death.

Over 100 million land mines remain in over 45 countries. Aresa's plans to spread seeds will enable ordinary people to detect land mines safely. The idea is still in development and Aresa, with the Institute of Molecular Biology at Copenhagen University, is seeking partners for further research and development.

→ **www.aresa.dk**

index each country's contributions to war and peace

168

The world needs a World Peace Index, similar in makeup to other indices such as the Human Development Index. This index will enable all people to see the contributions that individual countries are making to war (and peace) efforts. The Index could measure quantities like the amount of defense spending, number of conflicts, fatalities and injuries from conflicts, numbers of weapons of mass destruction and arms sold, counterbalanced by the number of peace programs, the advancement of conflict resolution, and peacekeeping work undertaken.

Ricky Chen

transform war zones into nature sanctuaries

169

The reconciliation between North and South Korea is an uplifting event, though the accord is fragile. A Korean-born entomologist, Ke Chung Kim, has long supported the creation of a peace park and wildlife preserve to transform the huge demilitarized zone between the two countries. He believes this will provide a fitting memorial to the dead and give the countries a chance to work together in creation not destruction.

The demilitarized zone is now a sanctuary for birds, mammals, fish, and plants wiped out elsewhere. The growth in South Korea's population has led to increased pollution and the destruction of habitats, while major deforestation in North Korea has caused flooding and soil erosion. The zone could restore an ecological balance in the area.

The sanctuary contains 1,200 different species of flowers, 83 species of fish (18 unique to the area), and two of the world's most endangered birds, the re-crowned and white-naped crane. So, a piece of land created by war is being used for the peaceful protection of rare native species and habitats, as well as for the peaceful reconciliation of the two Koreas: a blend of political and ecological harmony.

Border reserves have been established in other former war zones, such as the one between Costa Rica and Panama, so there is an established history of formalizing these accidental wildlife areas.

communicate city-to-city
to bypass bureaucracy

170

Where national governments remain in conflict, stalemated in failed negotiations, cities could become vehicles of hope, peace, and democracy.

This was eloquently proved in August 1999 when Athenians were so moved by television broadcasts of the devastating earthquake in Istanbul that they sent help and assistance to the afflicted, despite the deep-rooted antagonism between Turkey and Greece. Dimitris Arvamapoulos, mayor of Athens, went to Istanbul with a rescue team.

The next month, when an earthquake hit Greece, Mayor Ali Mufit Gurtuna of Istanbul paid a reciprocal supportive visit to Greece. Athens and Istanbul effectively bypassed the mutually distrustful state machineries of their countries and forged a hopeful alliance. This alliance, Arvamapoulos suggests, led Greece to drop its objection to Turkish EU membership.

This model of direct and unmediated ties between cities could lead to effective solutions for those who suffer from intense regional and ethnic conflicts.

Cities could cooperate with each other directly to solve shared problems of crime, drugs, unemployment, pollution, and illegal migration—bypassing nation states and their bureaucracy.

The rapid pace of globalization has failed to serve a growing number of the industrialized subproletariat in the great cities of Third World countries. They feel that national governments cannot provide them with basic necessities. Perhaps direct and local democracy could open up avenues for more pragmatic solutions. As nation states weaken and distrust with establishments (be they corporate, military, or national) grows, then city-to-city, people-to-people communication can be a powerful tool for shaping progressive accords.

balance the bills
for UN dues

171

My suggestion is that nations should be assessed to pay their United Nations peacekeeping dues in direct proportion to their exports of weapons and firepower.

Gregory Wright

journalists to join in conflict resolution

172

Dudley Weeks, a conflict resolution expert, has drawn attention to the role journalists might play in conflict resolution, utilizing their central and independent position.

His proposal is to make this potential more widely known and formalized by encouraging the media to tell the whole story, not only what has happened and what is currently happening, but also what might happen (which would encompass conflict resolution possibilities). Focusing solely on the causes of the conflict and the actions that ensure it continues, is not, in this wider sense, telling the whole story: the common ground between sides and the connections that can be found should not be ignored.

Weeks suggests a number of ways in which the current divisive approach can be altered. These include changes in interview technique, so that questions designed to enlarge and broaden the picture are included, rather than questions that focus only on the negativity between sides. For example, simply asking the question, "Have you had any cooperative dealings with the other party?" or "Are there any needs that you share with the other party?" can open up an entirely different area of understanding. Similar questions are asked by conflict resolution facilitators and mediators and, while Weeks does not suggest journalists fulfill their roles, he does state that they could adopt some of their questions and learn from such techniques. After all, a facilitator aims to get to the bottom of the problem and understand the issues in totality and from all sides: a journalist who aims to do the same would surely be a good one.

Dudley Weeks says: "Are these legitimate questions for a journalist to ask? I believe so. I ask such questions as part of a process that empowers conflict parties to discover together additional action steps for dealing effectively and in a sustainable manner with a conflict and improving the overall relationship. A journalist asks such questions as part of uncovering the complete story as a basis for telling the complete story. That is responsible journalism, not conflict resolution journalism."

→ **www.dudleyweeks.com**

debate potential conflict in the press

173

In many wars, the general public in the combatant countries did not have accessible in-depth perspective on the conflict as it developed in both countries. As an aid to understanding, the Security Council of the United Nations could require and finance both parties to an imminent conflict to place full-page advertisements in the main newspapers of both sides and other principal newspapers globally, stating their position in numbered points. Each side would then have to respond to these point-by-point in a second series of advertisements, with a final third advertisement responding to the reply. Then, so far as reason has a part to play in this sphere, it should be clearer to the general public and to world opinion which side has the better case.

Nicholas Albery

support sporting spirit to promote truce during olympic games

174

The Olympic Truce, an initiative started by the International Olympic committee in 1992, offers inspiration to leaders from around the world. Based on the truce of ancient Athens, the agreement is that for the duration of the Games, all global conflicts cease.

The Truce became the first resolution endorsed by all members of the United Nations in 2003. Through its connection with the Games, the message of peace reaches almost four billion people every two years in the winter and summer. Through its alliance with sports, it promotes values necessary for peaceful co-existence, such as respect and healthy competition.

This inspiring idea has already had many positive effects: leading to a ceasefire in Bosnia to enable medical relief; promoting solidarity between North and South Korea; causing a pause in bombing in Iraq in 1998; and obtaining a pledge by African leaders to halt hostilities in 2000.

Even though the truce only lasts for sixteen days at a time, it can nevertheless provide a respite, a time of peace, and the possibility of reflection for the warring parties.

→ **www.olympictruce.org**
→ **www.demos.co.uk/16days**

rely on remote cameras for virtual peacekeeping

175

In order to use the capabilities of Internet video technology fully, virtual peacekeeping could be put in place with cameras and monitoring rooms taking the place of armed forces. Whereas traditional peacekeeping has tended to have a token neutral force placed between the two warring parties as a symbolic buffer, virtual peacekeeping would use sealed remote transmitting cameras powered by solar cells to monitor a demilitarized zone.

The camera transmissions would be encrypted and checked and monitored to prevent spoofing or interference. The video could be transmitted anywhere it was desired, from a newsroom to a UN monitoring center. If anyone or anything wandered into the demilitarized zone, people would know instantly and be able to respond appropriately. Destroying the cameras or tampering with them would be considered a hostile action, just as an attack on a traditional peacekeeping force would be.

Clearly, there are difficulties with this idea, since most people are more likely to do harm to inanimate equipment than to actual human beings. Furthermore, some of the areas where the technology would be required would be extremely remote, making the employment and upkeep of any such equipment a problem.

Nevertheless, it may not be long before we see protest groups and campaigning minorities utilizing such technology to highlight their selected concerns, thus putting a check on any authorities who are thinking of clamping down on such activities. Virtual peacekeeping might not be far behind.

use conflict barometer to warn of war

176

A research team in America has developed a conflict barometer, which could provide early warnings of countries approaching civil war. Using a computer system that analyses and categorizes news stories, the inventors claim that they can predict when regimes and governments are nearing a fall. This barometer could enable other nations of the world to monitor those situations earlier than when they might otherwise do so, thus allowing for some peaceful (or other) intervention to avert an internal war. The barometer could also be used to forecast the collapse of threatened currencies, as the factors that lead to civil war are also substantially similar to those that lead to economic collapse (indeed, the two often go hand-in-hand).

The computer is fed with thousands of Reuters' news stories, which it then separates into approximately two hundred categories. From that point, Craig Jenkins and Doug Bond, of Ohio State and Harvard universities, calculate how many events involve civil protests, how many involve government repression, and how many involve violent outbreaks. These three factors are then entered into an equation that gives a result called a conflict carrying capacity (CCC). A national

CCC of 100 equals complete stability, while a CCC of zero equals complete chaos. If the figure remains below 85 percent for a number of months, there could well be a crisis in gestation.

Although the barometer is yet to be proven by any recent events, researchers have gone back and looked at ten years' worth of CCC levels for a number of countries. They found that their barometer would have predicted civil wars in Algeria and Sri Lanka more than six months ahead of them taking place. Equally, the system can chart a country's return to stability from civil strife. The Swiss Peace Foundation, meanwhile, uses the measuring system as a way of identifying countries whose currencies are at risk, thus demonstrating its usefulness in a number of areas. Although it is essentially a form of close observation of events, the conflict barometer speeds up the process (no human could process news stories as quickly as the computer does) and provides a figure that can be traced and tracked over a number of months and years.

→ **www.hiik.de**
→ **www.ngpsp.org**

swap citizenship for military service

177

In some nations, citizens are required to serve compulsory military service. This is deemed necessary to provide a cost-effective yet strong army to safeguard national security.

The author suggests an alternative to governments that still choose to maintain military service but do not wish to force their citizens to do time in the armed forces. Instead, the government could offer a military service for citizenship program.

This program would mean that anyone can bring as many family members as they choose into the country, provided that he or she serves at least five years of service per individual (up to the retirement age of the army). The family member must also give up all citizenships in any other country, effective immediately on entry.

Meanwhile, any citizen who wants to serve in any of the security services can still apply.

Eric Chen Yixiong

elect a peace prize panel for reconciliation

178

A panel akin to the South African Truth and Reconciliation system would benefit the world as a whole. An International Truth and Reconciliation panel would comprise (or be elected from) all currently living Nobel Peace Prize laureates, to ensure a sufficient mix in the political spectrum to avoid the risk of one-way thinking.

Such a panel would enable western countries to listen to the perspectives of countries of the developing world with the aim of learning about crises that have emerged there, without resorting to bloodshed or punishing the innocent through sanctions first.

The panel could also provide a forum for individual countries to resolve their own long-standing issues and conflicts, as occurred in South Africa.

Burt Kempner

ward off war through three steps

Our objective is not only to avoid conflicts before they become a problem, but also to ensure that if they do need to be settled by a form of competition, which war inevitably is, such competition would be a non-lethal game.

179

Avoiding war in this way would be a three-step process:

1 All countries must receive and pass a resolution class. This class would be run by a global council other than one from the United Nations. Not only would there be a governing body of counselors, but each nation would be mandated to have their own body of counselors that have graduated with a world resolution degree. These people would advise their leader in all aspects of world resolution, no matter the form of government or political ideologies. For example, if a dictatorship were instituted, the leader would not hold power over the counseling body; they would be on equal terms. Education is the most important long-term method for preventing conflicts, so conflict resolution would be a mandatory class throughout even the early years of school.

2 If the countries do not succeed internally with conflict resolution, then the countries must meet with the global committee. It is the job of the global committee to find equal ground without forcing the issue, and then provide an unbiased perspective. The global community would not represent individual countries; they would be a separate group, controlled by no other formal power.

3 Human nature makes conflict resolution difficult because of the passion of either side. In the event that both of the previous steps do not work, the countries will be allowed to go to war—a virtual reality war. It is the common man that dies on the battlefield or carries out the orders of leaders, and because of this it would be necessary to eliminate the middleman. The generals of the warring nations would show up at the world resolution headquarters and hook themselves up to the computer to fight a virtual war.

These changes (the education system, the global committee, the virtual conflict scenarios) would require a culture shift to support them, a world government to enforce them, and money to fund them, which could easily come from the amount saved on military and defense spending.

Jared and Kristen, Elon University

calculate terrorist data
to reveal violators

180

This idea is for the creation of a website called terrorismscorecard.org. Now that terrorism is on everybody's mind, it presents us with an opportunity to focus that attention toward ending terrorist policies (terrorism being defined here as political violence targeting civilians). The website would list terrorism-related data by country.

Data organized into a scrollable chart might include: financial backers of terrorism, arms suppliers, training, numbers of civilians killed, and so on. The data would put the present narrow discussion into a much broader context, revealing those countries which, though ostensibly fighting terrorism, actually contribute to or back terrorist groups. Other data included might be the aims of the terrorists and their backers, as well as current international efforts to end terrorist attacks.

Such data would reveal all of the countries that have been violating international laws against terrorism for years. Such a sight would lead to greater awareness of the inconsistency of some stated aims and actual policies, and would compel policymakers across the globe to live by the same rules they are demanding of others.

Todd Putnam

let letters
build bridges

181

Teachers in Western and Middle Eastern countries should organize children to become pen pals with each other. Lack of understanding is usually the basis of prejudice and hatred. If children come to realize, through writing to one another, that they are actually very similar, the other will be demystified. This is important, particularly in the United States and Arab countries, because the message children are receiving from their leaders right now is that people on the opposite side are inherently evil and are to be hated and feared.

Humanizing and personalizing these issues will work to overcome that paradigm, and direct correspondence is the simplest way of doing so.

Jennifer Scott

chapter 8

welfare

make music in unlikely places

182

I have taught cello for several years and wanted to find ways to boost the interest and progress of my students. At the end of a semester, I usually require that each student gives a public performance of some kind.

Ordinarily this might involve inviting all the students to my home and having them play for each other and their parents and siblings, and then a little reception afterward.

Or individual students might find their own venue for a concert, such as renting out a recital hall. It is hard to find audiences for such recitals. And in my experience, within certain sectors of society there are lots of people who for one reason or another would love to attend music recitals but cannot get out to do so.

I decided to require my students to arrange recitals at places where people were unlikely to be able to get out to enjoy a recital elsewhere. These locations included such places as nursing homes, hospitals, homeless shelters, and orphanages.

This idea helped bring about three things I thought were important:

1 It gave my students a venue for their musical performances to take place.

2 It gave musical enjoyment to people who were not able to go to concerts on their own.

3 It gave my students some experience in arranging concerts for themselves, which will be a valuable asset for them in the future, whether they eventually become professional musicians or apply their entrepreneurial experience to other endeavors.

Dianne Betkowski

give a glow-worm
a glimmer of hope

183

Families in the Italian city of Padua were asked to take reformed (and reforming) prostitutes into their homes as part of a campaign to help the young women rebuild their lives. Councilors in the city hoped that the initiative, called Adopt-a-Glow-worm (glow-worm means "loose girl" in Italian slang), would provide additional support toward reintegrating the women into society. Two human rights organizations helped prepare families for their new members, and the families also received significant support from the local authorities.

The initiative is an innovative approach to tackling the problem of prostitution, which is substantial in Italy: over 70,000 prostitutes are thought to live there, and 40 percent of those are underage. Giving them a home and a support network could very well help them find a permanent way off the streets.

let orphaned children
pick unplaced pets

184

The overcrowding of animal shelters is a pressing problem. Dogs and cats die everyday because there isn't enough room for them in the facilities and there aren't enough people coming in to adopt the animals. An uplifting solution would be for the shelters to provide loving pets to local foster families and orphanages, free of charge, to provide the children with love and support.

Both cats and dogs could be spayed or neutered for free as most adopted animals are, thanks to government funding and veterinary cooperation. Food and additional veterinary care could also be provided by the kind cooperation of companies, donors, veterinary offices, and government funding. The overwhelming cost of owning a pet would be significantly lessened so the orphanages and foster families could care for the pets.

The health and social benefits of pets on children are well documented: children with pets enjoy an improved resistance to disease and a primed immune system. Children receive love and self-esteem from caring for the pet that provide increased security.

Diane Dallos

police the mentally ill
with a holistic approach

In San Rafael, California, a policeman who is also a psychologist started a project called the Mental Health Liaison Program (MHLP). Joel Fay decided that the majority of his police work actually involved the use of psychology, rather than self-defense or chasing criminals down the street.

185

He noticed that a significant number of mentally ill people were having difficulty with the police. To address the problem of such people being arrested for minor crimes, placed in jail, taken off medication, and subsequently released again, Officer Fay went back to school to study psychology. He then founded the MHLP, which brings together law enforcement professionals and representatives from homeless and mental health agencies. Cases are studied on an individual basis by the MHLP team and decisions made on the best course of action. The team meets the following month to evaluate individual progress.

Officer Fay found that the collaboration process helped both camps find a middle ground. Previously, police were keen to deal with problems quickly, while the mental health agencies took a more considered approach, weighing the information available. Now that the two have started to work together, effective action is taken quickly, but not at the expense of specific options for each individual. Thus, for example, a mentally ill homeless man could be jailed for a few days to get him off illicit drugs before being treated with medication and assigned to an outreach program. Later, he can be helped to find permanent housing where his treatment can be monitored.

Thus far, none of the individuals integrated into housing and treatment have been rearrested, and the team has a 50 percent success rate in getting individual cases off the street. The police department in Marin County, which includes San Rafael, believes in the success of the program to the extent that it is giving 15 percent of its officers 40 hours of training to enable them to make general diagnoses about mentally ill people, and two additional officers will be sent to study for advanced degrees in psychology. The key has been cooperation across normal lines of involvement and a willingness not to prejudge any particular cases. The MHLP sets an example others could easily follow.

→ **www.srpd.org**

donate unused loyalty card points to causes

186

Much is wasted when people lose, don't use, or discard receipts in supermarkets offering storecard points. Why not implement a charity-loyalty card program?

→ Potential points that go unused could be collected on the store's charities card.

→ Such cards collect sums from purchases under the nominated cost of one point, cumulatively.

→ Points can be accounted per valid period and converted to vouchers or money.

→ This money will be given to nominated charities on a rotation basis.

→ The government can be approached to back the idea publicly.

→ The money donated is offset as a tax loss as it gains no interest.

Some places offer this option (in Canada, for example, the Hudson Bay Company has a store points donation program), but many places still do not, and supermarkets seem to be an obvious place for such an initiative. People could also choose to donate receipts, rather than having the points put on their own card.

K.D. Beheshtian

auction your personal skills for charity

187

An Auction of Promises is a novel fundraising technique that involves auctioning services and goods promised by members of a community.

The services and goods are priceless in the sense that they cannot normally be bought. For example, an English village church raised £1,537 ($3,000) for repairs, with promises including knitting a child's jumper (£5/$10), and two nights' baby or granny sitting (£20/$40). Larger charities have made the idea work on a grander scale. At Sotheby's, an auction in aid of the Samaritans included a guided tour of the Houses of Parliament, conducted by Baroness Thatcher.

The beauty of these auctions is that they create money from services people can provide free. Also, as the promises are fulfilled in the subsequent months, it can help to bring the members of the community closer together.

→ **www.globalideasbank.org/site/store**

make community service compulsory for graduation

188

There have been many suggestions to incorporate community (or voluntary) service into the educative process over the years. These have ranged from providing community service as a replacement for tuition fees to each student providing 320 hours of volunteer work every year. An element of community service has been mandatory in many American schools for several years, but this suggestion aims to take the idea to the next level: making community service a mandatory prerequisite for graduation from high school. Thus, students would have to complete a set number of hours in order to receive their diploma. As well as making a positive contribution to their particular community and the projects within it, students would also gain a wider view of the world, build their self-esteem, and possibly even gain insight into deciding on a career.

Another suggestion is that such a program will connect students to their community and give them the leadership skills needed to become actively involved in the future. With all students across the country doing compulsory community service for four or five years of their school career, the possibilities for change are significant: the extra hours put in by such numbers could well make a noticeable difference to many community projects and programs. Community service could also be a way of paying partial or total tuition fees at higher educational establishments.

If implemented, hundreds of thousands of students who would never have chosen to do community service would experience and learn a great deal from it, be that new skills, increased self-esteem, a broader perspective, or a view on their individual future. Many of these same students would not have chosen to perform community service, but many will be glad they did. That in itself may justify the introduction of such a law.

Garrett Breitbarth / Christy Gordon

get smart and
help the homeless

189

StreetSmart is a fundraising charity that raises money for homeless projects in UK cities by adding a voluntary £1 ($2) to the bill at participating restaurants during the months of November and December. At the end of each month, the restaurant passes the total money raised to the charity, which then distributes it to reputable homeless charities in that city.

The aim is to make it easy for people to help the homeless in their city, by giving them the option to add a small amount to a bill for a meal. Since the charity's administration and operational costs are all covered by sponsors, the donated money goes directly to helping the homeless.

The charity runs the initiative in November and December because it is during the winter months that homeless projects need the most support; the run-up to Christmas also often results in an upsurge in the number of people eating at restaurants. In 2002, the charity raised over £300,000 ($600,000) in 11 cities in the UK. It is trying to add new cities each year, and to add new restaurants willing to participate.

Over the four years it has been operating, StreetSmart has found that most customers are happy to pay the additional £1 ($2) after tax and service, with only 1 percent declining to participate. It has also found that normal tipping is not affected by the initiative, so restaurant staff members do not suffer from the charity's gain.

→ **www.StreetSmart.org.uk**

put fridges
in public places

190

Large self-service refrigerators could be installed in public places for homeless people to use to store items of food during the summer months. In a manner similar to lockers used at sports centers, users could be allocated closeable compartments within the fridge, fitted with a key they would keep. The food would thus be safe from theft and putrefaction.

David Bullock

bank on your baby
being safe

191

Desperate mothers who do not want to keep their babies can drop them off at the bank—the baby bank, that is—rather than dumping them in rivers or in garbage dumps. Thus the baby's life is saved while the mother's anonymity is maintained.

SterniParks, a charitable organization, created a system for mothers to drop babies through a 12- by 28-inch (30- by 70-cm) slot at a kindergarten next door to the New Apostolic church on Goethestrasse, Hamburg. The baby drops just a short way onto a soft heated bed, triggering an alarm at a nearby hospital. A video camera is trained on the bed so staff can keep watch on the infant until a nurse picks up the child. No attempt is made to identify or prosecute the mother. The abandoned children are given necessary medical care and held for two months, in case the mother should change her mind. The babies are then placed for adoption or foster care.

The first baby was deposited into the hatch at the baby bank by a teenage mother in Hamburg in June 2000. Nurses at the center named the two-day-old baby girl Ronja. The baby's arrival was not announced until after allowing the mother eight weeks to change her mind.

The baby bank in Hamburg is now at the center of a nationwide movement in Germany, with new banks now open in Munich, Leipzig, and Berlin. Similar banks have been opened in Palermo, Budapest, and Johannesburg. And while the system still has its critics, there is no doubt that it continues to save babies' lives.

Parents in the US who do not want to keep their babies can now leave them at a staffed hospital or fire station. In over 40 states, there is a safe haven law with a no questions asked policy for mothers or fathers who want to give up their newborn child. Instead of abandoning the baby somewhere else, they can safely bring him or her to either of these facilities to be cared for and adopted.

Although the grace period for leaving a child varies from state to state, it seems a better alternative for panicked parents who may otherwise leave their baby in a dumpster or on a doorstep to die of exposure.

→ **www.saveabandonedbabies.org**

break jail cycle
with self-build village

In Portland, Oregon, a novel village for the homeless is helping to break the cycle of jail–shelter–streets–jail.

192

In cities like Portland, shelters provide a necessary but flawed service: three out of four people seeking shelter cannot be accommodated, and space is allocated randomly or on a first-come-first-served basis. Job interviews and housing applications are not high on the agenda, nor often even possible. The village may change all this. The community, comprising about 60 people at any one time, is self-governing, with rules made by consensus, and has a strict drug-and-alcohol ban on the premises. Residents build their own shelters, with volunteer help, using donated and recycled material. There are unofficial systems to help people find jobs and places to live. Five hundred ex-village residents have found jobs and apartments so far.

The key to the village's success, says founder Ibrahim Mubarek, is that everyone has to pull their weight, which encourages the growth of self-reliance and self-respect. Now a permanent site is possible, as the council is helping in a pilot project.

→ **www.dignityvillage.org**

put a potato in a sock
for warmth and food

In the winter months, the homeless suffer greatly, particularly in countries where winter is severe: warmth and sustenance are equally hard to come by.

193

A charity in Toronto, Canada, has devised a novel solution: it gives baked potatoes in socks to homeless people to keep them warm and, when the warmth wears off, to feed them. In Toronto, temperatures fall as low as minus 40 degrees, and fifteen people die yearly from exposure. Ve'ahavta, the organization behind the Potato Tikun Olan program, says the potato–sock keeps sleeping bags warm for five hours, and pockets for about three. The potatoes then provide a good source of fiber, potassium, and energy.

→ **www.veahavta.org**

call a cab for help
with domestic violence

194

Cab drivers have been selected to offer help to victims of domestic violence, under a project backed by the UK government.

Women fleeing from violent husbands or partners tend to open up more in the back of a taxi than they would do normally: the anonymity of a cab serves as something of a modern-day confessional. A taxi is often the first port of call for a woman trying to get away from domestic abuse, and this makes the initiative all the more important. Taxi drivers may be trained in lending a sympathetic ear. Taxi receipts will carry helpline numbers for domestic violence, and advertisements with further information will be located on the tip-up seats in the back of the cab.

Domestic violence accounts for a quarter of all violent crimes in the UK, and two women die as a result of it each week. It is estimated that the annual economic cost of domestic violence in London alone is over £250 ($500) million, when court time, working days lost, and everything else is included; the emotional and psychological cost to families is incalculable. This initiative could get help to the victims more quickly by providing support in an unexpected way, although it is not meant to replace the professional services already in existence.

In a striking parallel to the UK project, San Francisco social workers and prosecutors have enlisted hairdressers to help women suffering from domestic abuse. As with cab drivers, hairdressers are another sector of the population with whom people often talk more openly. Therefore, they hear stories that even the victims' families and friends may not be aware of. Hairdressers are also in a position in which they can spot bruising or other signs of assault to the face or neck. As a result, officials in San Francisco have begun training hairdressers to look out for these signs of abuse, to offer carefully considered counseling and, when appropriate, to encourage women to report crimes or go to shelters for help.

As with cab drivers, there is a risk because these are not trained professionals, but if they act subtly to provide information and motivation, authorities believe they could make a real difference in helping abate one of the most underreported crimes. It is a measure of how difficult domestic violence is to tackle that legal agencies and social workers are looking at these kinds of radical, unorthodox projects.

→ **www.womenandequalityunit.gov.uk**
→ **www.cutitout.org**

join the brunch bunch
to halt hunger

A restaurant owner in Boston, US, holds a monthly brunch in which all the proceeds are donated to hunger-alleviating organizations.

195

The project has been such a success (raising $30,000 [£15,000] in its first year) that Frank Bell co-opted seven local restaurant owners to the initiative and this alliance (known as The Greater Table) now runs an annual weekend of brunches in which more than sixty restaurants participate. It is a simple idea and a neat one: a business that profits from people's desire for food gives something back to people who need food, but can't afford it.

The Super Hunger Brunch, as it is now known, works with three main hunger charities: the Greater Boston Food Bank, OXFAM America, and Share Our Strength. For three hours on each day of the chosen weekend, a representative of one of these organizations collects the payment for the brunch direct from the customer (generally $20–60/£10–30). The restaurants provide everything for free for a number of reasons. First, publicity. Second, the project often brings new customers who may return. Third, many food and drink suppliers donate their wares especially for the brunch, and staff members often volunteer their time.

→ **www.GBFB.org**
→ **www.Strength.org**

secure change
for charity

I n airports, we are asked to empty our pockets of metal objects before going through security. This often results in passengers holding a handful of change, providing the perfect opportunity for charitable giving.

196

At each security line, there could be a collection device where people could put their spare change while emptying pockets. The collection could be regularly emptied and given to local charities.

As well as raising money for charity, this would give the ever-more strenuous and lengthy airport security procedures a positive spin.

Gary Emenitove

save lives and landfill
by donating your phone

197

A not-for-profit organization is collecting unused and unwanted mobile phones in order to give them to domestic violence victims across the US.

A mobile phone is one of the most powerful tools in the fight against domestic violence, providing as it does the means for abuse victims to get instant help and support. As part of the Donate-a-Phone program, the phones are cleared and pre-programmed to dial 911, a hotline, or the number of a local domestic violence shelter. Free emergency airtime is donated by the Cellular Telecommunications and Internet Association, so no one who donates a phone has to pay for any calls.

It has been estimated that there are more than 24 million inactive phones in the US, due to the rapid changes in technology. As new technology comes on the market, users simply buy a new phone and either throw the old phone away or store it. Donate-a-Phone puts these old phones to better use and combines the need to help others with the need to recycle. Even phones that no longer work can be donated, either to be repaired or to be sold to raise funds for other domestic violence charities.

→ **www.wirelessfoundation.org/index.cfm**
→ **www.fonebak.com**

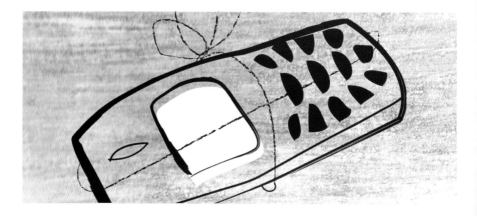

give homeless voicemail
for messages of hope

198

In Seattle, Washington, a non-profit group has provided free voicemail boxes for homeless people.

A person living on the street can get a private phone number and leave a personal greeting on the answerphone, so that potential employers responding to his or her calls can leave messages. For homeless people looking for work, this service overcomes what has been a big problem in the past: the inability of a potential employer to reach them, except perhaps at chaotic shelters.

The Community Voice Mail program goes from strength to strength. Thousands of people across the US have regained their dignity, by being able to send and receive messages about employment possibilities. There are now over 40 other cities with the voicemail systems, serving almost 50,000 people each year.

The French charity Emmaus has taken this idea to the logical next stage, by providing e-mail accounts and Internet space to homeless people. Their dedicated centers can help with technology training, as well as keeping people in touch with friends and family, and aiding their search for work.

→ **www.cvm.org**
→ **www.emmaus-france.org**

ramble with refugees
to aid integration

199

Rambling, or country walking, has emerged as an innovative way to integrate refugees into their new communities.

Because walks are informal and cost little, they provide an excellent way for newcomers to the country to meet people from their locality and to get to know them better. The branch of the National Ramblers' Association in the UK that is dedicated to this innovative venture is run on a small budget, mainly with the help of volunteers. It targets families who come from war-torn countries including Iran, Somalia, and Kosovo to three areas of the country.

→ **www.ramblers.org.uk**

create community corps
to boost the neighborhood

200

A neighborhood volunteer corps made up of youths, at-home parents, retired people, and anyone else who could give some time could coordinate activities to benefit the neighborhood, perform community service and, most important of all, have a great time together.

Imagine a neighborhood that works and plays together, in which every child has a mentor, no elderly person ever eats alone, and litter is picked up by the local walking group.

Classes could be taught and more ambitious neighborhood beautification projects undertaken. Providing companionship and support to those who need it most in the community would be at the center of the corps' work, from childcare help to grocery shopping trips. This simple idea could transform neighborhoods into extended families and bring back a sense of community. Indeed, it would make neighborhoods into communities.

G. Terrance Curry

support safer sex
with condoms in cabs

201

A Norwegian taxi firm, in collaboration with the local health authority, has been handing out free condoms to any client of any age who asks, and many have been taking up the opportunity.

In two weeks, 300 condoms were given out from the firm's twenty taxis, thanks to a sign on the back of the front seat reading, "Forgot condom? Ask the driver!" The Norwegian health authorities, who came up with the idea, decided

that taxis could play a part in the safer-sex drive they were undertaking in an effort to reduce the number of unwanted pregnancies and cases of sexually transmitted diseases. Jon Hilmar Iversen, promotions director with the health authority, said, "We want to give easy access to condoms to people where they are when they need it. Taxis are the perfect place, and the Norwegian public has not been shy in using the service."

log on for lowdown on multicultural help

202

A website at the cutting edge of multi-lingual technology is providing information and advice to minority communities in the UK on a range of key issues.

The Multikulti website provides culturally appropriate, accurately translated information on issues such as debt, housing, immigration, benefits, and employment. It hopes to widen access to such information for minority groups in the UK whose written English is limited.

Currently, the website provides information in Albanian, Arabic, Bengali, Chinese, English, Farsi, French, Gujurati, Somali, Spanish, and Turkish. It also provides certain information as PDF files, as many computers have difficulty with some language texts, and has a local agency finder to enable visitors to find a local adviser who speaks their language. As the website expands and becomes better known, it should effectively support citizenship through delivering this information to such a wide audience. It is also leading the way in cutting-edge language translation technology, opening up possibilities for other public sector and governmental websites that provide important information online.

→ **www.multikulti.org.uk**

count the pennies
to make money for charity

203

Ever since Australia abolished the one-cent coin, businesses have rounded up or rounded down the price of items. Thus if you buy something that costs $9.99, you will pay $10 (unless, of course, you use plastic, in which case the real amount is paid).

More beneficial would be to set up a system whereby the customer has the option of donating the extra one cent. This could be an extra feature on a cash register that, when a customer is paying for a $9.99 item, offers the option of rounding up for charity. Equally, the store could choose to round a $10 item down to $9.99 for charity at its discretion.

In this incremental way, such a system could purchase extra services for the community in which the business is situated. The business would be acknowledged for its role as a good corporate citizen and the community would benefit by having extra funds at its disposal. And all from counting the pennies!

John Töns

favor the homeless
with handouts of fur

204

In an initiative that aims to turn a negative into a positive, People for the Ethical Treatment of Animals (PETA) have been handing out fur coats to homeless people.

PETA receives many donated coats from people who no longer wish to wear fur, or be associated with what many perceive to be a cruel, unnecessary trade.

The act of donating the coats to those in need of warmth and protection does not of course give the animals their lives back, but it does mean that the clothes are helping others in need, rather than accentuating a supermodel's features.

While PETA has become best known for its catwalk protests at fashion shows, this idea displays its less antagonistic side. As well as handing out coats to those on the streets in the US, they also distributed some to refugees in Afghanistan, following the war.

→ **www.peta.org**

chapter 9

work

pursue pay principle
of the mondragon movement

205

The Mondragon Co-operative movement was started by José María Arizmendiarrieta, a young priest who arrived in Mondragon, Spain, in 1941.

He first set up a school in the 1940s, before establishing the co-operative's first manufacturing plant in 1956. He established the principles of the Mondragon Co-operative movement, still largely adhered to today. These include a restricted differential between high and low pay, which states that the highest paid person in the organization could not earn more than three times the lowest paid person. The co-operative altered this ratio to 4.5:1 in the 1980s and market conditions have led to further changes, but the principle remains.

The co-operative principles also include a democratic and participatory management structure, reinvestment of profits in community initiatives and job creation, an openness of admissions to all, and a principle that capital is subordinate to labor. Over its years of trading, only three co-operatives have failed, and unemployment has remained remarkably low. Mondragon has 23 plants, and is the eighth largest business in the whole of the country.

→ **www.Mondragon.mcc.es**

prompt employees
to perform publicity stunts

206

With the incentive of a free weekend trip to New York to be awarded to the best idea, Kaufman & Broad, a construction company in California enlisted its own staff to market their company. Every employee was presented with a T-shirt bearing the company logo and challenged to display it in the most attention-grabbing context possible. In response, one employee did a parachute jump in the company T-shirt, another posed as a mannequin in a department store window, and the eventual winner mocked-up a magazine with celebrities wearing the firm's logo.

→ **www.kbhome.com**

throw an unemployment shower to create confidence

207

Today's employment climate means that redundancies, even of competent and valued staff members, are unavoidable. Some particularly cruel ways of getting the boot have emerged in the modern era (including, recently, the clinical termination by text or recorded message), but there is a way to turn an unexpected job loss into a positive milestone: the unemployment shower.

The brainchild of Sharron Kahn Luttrell, who has herself experienced redundancy, unemployment parties or showers are fashioned on bridal and baby showers thrown in the US, and encourage the recently redundant to kick-start their job hunt and hail the end of a job as the dawn of a new life.

Instead of bringing a bottle of wine, guests offer gems of advice, lists of contacts, and examples of stand-out résumés, arming the fresh job-market fodder with a surge of confidence and a forward-looking way to deal with the psychological blow of being laid off.

The idea came to Luttrell when her boss threatened to throw a stagnant conference room buffet to mark her departure. Viewing this as a well-meant but depressing confirmation of her imminent ousting from the world of work, she decided an event of real use that addressed her predicament, rather than avoiding it, would be preferable. Luttrell wanted a "really practical occasion that would send me off with something to help me build my future." While an in-house unemployment shower would not be possible in the case of abrupt layoffs, social gatherings with friends and music would provide an equally useful alternative.

Author of *The Layoff Survival Guide*, Nancy Collamer suggests cathartic activities such as pin the tail on the boss to be included at such events, and suggests these would help re-empower the recently disillusioned. With job loss being among the most feared of modern phenomena, unemployment functions, parties, or showers could prove to be a positive and useful way of dealing with a major life event; an event that has up to now been marked principally by kindly but impractical offers of commiseration or simple references to bad luck.

→ **www.LayOffSurvivalGuide.com**

eliminate e-mails
to enhance interaction

208

Companies in the UK are now introducing e-mail-free Fridays to try to reduce the amount of unnecessary material sent out, and to foster greater interaction between employees.

E-mail has swiftly become the staple means of communication in the workplace, but this has had a downside: overloading of servers, overloading of people with information, reduced face-to-face interactions between employees, and reduced productivity.

A survey in the UK showed that 80 percent of workers use e-mail politically to cover their backs, while a third admit to using e-mail to avoid resolving a difficult situation face-to-face or over the phone. It is also common knowledge that up to half of all e-mails sent by workers are jokes, quizzes, and forwards from friends, which have become known to some in the communications world as "productivity viruses." E-mail-free Friday, a ban on e-mail communication on that day of the week, forces employees to take a different approach and to use their time more appropriately.

Nestlé Rowntree was the first company in the UK to introduce such a policy, after management discovered that employees were spending more time typing than talking to each other; they also found examples of people sending e-mails to colleagues who were just a small distance across from them, rather than just speaking to them directly.

As Andrew Harrison, marketing director at the company, points out, "A no-e-mail Friday removes needless information flow across the organization and forces people to talk face-to-face and agree on plans mutually. An e-mail ban begins to build a culture of designing and delivering ideas together."

The Friday ban also reduces the pressure on employees to spend time responding to everything that flows into their inbox, and enables them to escape the pressures of what work analysts have identified as information overload associated with many e-mails. Approximately 35 billion e-mails are sent every day and having policies in place to make sure the benefits of e-mail outweigh the disadvantages will be increasingly important for all organizations, big and small.

While some might not wish to go as far as Nestlé (or Computer Associates, who actually shut down their systems for an hour in the morning and an hour in the afternoon to prevent gossiping), placing a ban on all non-essential e-mails, or drawing up guidelines of what should and should not be sent by e-mail, should be things considered by all organizations.

pass go to get a job

A supermarket chain in Thailand introduced a new element to help assess its job applicants: the ancient Chinese board game, Go.

209

The company had grown tired of employing top graduates who proved incapable of being effective team players. So the 7-Eleven chief executive Korsak Chairasmisak, himself a keen Go player, introduced the unusual technique as part of the assessment of candidates' suitability. The company believes it helps them select people who can see the whole picture, who can strategize, and understand the way individual actions impact the whole.

In addition to including the game as part of their interviewing process, the company has a successful Go club with over 1,000 employees taking part (about 5 percent of the workforce). Employees can improve their skills and even receive coaching in how to become a better player.

The game originated in China 4,000 years ago, and is played on a square board with black and white pieces that players use to gain territory from their opponent. Its appeal and usefulness may last for many more years.

→ **http://gobase.org**

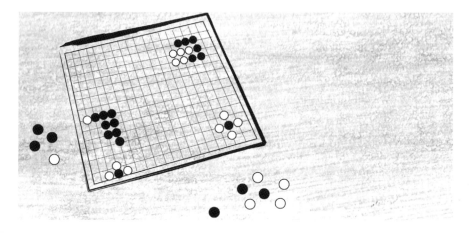

enter the workforce in a way that suits you

Laurel Baer heard a story on public radio about a woman struggling to get off welfare. After feeding and clothing her children, she had no money to afford a suit for herself; this one thing was keeping her from going to interviews. Laurel's instant reaction was that she could "go home right now and dress her out of my own closet." Soon after, she became the founder of Bottomless Closet, a not-for-profit organization that provides interview suits and career advice to women on lower incomes.

On a client's first visit, a volunteer assists with the selection of two interview-appropriate outfits. The outfits may include a suit or dress, hosiery, shoes, handbag, coat, and jewelry. If the woman is successful in getting a job, she may return to select three additional outfits and related accessories, resulting in a week's worth of professional clothes. She may also attend workshops on personal development, receiving training in key skills such as résumé (CV) writing and interviewing.

The Bottomless Closets achievements since its inception are impressive: over 13,500 women assisted, of whom 65 percent found employment. Over a thousand more a year are helped in the Chicago area alone, and there are branches of the organization in several other US cities. Similar initiatives have sprouted up across the US and internationally, most notably Dress for Success, which has operations in over 70 cities. There is also a network of such organizations under the umbrella of the Women's Alliance.

→ **www.bottomlesscloset.org**
→ **www.dressforsuccess.org**
→ **www.thewomensalliance.org**

210

encourage creativity
to keep workforce

211

Possibly the best way to keep talented staff, promote creativity, and better use company resources is through the concept of *intrapreneurship*.

Intrapreneurship is when a company uses the talents and abilities of its employees to develop innovative in-house projects and services. It allows the entrepreneurial, innovative, and dynamic outlook associated with smaller, newer organizations to flourish in large, established corporations and businesses.

Companies often lose employees who feel creatively suppressed and ignored. Eventually, not even the money is worth the efforts of the job. But if companies value and listen to the opinions and ideas of employees, rather than just hiring new people, the situation improves for both parties. The impetus is for creators, rather than followers, and intrapreneurship is a means of unleashing hidden talent while also creating new opportunities and greater job satisfaction. The best ideas do not always come from outside: giving organizational support and resources to those within the organization has the potential to be equally, if not more, beneficial.

→ **www.intrapreneur.com**

have a hibernation day
for national regeneration

212

Due to the way the world works today, with businesses and corporations, people must work or go to school to make a living and to survive, all of which can get very stressful at times. We need a break! I believe that we should have another national holiday and call it Hibernation Day, when students and employees are allowed a day off to just rest in, thanks to all of their hard work. No businesses, schools, restaurants, or shopping areas would be open, so everyone would be ensured a day off to relax. If the proposal for this holiday is passed, it will prove a useful breather for all and allow nations to recharge their collective batteries.

Ashley Biscoe

provide a job reference for your previous boss

213

Bullies and bad managers abound because their bosses neither know nor adequately care about their behavior, or because they misrepresent conflict between themselves and their subordinates. Even if they are aware of this, when people leave an organization many employers still give them a good reference (sometimes to ensure they leave).

A very different picture would emerge if it were standard practice for a person seeking a new job to supply names and contact details of everyone who had worked under them at their last job. The prospective employer could randomly contact (in confidence) one or more employees to satisfy themselves that the smooth talker at the job interview was the team leader he or she claimed. How differently your boss would treat you if his career hinged, at least in part, on your opinion!

Philip McLeish/Ashley Biscoe

choose a career with a fairer future

214

A service run by the charity People and Planet in Oxford focuses on ethical careers, opportunities, and lifestyles. It aims to help UK graduates and students make informed choices about socially and environmentally responsible careers. They provide information and advice and highlight the range of opportunities in charities, not-for-profits, and ethical companies. The website includes hundreds of links to employers and agencies, and information on how to make an impact in whatever office you are in: green electricity tariffs, fair trade producers, ethical suppliers, and recycling information.

Students can also receive the organization's magazine, *yOUR FUTURE*, which includes an ethical advice column and dream job profiles, as well as listings of fairs, seminars, events, and vacancies. Those running the service stress that their intention is not to preach, but to outline issues involved in particular sectors and possibilities for change in all occupations.

➜ **http://peopleandplanet.org/ethicalcareers**

reward recruits and recruiters for staff stability

215

Many companies struggle to recruit the kind of staff they want and, as importantly, to hold on to them once they have employed them. Rewarding current employees who recruit new people to a company is one way to avoid both costly recruitment fees and high staff turnover.

Carlson Companies in Minneapolis offered a program in which employees who referred IT workers received $2,000 (£1,000) when the person was hired and another $1,000 (£500) every year for four years, providing that both employees stayed with the company. This not only encouraged employees to refer friends or acquaintances, but also gave them an incentive to look after their referrals once they got the job.

This innovative combination of a lump sum and a deferred payment (tied to both employees remaining with the company) made Carlson's initiative a great success. More than one-fifth of newly hired IT employees came from such referrals once the incentive idea was underway. The program also affected people's attitudes within the organization more generally; as Lynne Carroll, one IT recruiter with the firm, pointed out, the initiative "keeps everybody involved in making sure that people are happy with their jobs."

Such an idea can work for everyone: the organization saves on advertising and recruitment costs while developing a greater sense of company loyalty, the original employee has a chance for personal financial gain, and the new hire instantly feels more settled in a place where they know someone.

→ **www.carlson.com**

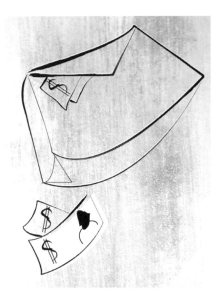

swap jobs to learn new skills

216

Councillors and other employees who work for the municipal council of Fet, a small municipality in Norway, east of Oslo, swap jobs with each other one day of the year as part of an annual event called Skills and Fun.

The idea is to give everyone some training in general skills, in addition to providing an opportunity for a party afterwards.

People on the council payroll have enormously varied jobs. In Fet, there are about thirty different occupational groups with little in common but their employer. The topic in one year was "adaptability to new situations," and job swapping was a way of testing the ability to handle change.

By doing someone else's job for a day, you get an insight into how different parts of the council organization work, as well as a better understanding of how priorities are decided on and how resources are used. Another objective was to encourage cross-sector cooperation and to highlight different job opportunities within the council.

So if you had tried phoning the Mayor of Fet on August 24, 1999, you would have received a reply, but not from the mayor. The mayor for the day was a plumber, and the real mayor was out conducting tests at the sewage works. In fact, it would have been hard to find any council staff at their ordinary workplaces that day.

Each year they add some unusual training, but the format always changes. In 1998 there was a conference on teamwork. Nothing was prepared when people arrived, and the participants were given 36,000 Krone ($6,000/ £3,000), twenty-one tasks (such as getting food, organizing speakers) and three hours to get the job done.

The conference had to be organized in this time and it was left to the employees to solve the tasks as a group. The goal of the exercise was to encourage cooperation as well as to show participants the importance of delegating and giving away responsibility to other members of their team. Three hours later, everything was ready, with Japanese-style mats to sit on, a delicious lunch, and, as usual, a party that night.

→ **www.fet.kommune.no**

set your own sales targets for staff satisfaction

At Semco, a Brazilian manufacturer of industrial equipment, most employees decide their own salaries. Their bonuses, which are tied to the company's profits, are shared as they choose.

217

Everyone, including factory workers, sets his or her own working hours, and groups of employees set their own productivity and sales targets. There are no controls over travel or business expenses. There are no manuals or written procedures. Workers choose their own boss and then publicly evaluate his performance. All employees have unlimited access to the company's books and are trained to read balance sheets.

Everyone knows what everyone else earns, and some workers can earn more than their boss. Big corporate decisions, such as diversifications and acquisitions, are made by all employees. In 2003, there was a tenth anniversary party celebrating a decade since Ricardo Semler, the majority shareholder and catalyst for the change, last made any sort of decision.

Other measures include the contracting out of employees: encouraging them to leave the payroll and start their own enterprises (and making the transition easier wherever possible).

Half the manufacturing of the company is now contracted out to these satellites, which has allowed the cutting of permanent staff at Semco itself to save costs. Among those staffers who remain, job rotation is encouraged every two to five years to prevent boredom, which also helps to ensure that there is no pyramidal hierarchical working structure.

Ricardo Semler's experiment in employee power seems to work largely because it is allied with some old-fashioned, financial hard-headedness. Budget controls are not only transparent, but also strict.

As owner of the firm, Mr. Semler demands healthy dividends. And because a large proportion of the earnings of all employees is also tied directly to the firm's profits, peer pressure on employees not to abuse their freedom is enormous. "It's all very simple," says Mr. Semler. All we're doing is treating people like adults."

→ **http://semco.locaweb.com.br**

pin pay-rise request to noticeboard for colleagues to vote on

How would you like it if the next time you asked for a pay raise, your boss said, "We'll put it to a vote of your fellow workers"? Romac Industries, a company in Seattle, introduced this unique pay initiative and its president, Manford McNeil, reports: "Our workers are happy and productivity has been increasing steadily." He didn't think they would have the kind of production they had achieved with a conventional wage system.

All production workers at Romac, which makes pipefittings, begin at the same wage and get raises from management during their first six months. After that, a worker who wants a raise gets a slip from the plant manager, writes his name on it along with the raise he wants, the new rate he would earn if it were approved, and the reason he deserves more money. The request and a picture of the worker are then posted on the bulletin board for five days. There is then a secret ballot of the worker's fellow employees, with the worker needing a majority vote to achieve the raise.

About 95 percent of raise requests are granted; most increases average 20–40 cents (10–20 pence) an hour. The company's 80 production workers average about $12 (£6) an hour. Management has the right of veto, but "we've never had to use it," said McNeil.

218

"Nobody has asked for a ridiculous rate for the job he's doing."

One worker, Don Past, says: "If management was giving the raises, some would think, 'The boss isn't here, so I can take it easy.' But the boss is always here; he's your fellow worker."

Another worker, Pat Ferguson, said he was once turned down. "I said to myself, 'Hey, you better start working harder, the guys are telling you something.'" He did—now he's a foreman.

→ **www.romacindustries.com**

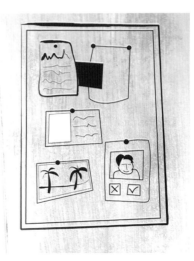

stick to stress code
to avoid overwork

A six-point stress code helps ensure that employees avoid overwork and that they receive enough support. The code means firms can fail assessment by the Health and Safety Executive in the UK. It provides a firmer basis for employees to launch legal action and encourages companies to act on the issue and so reduce the estimated 13.4 million working days lost to stress each year.

219

The six points of the code are:

→ Change: 65 percent of employees must be involved in organizational change

→ Control: 85 percent must feel they have an adequate say over their job

→ Demands: 85 percent must say they can cope with the demands of their job

→ Relationships: 65 percent must say they do not have to face unacceptable behavior

→ Role: 65 percent must say they understand their roles and responsibilities

→ Support: 85 percent must say they have the backup they need

→ **www.hse.gov.uk**

bank on a bonus
through performance profits

Svenska Handelsbanken in Sweden has a unique profit-sharing initiative that encourages staff to cut costs and to increase revenue: each branch of the bank has a bonus payout that depends upon the extent to which Handelsbanken outperforms its competitors.

220

The money does not go directly to staff, however, but into a fund that provides a lump sum on leaving or on retirement, with the amount depending not on salary but on length of service. An employee leaving after 25 years would receive about £200,000 ($400,000) from this fund and thus has a big incentive to help the branch flourish. This profit-sharing foundation, called Oktogonen, is central to the bank's efforts to improve its profitability consistently.

→ **www.handelsbanken.se**

take a team-building walk

221

A team of employees at an IT firm takes short group walks outdoors during work breaks. Aside from being much healthier than the normal tea break, the workers claim that their stroll is excellent for teambuilding and helps enhance the way they feel about their jobs. Fresh air and exercise provide a needed physical stimulus after a number of hours in an enclosed office. The only problem they have come up against is walking past the offices of some senior managers, who complained that they looked much too happy. Perhaps the next time the managers will join them!

win cash and prizes for your good health

222

The Electric Boat shipyard in Groton, Massachusetts, tackles the problem of absenteeism head-on by offering cash prizes to all salaried workers who have not used their sick days. The number of employees taking days off sick has halved as a result.

Each salaried worker at the shipyard is entered into a lottery, with prizes including $2,500 (£1,250) cash prizes, gift certificates, and free parking spaces. At the end of each year, the company hands out the prizes to the lucky few who haven't been off sick all year. In December 2000, for example, twenty workers received the top cash prize, having been drawn from a pool of 955 workers who had not called in sick for two years. A further 75 prizes of $1,000 (£500) were awarded, plus free parking spaces and many gift certificates; no one went home empty-handed. The result? The average number of sick days taken by workers at the shipyard has fallen from 7.2 to 3.5 per year, and 41 percent of workers did not use a sick day in 2000.

Other companies are starting to implement innovative approaches to the problem as well. Another company, Aetna of Hartford in Connecticut, no longer gives workers sick days. Instead, policy pools together vacation and sick leave into one big paid time-off grouping. That gives the workers the option of using the days in the ways they see fit, and the added flexibility is proving very popular at the company.

enjoy midlife retirement to care for children

Instead of retiring when they are 60 to 65, when they might be too old to enjoy the benefits of retirement, people should take a five- or ten-year-long midlife retirement between the ages of 30 and 40. Benefits would include the following:

→ People would still form the basis of their career and skills at an early age.

→ This mid-life retirement period might coincide with the raising of children, which could prove to be very important for society— imagine a situation where both mum and dad could devote 100 percent of their time to the kids during their most formative years.

→ Ageism may decrease among employers, who would no longer see someone of 45 or 50 as a risk.

→ Enthusiasm for work would be maintained longer with this midterm holiday break.

→ People's working lives could be extended (if they wish) so that the standard retirement age would be 70 or 75.

→ This would promote saving money, especially by younger people, eager to make the most of their temporary retirement.

→ Young people would be prompted to think about their careers at an earlier age.

→ People would be taking career breaks at a point in their lives when they still have

223

both the energy and the enthusiasm to make the most of such a break.

Of course, the break would be optional and people could use the time to learn new skills or to earn new qualifications if they so desire.

The government would need to help fund these pre-retirement breaks, although this could be enabled in part by the extension of the standard retirement age. A break with tradition might well breathe some fresh air into people's lives.

Dave Morgan

ring the bell
for job-winners

224

Performance statistics place Training, Inc. among the best employment-training programs in the US. Its Indianapolis site was the first job-training program to rely on performance-based funding. Of candidates who start in the Boston program, for example, 90 percent complete the demanding 14-week schedule and 85 percent of those get jobs soon after graduation. A year later, 80 percent are still on the job and almost all have won a raise or promotion.

The key factor is having the trainees act the part. Their activities mirror the real world six hours a day, five days a week. They are expected to dress for work, to arrive on time, and to interact professionally with the staff and fellow trainees. The office has departments, not classrooms. Every day one of the trainees rotates into the role of receptionist for the entire office. Simulated work projects provide the feel of the professional world. In a typical site, 36 people work on typing, word processing, data entry, filing, or book-keeping in learning groups of 12 or 13, using materials that simulate business content.

Rather than training people in a union hall or community center in the trainees' neighborhoods, the program highlights the potential work environment. The professional office with beautiful rooms for the various departments tells the trainees clearly from the start that they are worth the investment.

The preparation for job search involves individual work detailed through a manual, and seminars on wardrobe and first impressions, followed by mock interviews: by pairs, before a panel of peers, on videotape, with outside interviewers, with professional human resource people, at a job fair, and in other offices.

When it comes to looking for a job, however, the trainees do it on their own. A job developer may help with leads, but the trainees set their own appointments and get the job (or not) themselves. They debrief after every interview, with a staff person and sometimes with a team of other trainees. Whenever someone gets a job, the placement is added to the job board, a bell is rung, and work stops so that everyone can hear what happened.

Training, Inc. offers strong follow-up. Graduates feel free to return, rejoice over victories, discuss their failures, and seek advice for further career steps. Under a peer mentoring initiative, graduates who have been employed at least a year can volunteer their time to work with current trainees during the program.

→ **www.traininginc.org**

perfect your purpose
in the workplace

225

The root cause of many social problems is low self-esteem. Many people who are gainfully employed, after working 40 or more hours a week, come home overstressed and unfulfilled, even when doing their job to the fullest. A job should be a perfect opportunity to increase self-esteem, though.

This can be accomplished by having a job purpose within a job description. Most of us are trained how to perform a job and fulfill its responsibilities, but the actual why of a job is rarely explained. Within the training or explaining of a job function, one needs to be enlightened to the effect of an expected performance of a task and, better still, what benefits occur when the job is performed beyond expectation.

Similarly, the consequences of the reverse situation will also be clear. In this way, a job purpose will not only enable people to achieve greater fulfillment at work, but also help clarify aims and goals at the place of employment, thus improving employer–employee relations.

Anthony R. Dziedzic

make a living Long Now style:
generational employment and income

226

Pride in work may fall by the wayside: an oversimplified analysis is that this is partly due to cultural distrust between employer and employee, and partly to lack of widespread concern for the future. A simple example would be: quality of food produced by a farmer and the condition the land is left in compared with its original state.

Wages earned could be offset by one generation and pro-rated according to quality of work. That is, if a woman/mother does a lifetime of work, her wages would be paid to her descendants. This encourages people to do their best knowing that descendants depend on their effort for quality of life.

These and similar ideas are promoted by The Long Now Foundation, established in 1996 to counter today's "faster/cheaper" mindset and promote "slower/better," long-term thinking.

Tim Gerwing

→ **www.longnow.org**

discover your dream
vocation on vacation

227

An initiative that allows people to try out their dream jobs without having to leave their current position aims to help people to find their true calling.

Vocation Vacations is an innovative travel company based in Portland, Oregon, that lets people try out their fantasy jobs while they are on vacation from their real work. "The time has come when people are ready to start thinking outside the cubicle," says company founder Brian Kurth. "This idea allows people to test the waters in a safe way. These are baby steps into a possible new life."

During Vocation Vacations, people can explore careers such as winemaker, gardener, innkeeper, rancher, cheese maker, or brew master. Most vacations include hands-on work with an expert mentor. The average trip lasts a weekend and costs $500 (£250) to $1,000 (£500), which includes a follow-up session with a career coach.

Kurth is looking into creating new packages, including stints for possible chefs, golf pros, news anchors, and even wedding planners.

➔ **www.VocationVacations.com**

clean up cleaning to help
health and environment

228

Many professional cleaners suffer from rashes, headaches, dizziness, and nausea as a result of the products they use. People suffering in this way are often the poorest in society, who have little recourse for complaint. A project in California is helping women cleaners address these problems by helping them set up eco-friendly cleaning co-operatives. The results are impressive: improved health, reduced environmental impact, and

improved financial security, working conditions, and support. Least-toxic cleaning is generally becoming more common in the US, but it is the combination of this eco-cleaning with co-operative principles that is helping turn lives around.

The project is run by Women's Action to Gain Economic Security (WAGES), which has helped women start up three such co-operatives thus far. They use products such as vinegar to clean windows, baking soda to scour, and eco-friendly products for general cleaning. Each of the owner-members works 20–25 hours a week, earning $12 (£6) an hour.

The co-operative structure enables women to share stories and work responsibilities. WAGES also trains each of them in eco-safe cleaning and business practice to ensure long-term sustainability.

WAGES has calculated that two of their co-operatives will have prevented 3,863 pounds (1,752 kg) of hazardous or toxic materials being released into the environment each year. The owner-members are now seen as leaders in their community, and their own self-esteem is justly sky-high as a result.

→ **www.wagescooperatives.org**

try out text messages for jobs and wages

Mobile phones are being used in Australia to alert the long-term unemployed to seasonal vacancies as crop-pickers in fruit and vegetable harvests.

Having started in March in South Australia and Victoria and moved on to Queensland in May, this method of recruiting harvest workers is now being used in Australia's Northern Territory to recruit pickers for the mango harvest. Thousands of text messages are sent by mobile phone to the long-term unemployed, encouraging them to take up the vacancies.

Max Polworth from Australia's National Harvest Labor Information Service says that when they first started the initiative the response was huge: "It's putting [on] more Australian job seekers and putting it in their minds that they might join in the harvest trail."

In New Zealand, meanwhile, it is the workers who are turning mobile technology to their advantage. To gain leverage with employers, seasonal workers are exchanging messages about rates of pay at different farms. Once they know what the price per basket is at different farms, they can try to bargain with the farm they are at to get more pay or move to better-paid work elsewhere. Fruit pickers are traditionally limited by geography and timing in gathering this wage information, which can allow farmers to distort the market in their favor. Using technology in this way empowers individual workers and allows the market to function on a fairer basis.

→ **www.australia.gov.au**
→ **www.jobsearch.gov.au**

take a seventh-year sabbatical
for the benefit of all

230

Advances in technology are reducing the amount of work required to sustain society. However, rather than capitalizing on increased leisure time, the workforce has become divided into those with skills in demand, who often work excessive amounts of overtime, and those without skills, who cannot find any work whatsoever.

This problem can affect everyone, as even those with work may live in fear that their skills will become outmoded, or that someone with equivalent skills and the ability to work even more hours will take their job. Company and employer loyalty is a thing of the past.

In addition, people find that their best earning years, those when they have to keep their noses to the grindstone, are also the primary child-raising years, adding even more stress to families and the social fabric. As a result, we see stress disorders, broken families, a lack of consumer confidence, and a great deal of cynicism at every level of society.

A possible source of relief would be to extend the concept of sabbatical years beyond the borders of academia, to the working world at large. Workers of all types would work for six years, taking the seventh as a sabbatical. This time could be used for upgrading of skills, family time, vacation, or whatever. In conjunction, the retirement age would be moved ahead, perhaps to 71, thus giving each person the same number of potential earning years that he or she has now.

To compensate for the sabbatical, the worker would take a pro-rated part of their earnings during the working years—six-sevenths of their salary. To some extent, this rollback would be offset by a reduced burden of payroll taxes, as the number of unemployed would be dramatically reduced. These former unemployed would be required to fill in for the first batch of people taking the sabbatical. When they return, another one-seventh of the population would go off, and so on. Workers taking time away for other reasons (e.g., maternity leave) would stop accruing time while off work, but continue on return.

The initiative's advantages are that it:
→ creates a proactive cycling of all workers through employment/unemployment;
→ gives workers time to upgrade their skills;
→ changes unemployment from stigmatizing tragedy to a time of personal development;
→ reduces the level of despair and fear;
→ increases the opportunity for family time;
→ increases consumer confidence;
→ reduces amount of time able workers spend in retirement.

Evelyn

chapter 10

spirituality

choose change with earth democracy's primary principles

231

Transforming the negative campaigning against globalization and corporatism into a positive movement for something is one of the biggest challenges faced by social activists.

To combine this energy and passion with the many projects in place globally, the idea of Earth Democracy has been proposed. It is, ostensibly, a way of uniting people working in different sectors by identifying key common principles that underlie what they are doing. It is an idea aimed at giving the pro-movement a spiritual core to rally around—a set of principles and visions that bring disparate groups (all working for positive change) together into a coherent, and therefore more potent, force. It is also a way of signaling the need for humans to work together with nature: hence, Earth Democracy, rather than New Democracy, with the emphasis on respect and understanding.

The Gaia Foundation outlines some emerging principles:
→ Respect for all life
→ Responsibility for non-violent resistance
→ Responsibility for creating alternatives
→ Communicating values through the arts (and celebration)
→ Reaching out into new sectors, beyond those already converted

→ Committing to a decade of Earth Democracy and Justice.

Vandana Shiva thinks of Earth Democracy as a commitment to go[ing] beyond the crisis of economic injustice and inequality, ecological non-sustainability, the decay of democracy, and the rise of terrorism. The emphasis is on a progressive move forward, on a new world in which humans coexist with the rest of the Earth's inhabitants, rather than at their expense. It can unite people around common causes.

The ten primary principles of Earth Democracy that Shiva proposes are:

1 Democracy for all life—protecting the welfare and rights of all species

2 Intrinsic worth of all species—no humans have the right to own other species

3 Diversity in nature and culture—defending diversity to be viewed as a duty

4 Right to sustenance—all have rights to food, water, clean habitat, and security

5 Economic democracy—economic systems protecting people and nature

6 Local economies—reducing reliance on long-distance trade

7 Local living democracy—local communities deciding things of importance to them

8 Living knowledge—knowledge that renews living processes (community-centered)

9 Balance of responsibility and rights—decision-makers must face consequences
10 A globalization of compassion and care—in other words, a method of connecting people, not crushing people.

While some of the principles and ideas discussed above may seem like recapitulations of old ideas or woolly attempts to draw disparate strands together, the possibility that Earth Democracy can provide a central core of commonality for people to unite around is reason enough to pursue it. If nothing else, it serves to remind us that the world needs to change in radical ways in the future for the well being of everything on the planet, and that there is a belief system that underlies that change.

→ **www.theGaiaFoundation.org**
→ **www.VShiva.net**

take tea with other faith families

232

Religion at national and international levels is seen as a source of strife. At a local level, however, it can lead to acts of good neighborliness and helpfulness. This simple idea aims to extend the interaction of ordinary families across faith communities.

Initially six voluntary coordinators, each from a different faith community, would recruit ten members or families from their community. The members commit to accepting one invitation for tea from a member of another community, and to reciprocate once a year.

Coordinators meet in pairs to match community members, exchange phone numbers, and give support in the form of a brief guide and possibly an evaluation. One central organizer in each town could choose the six coordinators from the major faith communities of the town (e.g., Anglican, RC, Quaker/Free Churches, Muslim, Hindu). By connecting these faiths at a grassroots level, we can work toward common solutions and to cut intra-religious conflict in the long term.

Richard Thompson

support selflessness
for the common good

233

Swadhyaya, a religion-based community movement, is sweeping across India and revitalizing society as it goes.

Its central tenet is that one's primary responsibility is to do one's duty to the best of one's capability for God and without attachment to the fruits of labor. Projects are undertaken to help people achieve this goal and change the way they view the world. Further, the movement emphasizes the fact that all humans are related by virtue of divine creation, and this interconnectedness is at the heart of their work. Dada, the movement's leader, advises that this is an equalizing creed: there is no discrimination because of gender or caste among Swadhyayees because all individuals are viewed as creations of a higher power.

One of the primary methods by which Swadhyaya is changing society is through devotional visits, or *bhakti pheris*. These visits involve visiting villagers (often of a lower caste) in order to establish connections with them with no other motive, talking and getting to know them without trying to convert them. The process of change begins to occur when the people being visited accept that the visits are entirely selfless and that the Swadhyayees are asking nothing except friendship—this helps to rebuild a basic trust in humanity.

Swadhyayees work in a more tangible way as well. One project turned a wasteland into fertile farmland as villagers worked together to build wells for water. Elsewhere, land sharing takes place under the aegis of the movement. A piece of land is shared between twenty villages, and each day a different person from each village works on the land. In this way, twenty people are always working the land, providing their own tools, labor, and seeds. Produce is sold at market prices, with any profits from sales going to the foundation to purchase more land or help more people. These projects expand notions of community, allowing individuals to give time and effort with no thought of reward or gain.

The ethos of Swadhyaya is Hindu, and some Muslims have taken offense at the worship of idols, while Buddhists reject the acceptance of God as a central figure. Nevertheless, people from all religions are gradually accepting the movement for its social, rather than religious, ideals. This movement is not seeking conversion, but to spread a message of the innate good of humans. And in an increasingly dysfunctional, isolated world, it is reconnecting people irrespective of their differences.

→ **www.swadhyay.org**

restore ritual
with a naming ceremony

234

In the UK, as society has become more secular, the numbers of church baptisms have fallen dramatically (from 68 percent in 1950 to 29 percent in 1995), so far without being replaced by anything else.

People often feel something is missing: rituals ease transitions by honoring the arriving or departing people, by strengthening relationships of group members so that they can stand the strain, and by using the occasions for re-dedication to the moral values that hold society together. A child awakens feelings of love and gentleness, and these feelings need to be spread into ordinary adult life.

A secular baptism ritual would have five main functions: naming the newborn child, welcoming the child, expressing solidarity with the parents, marking a commitment by the parents and others, and expressing a sense of wonder for the miracle of birth. As a complementary step, for those marrying in church, the marriage vows could be modified to include specific account of parental duties toward children. For example, … "and I promise to love and to cherish all children of ours, to care for them and to encourage them, all my life long, till death do us part, and this is my solemn vow."

For unmarried cohabitants, a secular baptism ceremony might be the first occasion on which the parents commit themselves to each other and to their child in the presence of others. The ceremony could include a party and possibly other formal features, such as a candle at the head of the cradle (from which other candles would be lit); live or taped music; the exchange of rings, with a tiny ring (just for the occasion) for the baby's finger, to symbolize the fact that the child is now very much part of the circle.

Godparents could give their commitment verbally on the day of the ceremony as well as in writing. They could undertake to keep in touch with the child, to take an interest in the child's progress, to recognize the child's birthdays, and to lend support in times of illness or other setback. Godparents in this way would become like an extended family for the child.

While religious rituals remain strong in other countries, such ceremonies could prove to be important and viable options. Indeed, in a world where parents often have children without being married, the naming ceremony could prove to be the first major event that brings all sides of the family together, and, in doing so, shores up what has become the crumbling institution of the family.

→ **www.civilceremonies.co.uk**

participate in
an online parish

235

Under an initiative to widen its access to new people, the Church of England launched i-Church, a virtual parish in which people can communicate via the web. The online community can gather at the website for e-mail chat, webcast services, and prayers in chat rooms. The new parish also has its own pastor, who will oversee the community. Those behind the scenes say that it will help a wide range of people who do not usually come to a traditional church. This could include those working overseas, those whose mobility is limited, and those dissatisfied with the church in their locality.

It is part of the Archbishop of Canterbury's desire for modernity, what he calls "a mission-shaped church." It is hoped young people, who prefer to deal with groups on the web, will find i-Church a good discussion forum and meet like-minded friends in a supportive community.

→ **www.i-church.org**

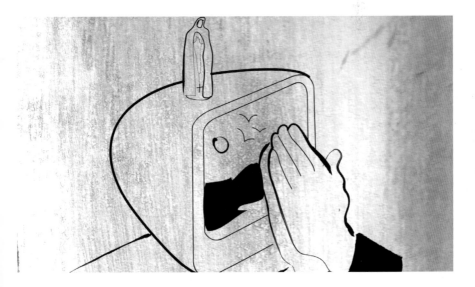

teach meditation
to tackle testing times

236

The possibilities for incorporating meditation into your daily regime are numerous and potentially life-changing. Teaching meditation to children could become an established educative staple in the future. As examinations and testing have increased in schools, so levels of stress have risen among pupils. Levels of concentration are also hard to improve, as children live in a world of instant gratification via video games or the net.

Meditation can have an impact on these problems, not only in reducing stress, but also in preparing a student for the day ahead.

The evidence from those schools that have introduced meditation (in whatever form) to their students is certainly positive and could become a useful tool in the changing pedagogical world.

Leslie Gilsdorf

pledge allegiance to matriotism

237

Matriotism is a new kind of spirituality that crosses all borders and barriers. The concept of Matriotism has been growing as a great philosophy that could revolutionize the peacemaking activities of individuals, organizations, and governments throughout the world.

Matriots could be drawn from all countries, continents, and spiritual paths to embody and envision fresh and creative approaches and solutions to crisis points anywhere. In this sense, matriotism would be a type of spiritual United Nations, yet with the benefit of being unattached to any particular ideology or cultural expression, undeterred by patriotic needs to protect and defend any one piece of land. It could also be viewed as a peace corps of the heart, but with a long-term commitment to responding calmingly to conflict everywhere. Definitions of the key terms are as follows:

→ **Matriotism**: *The practice of the philosophy that all life on the mother planet called Earth is sacred and deserves respect, honor, and care regardless of location, life form, or cultural circumstance on the globe. A deep, indigenous, native sense and experience of being grounded and rooted here—of being home.*

→ **Matriotic**: *To pledge allegiance to One Earth, One Spirit, One Humanity, One Community of human, animal, and plant. To salute and seek unity under only one flag, the green (plants), blue (water and sky) and red (blood) banner of peace, justice and well-being of all.*

→ **Matriot**: *A person who lives as a planetary citizen without separating people from people, creature from creation, human from divine. An interrelated individual who actively cooperates to expand fields of view and works creatively to dismantle real or imagined barriers, walls, and borders.*

Also, we are matriotic, not patriotic, if patriotism means blind and unquestioned allegiance to one government, religion, way of life, or authoritative voice as opposed to another government, religion, way of life, or voice. We are matriotic if we are guided by our common ideas and breath and vision. Mother Earth is inviting us to join together as co-creators of new paradigms for social and ecological healing.

Practical matriotic steps can be taken by all of us now, in our communities and in our lives.

Chris Highland

let your spirituality evolve and grow throughout your life

238

The Nigerian playwright Wole Soyinka has written of the secular temper as being humanistic and has also referred to an age-old belief in the unity of the human community.

"Age-old" is apt, because *secular* comes from the Latin *saeculum*, meaning a "lifetime" or "generation." Secularism is about universal human beliefs dating back lifetimes, beliefs concerned with unity among humans. The idea of the secular deity is proposed in response to the divisive dogmas and intolerances of existing religions. The premise is that the religions that dominate the world fall all too easily into dogmatism, absolutes, and binary oppositions, and that a more open, tolerant, and human spirituality could help avoid the conflicts and problems arising from those oppositions.

For his example of a secular deity, Soyinka goes back to his homeland Nigeria, and the world of the Yoruba. The Yoruba believe that when a child is born, he or she brings an individual destiny (*ori*) into the world, and that it is useless to try to change it or to impose a different one on the child. This destiny can change with the child's growth and life in the world: other guardian deities may be added or replaced. The Yoruba believe that all gods are different parts of the giant, universal whole of which humans and humanity are a part. Similarly, their Bible equivalent, in the form of prognostic verses (*Ifa*), is filled with signs and parables, and mentions those who decided not to follow the Yoruba path: these people are not criticized or punished; if they suffer misfortune, that is their own destiny.

It is this concept of truth as being different things to different people that is key; Soyinka quotes from the ancient India Vedic texts: "Wise is he who recognizes that Truth is one and only, but wiser still the one who accepts that Truth is called by many names, and approached from myriad routes."

Our beliefs should unite us and be accommodating in spirit, not divisive in their effects. The search for truth should not be confused with the veneration and validation of particular propositions of truth: there lies the path to absolutism, dogmatism, and religious conflict. An acceptance of others and other truths should be paramount in our spiritual lives, and our deities should be elastic and dynamic: able to change to our own constantly evolving perceptions of the world, and to be molded into a personal system of tolerance, faith, and understanding.

Of course, this is not so much a new social invention as the rediscovery of a much older one: a unifying, non-competing spirituality from generations ago. Those who believe in these religions would rightly point to the teachings that urge tolerance of others, loving thy neighbor, and so on. The issue is more with the institutions and the texts. The former often inexorably lead to factionalism and a concentration on internal politics rather than the religion's ideals (helping others, supporting fellow believers, providing a sense of belonging and a place in the world, helping things make sense). The latter are, like any text, open to a huge variety of interpretations, allowing any particular group to cite parts of them as justification for their own particular version of the religion—this is then reinforced by institutionalizing this version. The arguments over who is right, or who follows the one true way, inevitably follow.

I would like to see something close to transcendentalism—a belief in spirituality, in the divine in all things, in communion with nature and others, but with no regulations, texts, canticles, absolutes, buildings, or intermediaries. It would be a personal spiritual connection on individual terms that is ever changing yet holding unity at its core.

This may be removed from Soyinka's secular deity, but there are similarities: openness, understanding, the ability to evolve, belief in unity, tolerance of other opinions, and strong faith in a world above and beyond our own. It would be a religion that accommodates not divides; a spirituality that strengthens and evolves, not dwelling on one path followed for centuries.

Nick Temple

create cyber karma
to cut out carping

239

Some people constantly carp that the world is unfair, or that they have been hard done by. In some cases, these individuals do seem to have a particularly poor run of luck. So here's a suggestion that might help them alleviate those feelings and move on positively: a karma website that allows people to network and equalize society's karma to get things done.

Whenever something bad has happened to you, log on and find out if someone is willing to help you: perhaps there is a networking opportunity just around the corner. Perhaps someone who has landed a job through a stroke of good fortune wants to give something back, through a placement or an interview.

Matching up the bad and good karma in society could enable us all to make progress and promote greater feelings of fairness in the world.

Greg Deacon

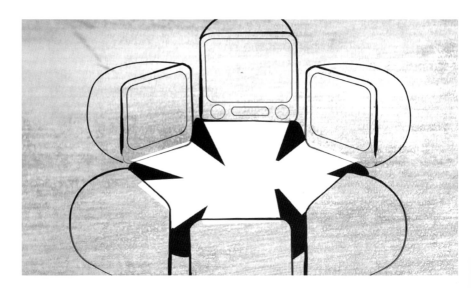

customize your own commandments

240

As part of their religious education, every schoolchild could be encouraged to design their own ten commandments. Adults might choose to do the same. Quakers, one correspondent suggests, might prefer questions to commandments. Here, to get you thinking, are ten contemporary commandments:

1 Show reverence toward creation in all its manifestations.

2 Maintain and care for your network of family, friends, and neighbors.

3 Preserve your health for old age.

4 Procreate with respect for population limits.

5 Choose work that is life-enhancing.

6 Resolve disputes without resorting to violence.

7 Resist enslavement to television, computers, and similar virtual realities.

8 Refrain from acts that seriously impinge on the well-being of others.

9 Create human scale societies of small neighborhoods, small firms, and small nations.

10 Preserve the beauty and diversity of the planet for future generations.

You might also consider a secular version of the Ten Commandments, on the other hand, which might contain some or all of the following suggestions:

1 Do your best to mitigate human and other suffering.

2 Observe the Golden Rule: Do unto others as you would be done by.

3 Be tolerant, avoiding tribalism, sectarianism, and other hatreds of those who are different.

4 Be a wise steward of the earth for present and future generations.

5 Be a lifelong student—never cease to learn.

6 Remember that you have not only rights, but also responsibilities.

7 Be industrious. A full life is a happier one.

8 Do not conceive children who may not be loved and cared for adequately.

9 Try always to do your best and respect others for doing the same.

10 Try to maintain equanimity as well as cheerfulness.

Nicholas Albery and Peter Tod

ponder the purpose
of angels

241

Rupert Sheldrake and Matthew Fox, in exploring the realm where science and spirit meet, looked closely at the physics of angels.

They pondered questions such as: Does each galaxy have its own angel? Can angels evolve? Can they guide us through the evils that beset us? They examined the role of angels in the Bible and in the works of Dionysius the Areopagite, St. Thomas Aquinas, and Hildegard of Bingen.

The resulting speculations and conclusions are as follows:

→ Angels exist in astronomical numbers. There are many other kinds of consciousness in the cosmos besides human.

→ Angels have been present from the origin of the universe.

→ They exist in a hierarchic order of nested levels within levels.

→ They are nature's governing intelligences.

→ They have a special relationship to light, fire, flames, and photons. There are astonishing parallels between Aquinas and Einstein with regard to the nature of angels and of photons: in their locomotion and mode of movement, their agelessness, and state of being massless.

→ Musical in nature, they work in harmonious relationship with one another.

→ Most are friendly, but not all. Christ has power over the angels.

→ They have a special relationship to human consciousness. Humans help link the earthly world with cosmic intelligences.

→ Angels may have played a special role in the birth of language.

→ They inspire prophets and awaken human imagination and intuition and thus befriend the artist in a special way.

→ Angels are amazed at us, and our actions through the angels can affect the entire cosmos.

→ Their primary role is praise.

→ They have a variety of functions in their relationship with humans, including inspiring, message bearing, protecting, guiding.

→ They are present at holy worship.

→ Both good and bad angels act in the arena of our conscience and decision-making.

→ They do not have material bodies but can temporarily assume the appearance of human or other bodies for the sake of communicating with and helping human beings.

→ They accompany people from this life to the next.

chapter 11

communication
and the internet

stay focused with internet blinkers

242

Jobs with permanent Internet access are arguably among the most difficult in the world. Why? Distraction. The Internet is perhaps the single most distracting thing humankind has ever developed, and has the added danger of being more interesting than any combination of CSS (Cascading Style Sheet), XML (eXtensible Markup Language), and PERL (Practical Extraction and Report Language).

Distraction of this type costs businesses both big and small a lot of money every year, with countless wasted production hours. One solution could be a piece of software called Internet blinkers. The person using the computer would inform the software which piece of work it is meant to be working on, and then set a tolerance level. The program would keep tabs on the individual's activities and issue reminders if he or she seems to be straying from the task at hand. In extreme cases, for those who find the Internet particularly addictive, the tolerance level could be set so that the software could force a browser window or e-mail client to close, or even e-mail a colleague and ask for help.

Chris Kemp-Salt

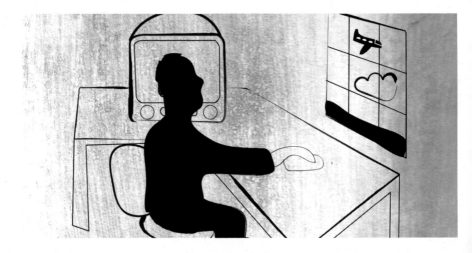

share your work without losing all your rights

243

A not-for-profit organization called Creative Commons has developed an idea to help those who are willing to share work but don't want to lose all rights to it.

Creative Commons aims to provide people with some rights reserved or no rights reserved licenses which will stand up in court, so they can distribute, reuse, or modify work, depending on their own stipulations. The idea is aimed at those who use the Internet, and is based on the open source ethos of programmers and software developers, such as those with online artwork, or musicians with MP3 files available. The Creative Commons licenses, which are free, enable these people to let others know exactly what can be used and how, and covers websites, scholarship, music, film, photography, and literature, rather than just software.

At present, creative works are automatically copyrighted as soon as they are in a tangible medium of expression, but many wish to share their work, to use distribution to gain exposure, or because they are of a generous spirit and enjoy being part of a collective. The new licenses are an easy way to inform others that a person intends to enforce only some or none of their intellectual property rights.

The free licenses were developed with the law schools at Harvard and Stanford in such a way that they can be identified by web applications (search engines, browsers), thus ensuring that they work in the Internet environment. So, if a musician wants to allow people to copy and download his MP3 file, he can specify in the license that he permits people to distribute it and to copy it, but not to use it for any commercial purposes (without specific permission); or he can add a caveat that allows people to derive other works from his original. Others may prefer to simply let their work enter the public domain, using the licenses to declare, No rights reserved.

The Creative Commons organization also hopes to build "an intellectual works conservancy." This will work like a museum or nature preserve, to protect works of special public value and prevent them from falling into private hands. It intends to encourage donations and, ultimately, to purchase some important works. "Our ultimate goal is to develop a rich repository of high-quality works in a variety of media, and to promote an ethos of sharing, public education, and creative interactivity." In that way, as with their free licenses, they will continue to dismantle the barriers that presently hinder collaborative creativity.

→ **www.creativecommons.org**

get smart for collective action

244

Smart mobs, a term devised by the author Howard Rheingold, are groups of people who do not necessarily know each other, but who use mobile media and computer networks to organize collective action.

Rheingold has predicted that the speed and ease of connecting large numbers in this way may have hugely positive, or negative, effects in the future. For example, demonstrations against President Estrada in the Philippines in 2000 were primarily organized with text messages and were credited with helping to bring down the government. On the flipside, anarchist and terrorist groups are making use of the technology to further their ends.

The powerful thing about smart mobs is that members do not have to know each other to become engaged in a collective action, which amplifies the possible numbers beyond traditional protest groups or campaigns that organize themselves via phone calls and leafleting. The organizing capabilities of the Internet and mobile phones, and the increasing ubiquity of both technologies, provide the potential for huge groups of people to engage in activity together, whether in protest, in play, in flirting, in gaming, or in causing trouble.

One example of a smart mob is the collective of millions of people who give their computer's processing capability to the search for extraterrestrial intelligence. Another example, arguably more useful, is the group that enables the Fight Aids at Home project. These groups have shown how individual technological resources can be pooled effectively for a single aim.

As Rheingold says, "Combining the data storage, computation, and communication power of millions of PCs makes possible entirely new kinds of science, business, and social enterprise, based on the emergent power of millions of individuals."

When smart environments and smart clothing are thrown into the mix, there could come a time when a person walking down a street could wirelessly communicate with any number of ad hoc networks based practically anywhere. A single e-mail could be forwarded a million times in minutes, reaching a massive number of people on one issue or one event. The potential for social and cultural change is huge.

Rheingold's vision is one of cooperation on an unimaginable scale and, when cooperation breaks out, civilizations advance and the lives of citizens improve.

→ **www.smartmobs.com**

hear the hard truth
from hard tortilla

245

The Mexican government has funded a radio soap opera called *Hard Tortilla* in an effort to educate its people about the hardships associated with crossing over to the US. The 30-part drama gives an unbiased portrayal of what migrants crossing the border can expect when they arrive.

The program is part of an effort by Mexican authorities to persuade more people to stay in Mexico rather than pursuing the American dream, which often proves elusive or, in the worst cases, closer to a nightmare. The drama covered issues including drug abuse, AIDS, employment rights, and prison conditions, and broadcast positive stories as well as negative ones. It is hoped that the medium of radio will allow the stories (and therefore the message) to reach people who may not otherwise receive the full body of information.

The program was broadcast in those Mexican states with the highest numbers of migrants to the US, as well as on Spanish-language radio in California. While the Mexican government is aware that it needs to improve employment and economic prospects in its own country to keep people from emigrating, they also hope the radio program will have an effect.

It is not the first educational radio soap opera to be broadcast in the country: Johns Hopkins University produced over fifty such dramas that were aired in Mexico and other areas of the world, covering topics such as family planning and health information. Surveys conducted on the efficacy of programs have shown that listeners are significantly more likely to change their behavior accordingly than those who do not tune in. Whether the same will prove true in the case of *Hard Tortilla* remains to be seen, but it is an innovative approach to information dissemination that may just begin to affect public opinion.

allocate mail codes
to individuals at birth

One problem of modern life is that, as populations have become more mobile, postal addresses have changed with increasing frequency. While forwarding services exist, they are far from perfect.

One method to solve this problem is with lifetime mail codes. Modern post office letter-sorting technology could allow each individual at birth to be allocated one mail code to last a lifetime. Whenever people moved to new homes, they would simply need to inform the post office of their new address: the corre-

246

spondents would not need to be notified. People writing to the individual (or organization) need only put the particular code on the envelope (e.g., Austin28748STA), with no further name or address, and it would reach that person wherever they were. People could give out their code without fear of any unauthorized individuals knowing where they live or coming to their house. The only issue would be to ensure the security of the information in its centrally held place, the post office.

Barry Austin

investigate an
interplanetary internet

247

The Internet revolution that has spread like technological wildfire across the world may not stop at terrestrial domination.

Vint Cerf, who co-invented the TCP/IP (Transmission Control Protocol/Internet Protocol) system, which allows the Internet to work, has raised the possibility of an interplanetary Internet.

Until now, NASA (National Aeronautics and Space Administration) had no standard procedures for outer-space communication and Cerf thinks it is time that they did. His vision is of a time when every satellite, space station, and explorer probe will have the ability to send and receive Internet data. Not only would Earth to space communication be made much simpler, but satellites could even communicate with each other, perhaps eventually engendering a traffic system that needs no administration from Earth.

For now, Cerf is aiming to extend the Internet's many advantages to outer space, with Earth-space communication at the heart of that project. For example, NASA staff on Earth could communicate much more easily and reliably with a probe looking at Jupiter if the messages were traveling on an Internet system: from Earth to satellite to space station to a satellite near Jupiter and down to the probe itself. This system would be simpler, quicker, and probably cheaper than a massive radio dish or hundreds of transmitters on every planet.

Furthermore, with each new space satellite or station launched with Internet capabilities, the possible routes for messages to travel increases, simultaneously increasing the power of such an interplanetary Internet. Therefore, if one device fails, contact back to Earth would still be possible via another route in the solar system. The more Internet-enabled equipment that is launched into space, the better the system becomes, or so the theory goes. And as space traffic continues to increase, with orbiting debris from previous missions a growing problem, a system by which the space vehicles can communicate with each other could be both useful and crucial to future exploration.

→ **http://global.mci.com/us/enterprise /insight/cerfs_up/interplanetary_internet/**

scan ancient artifacts to create clones

248

Three-dimensional laser scanning technology used in medicine and aircraft design is being employed to make virtual copies of fragile historical relics; these copies can then be used to create physical clones of the original objects.

The availability of digital replicas could revolutionize the way we view the revered ancient artifacts, which have previously been available for the public's gaze only behind glass in museums. In the future, 3-D digital equivalents of entire museum catalogues could be made available to a wide audience on the web. Laser scanning fragile and ancient pieces, a process that is harmless to the object's surface, began when museum curators from Iraq asked the British Museum to make copies of 1,000 clay tablets dating from the seventh century BC. While using the traditional method of making resin moulds would take a number of years, the museum decided to employ the most cutting-edge techniques available, and obtained digital blueprints of the delicate tablets through scanning. The 3-D data was then fed into specialist robotic machinery, which uses the virtual dimensions of an object to create an exact replica. This quick and smart method has obvious benefits for museums, which could utilize the technology to display perfect copies of artifacts without compromising the fragile original structures themselves.

"It's a bit like a photocopier but a million times more powerful," says Dr. Irving Finkel of the Department of the Ancient Near East. "Imagine that you have a block of cheese. You turn on the machine and the laser cuts out this cheese in three dimensions. With this method, it takes only a few weeks to prepare immaculate replicas for exhibiting. Used in instances of objects so fragile that the originals could never otherwise be displayed, or to provide numerous museums around the world with one-off objects of significant historical worth, the technique has far-reaching possibilities."

The only downside to this is the argument that a museum's artifacts inspire awe specifically because ancient air once touched them. How satisfying would it be, for example, to view the Rosetta Stone in the knowledge that it had been crafted last Thursday?

The idea of web catalogues bearing 3-D images of the world's treasures for anyone to download in an instant is perhaps of even greater significance. Despite moves to waive museum entrance fees to encourage a more varied mix of visitors, the establishments are still viewed by many as occupying the inaccessible realms of high culture.

An Internet-based way of viewing and learning about objects would bring history to the general population in the click of a mouse, while overcoming geographical boundaries which normally prevent access to certain objects. If 3-D data was gathered from all the major museums worldwide and entered into a network of sites, the resulting web-bank would be a virtual museum of huge proportions—an extensive compendium of civilization. Not only would this be a valuable resource in itself, it might serve to extend, rather than replace, the traditional educational and inspirational role of the museum, and could instill a renewed enthusiasm for visiting those buildings that house the real, ancient objects.

→ **www.thebritishmuseum.ac.uk**

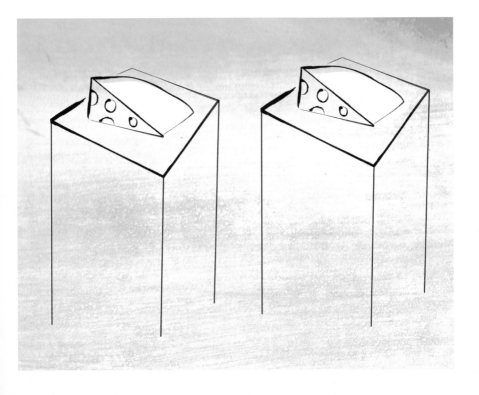

start a social epidemic
with the tipping point

The tipping point is a concept that describes how changes can come about quickly and unexpectedly.

249

Malcolm Gladwell uses the term to try to explain how these social epidemics take hold: how an unknown book becomes a bestseller, how viral marketing works, how word of mouth has such power. The phrase *tipping point* has its origins in epidemiology, the study of illness epidemics, and is the point at which epidemiologists label a virus as having reached critical mass: the moment when numbers begin to increase very rapidly.

Gladwell's argument, essentially, is that there is a similar tipping point in all areas of life, from TV to selling shoes or teenage smoking, and that ideas, behaviors, and products move through a population much like a disease does. The theory has immense potential for all sorts of people, be they involved in charities working on a limited budget or working as educators trying to reach a great number of students.

An interesting aspect to Gladwell's theory is that a very small adjustment can mean the difference between obscurity and ubiquity. As an example, he recounts a tale from the creators of the children's TV show, *Blue's Clues*, putting clues together for children to solve. The answer to the question was *penguin*, and the produc-

ers had stipulated three clues to be given in order: *ice*, *waddle*, then *black and white*. In a test on seventeen children, four guessed it after the first clue, six after the second, and four after all three. But when a teacher gave the clues to nine children in her class in the order *black and white*, *ice*, then *waddle*, the results were very different. No children got it right after the first clue, only one after the second, and six more after the third clue. Simply by changing the order of the clues, the teacher had kept suspense in the guessing game and had also allowed the children to think more broadly after earlier clues: *black and white* led to guesses of pandas, cows, and dogs, while *ice* led to polar bears. This small change led to *Blues Clues* being a hugely successful educational TV program that children loved.

Gladwell also has interesting things to say about the effectiveness of groups in magnifying the epidemic potential of a message or idea. He uses the example of book groups to show how this can occur, and then elaborates on this concept with the rule of 150. This rule suggests that groups with numbers greater than 150 lose the community ethos and can become divided and alienated, which prevents the spreading of an idea or method or message by the groups. Gladwell focuses, in particular, on the example of the Gore Associates Company (which makes Gore-Tex fabric), who limited all their plants to 150 employees. This led to strong bonds between workers, effective informal relationships, and no need for middle management. The size helps encourage peer pressure for those groups to be successful; because each of the 150 knows everyone personally, they know their strengths, weaknesses, ways of working, and how best people interact; and they also know that information and ideas can filter much more swiftly among them—the size enables the tipping point to take effect more easily.

The above demonstrates one of three rules that Gladwell claims is crucial to reaching tipping point: the power of context (environment is important). The other two rules are the law of the few (it only takes a small number of people to make a big change) and "stickiness" (as illustrated by the clues on the TV program). In addition to these rules, Gladwell also identifies three main personality types that are crucial to the spreading of a social epidemic: connectors, mavens, and salesmen. *Connectors* are the people who know lots of other people, the people with the fullest address books. *Mavens* are the accumulators of knowledge (on particular topics) who then share this understanding with others. *Salesmen* are those who convince others that this information is valuable, relevant, or important. All three play a key role in tipping an epidemic.

Essentially, what Malcolm Gladwell has done is take a scientific theory and made it relevant to our lives. In doing so, he has shown why the public should no longer be surprised at unforeseen runaway successes or word-of-mouth bestsellers. In addition, more tellingly, he has demonstrated how people might attempt to start their own positive epidemics for social good.

install cell phone jammers for cinema silence

The French government has brought in legislation that will surely meet with the approval of cinemagoers everywhere. This legislation allows cinemas, concert halls, and theaters to install cell phone jammers in order to ensure silence in those arenas.

The approval came with the caveat that emergency calls could still be accessed. The president of the National Federation of French Cinemas, Jean Labbe, said that the measure was a response to a longstanding request from cinemas of all sizes.

relish the real world on international internet-free day

251

A not-for-profit website for participatory events in every city in the world, www.GlobalIdeasBank.org, promotes the last Sunday of January as International Internet-Free Day, a day for doing and being out in the real world.

The Global Ideas Bank proposes:

"It's a matter of reclaiming the web, using it for a different message. The Internet did not start off as a vehicle for social isolation and damaged eyesight. That is what big business has done with it. It began as a medium for communication between researchers, a quick and simple way of exchanging information.

"But it's so easy nowadays to get addicted to a half life in a virtual world, and to lose touch with your family, friends, and neighbors. Yet we're creatures evolved from a tribal past and an annual Internet-Free Day on the fourth Sunday in January is a recognition of our need for contacts out in the real world. E-mail and the Internet are just not enough."

The slogan for the day is:

"Log Out! Get Out! Get a Life! The real world needs you!"

Have you started tilting your head sideways to smile? When you check your e-mail and it says "No new messages," do you immediately check again? Do you dream in HTML? You could be spending too much time on the Internet. Here are a few good reasons to join the real world on Internet-Free Day:

→ Because it's all too easy to miss out on face-to-face interaction with your family, friends, and neighbors.

→ Because the net can be addictive and one day of cold turkey won't hurt.

→ Because blogging doesn't provide your daily vitamins and minerals.

→ Because you've got repetitive strain injury (RSI) coming on in your mouse arm.

→ Because we all need time to reflect.

→ Because the real world is a wonderful place.

→ Because if the mere idea of it enrages you, you definitely need it.

We're not alone in our opinion. There are companies who have e-mail-free Fridays (see page 178), there are Internet addiction courses and camps, and there are studies into the psychological effects of excessive Internet use. And we're only suggesting one day off from the Internet (including e-mail) and it's a Sunday.

Obviously, there is a certain irony to a web-based project promoting an Internet-free day, but this is not an anti-Internet campaign. The web has brought numerous benefits to hundreds of thousands of people through easier communication, networks of support, consumer choice, access to news and information or, as the recent tsunami relief effort has shown, coordinating campaigns and donations to help others. Nevertheless, recent events should remind us of what is truly important: friends, family, health, and freedom.

→ **http://members.aol.com/Iainmacn /addicts/ (Internet Anonymous)**
→ **www.globalideasbank.org/site/bank/ idea.php?ideaId=4312 (e-mail free Friday)**
→ **www.netaddiction.com/resources/ internet_addiction_test.htm**

track news topics
for complete picture

252

News sources, whether newspapers, television stations, or magazines, all lack story follow-through.

The general public is fed newsworthy topics in often small, incomplete pieces. The sources determine which topics will be covered and how, and are rarely committed to educating the general public on a subject, or to following through. You can spend a lot of time reading and listening to many news sources to become well-informed, and can still be left with the question, "What ever happened to…?"

The idea, therefore, is to create an Internet-based news source that is committed to following a story to its completion. The site could be set up with categories or themes, and also divided by country and region where applicable. The news should be delivered by qualified investigative reporters who are committed to reporting the story from a holistic perspective and who are committed to seeing the story to its end.

Users of this source would be able to track the stories of their choosing and receive e-mail notices when an update to the story is listed on the site. In this way, whenever the "whatever happened?" question arises, they will be able to find the answer. The website, which would ideally be cooperatively owned by its members, could be called Tracking The News or The Long Run.

The site could even have a quarterly newspaper offshoot that gives detailed reports and updates to the bigger picture that much of daily news ignores or overlooks. Such a periodical could also serve to remind the public about big issues that are ongoing: Aids in Africa, or the devastation of the rainforests. It could also show how positive moves are being made, and how changes have occurred over time. Such a journalistic initiative could even be funded by a major organization such as the United Nations.

Janet DeLapp / Floris

teach computers common sense

253

Doug Lenat has been amassing a database of human common sense for over twenty years, in an attempt to give computers the ability to understand language in the way that humans do.

His vision is that applications incorporating common sense will be less likely to fail in the real world. So, over one-and-a-half million facts about the everyday world have been put into Cycs (short for encyclopedia) memory banks. This means that Cyc knows that a glass is held with the open-side up, people stop buying things when they die, and trees are generally found outdoors. This common sense, or *consensus knowledge* as Lenat's company prefers to call it, enables the computer to reason as a human would, using applications and documents. This could eliminate one of the differences between humans and computers.

As an example of what Cyc can presently do, it is being used to improve the quality of retrievals for the Lycos search engine. Thus, when a term such as *Guatemala* is entered, the search engine will not immediately pop up with several "Would you like to buy a Guatemala?" or "Where can I get free Guatemala online?" offers. In the same way, but on a more positive note, if a term such as *dime* is entered, the engine will offer Franklin D. Roosevelt as a topic, because it knows his picture is on that coin. Common sense ensures a greater relevancy and accuracy.

Lenat believes that all software will eventually incorporate common sense, although it is taking him longer than originally thought to amass the facts needed. This is due to having to enter not only facts into the computer, but also the context for those facts, without which some of them can be misleading, ambiguous, or just plain wrong.

The potential uses for such a database will be massive. Imagine an internal security system that takes account of disaffected ex-employees, or a spreadsheet that notices hourly and monthly figures mistakenly added together. Imagine a computer with common sense.

➜ **www.cyc.com**

seat groups in circles
to step up support and safety

Taking part in a Community Counseling Circles group led by the unorthodox Freudian analyst John Southgate is an enlivening experience. It is the most dynamic advance in working with large groups since pioneering Dr. S. H. Foulkes devised the Group-Analytic method in the 1960s.

Community Counseling Circles were designed for training large groups and addressing the main problem with working with large groups: the lack of feelings of safety and mutual support. Under this system, the atmosphere in the group is improved by seating members in four concentric circles.

The innermost circle is treated as a single person "client," and this group free associates with all the other circles as its therapists; the second circle concentrates on noticing the emotional climate; the third circle on any material that might relate to parental and family relationships; and the fourth circle on organizational problems in life and work.

The whole group resembles an individual's psychic world, and the members learn about the innermost dynamics of individual people while at the same time being educated in group dynamics and the way communities operate.

Community Counseling Circles have been used in area health authorities, social work train-ing, and at universities in the UK. Settings where they have been tried include group and management training; among psychiatric workers and district nurses; in cooperatives and communities; in local government groups; and in women's and ethnic groups.

→ **www.globalideasbank.org/site/store**

254

make media labs from
cost-free computers and software

Although the Internet has opened up many possibilities to people across the world, it does have one major drawback: online access costs.

255

A group of artists in Sheffield created a media lab with computers and software they obtained completely for free. They managed to create web pages, process images, publicize creative projects, set up networks, and much more, relying particularly on Linux, the free operating system.

They created an exhibition with a video wall (which cost them nothing), and also a drop-in lab that allows access to creative technology for local people. The beauty of it is that people are constantly updating their system, so the quality of the free technology also constantly improves. With recycling regulations set to become more stringent, such re-use programs could become increasingly common.

The UK's Redundant Technology Initiatives founder James Wallbank put the project in these terms: "What we've shown is that you simply don't need a capital budget to get involved with digital media—you just need a small group of committed people prepared to learn new skills." Now they hope to help others use the knowledge and expertise they've gained.

→ **www.lowtech.org**

encourage international body
to supply free antivirus software

If an international body were to provide regularly updated antivirus software for free on the Internet, developing countries would be less likely to be crippled by the effects of rogue computer viruses.

256

As a scientific adviser who worked for a government office in Tanzania, Matti Nummelin found himself spending much of his time removing viruses from machines. Thanks to the constantly updated software sent by the Finnish home office, he had excellent tools and could deal with the problems quickly. He proposes that a body such as the UN Development Program coordinate the creation of antivirus software that anybody can download for free on the Internet.

foster patriotism and togetherness with open source software

257

Open source technology has been heralded as a force for liberation from big business and lauded, with its free distribution and collective improvements, as effective social and virtual collaboration.

The Spanish region of Extremadura has now taken open source into new territory: a regional operating system provided free to all residents. The objective of this act of digital socialism is to empower the local people and to foster new growth and new business in the area, thus preventing many people from leaving the area for employment, since it is the poorest region of Spain in economic and technological terms. The power of the Internet and other applications could, the local authorities believe, reduce Extremadura's traditionally peripheral nature in the country. Alongside this provision of resources, and inexorably contained in it, is the hope that the project will also help foster patriotism and a loyalty to the region itself.

The local authority, under the auspices of regional president Juan Carlos Rodriguez Ibarra, produced 150,000 CDs that contain a customized version of Linux (the widely known open source operating system) called LinEx. The free CD includes a package containing a word processing package, an e-mail client, an Internet browser, a spreadsheet application, and even an MP3 player. The package in itself is nothing new; what is novel is the customization of the system to make it specific to Extremadura. The e-mail application logo is the stork, the bird of the region; the word processor is named after a local poet; and the system contains countless other symbols and references to the region. In this way, the distribution of the LinEx package to its residents not only empowers them to take part in the information industry (or the digital revolution), but also encourages allegiance to their homeland. The system has been installed in 40,000 schools and is used by twice that number of students.

The region also took this approach because it was by far the most cost-effective and flexible for the sweeping changes they wished to introduce. It has proved a low-cost way of raising technological literacy in the area and in providing services to educational and business institutions. If others follow the lead, there could be a world of digitally and globally connected regions, working from free software for a better future.

→ **www.linex.org**

get peace of mind from text messaging service

A text-message-based service called AmberResponse aims to provide peace of mind for friends and relatives for those taking journeys or traveling alone.

The person who is traveling simply sends details of their journey to AmberResponse (where they are going, how they are traveling, who to contact if they don't arrive) via simple text messages. A text is then sent to start the service, and another to stop it, all for just 50p ($1) a time. The innovative part occurs if the journey is not completed: if AmberResponse does not receive the second text message confirming arrival, it automatically sends a text message to the emergency contact. That person can then contact AmberResponse via phone or web to find out more information about the journey, quoting a PIN number sent as part of the emergency text. The contact can then take appropriate action, taking into account the person involved and the nature of the journey.

AmberResponse is the brainchild of Hugh Douglas-Smith, who was involved in a scuba-diving incident during which he became aware

258

of the fact that no one knew where they were or when they were expected back. Thus, no one would raise the alarm until it was potentially too late. Having survived that incident unscathed, he set about using a flight plan model for personal safety: a simple plan is submitted by text message, and if the journey is not completed, the authorities (in this case, the emergency contact) are alerted.

Clearly the system could be useful for anyone undertaking activities such as sailing, climbing, walking, and so on, and could help reduce search and rescue times where the circumstances could be serious.

On a day-to-day level, the system could be used by teenagers going out for an evening (to alleviate concern of parents), by someone walking home alone, or by a driver taking an unfamiliar route home. The system is ingenious because it is simple, cost-effective, and makes use of technology that is widely used.

→ **www.amberresponse.com**
→ **www.safetytext.com**

learn linguistic evidence of truth and fact

259

An Amazonian language that is threatened with extinction may hold valuable lessons for us all.

Tariana is particularly rich in what are called evidentials—markers used in a statement to denote the evidence on which the statement is based. For example, rather than the statement being simply "Simon kissed a woman," it would translate as "Simon kissed a woman, visual" or "Simon kissed a woman, reported." Evidentiality is obligatory in Tariana: it is a grammatical error not to use evidentials, which means that inherent in the language is the requirement to tell the truth. Liars and equivocators do not prosper in Tariana, as their use of the language makes it obvious that they are omitting details.

Alexandra Aikhenvald, an Australian expert in Tariana, has made a suggestion that could change society. As she puts it, "Wouldn't it be great if our politicians had obligatory evidentials, and were compelled by the language to say exactly how they knew that children had been thrown overboard?" This is in particular reference to the Australian furore where government officials claimed that refugees were throwing their children overboard in order to procure asylum, a claim later alleged to be false.

The same could also apply to the debate over weapons of mass destruction; imagine if each politician (and journalist) had to say how they knew about each piece of evidence. The lesson of Tariana is that precision in language is important, and that languages can be extended to communicate more than is often thought possible or viable. The obligatory evidentials legislation is eagerly awaited.

It is also worth noting that speakers of Tariana, who live in the northwest of the Amazonian jungle, traditionally marry someone who speaks a different language. As a result, most speak five or six languages. This multilingualism makes the area unique and also preserves the individual languages. Again, though, there is a lesson for the wider world in their practice. Imagine the changes in people's outlook if it were a tradition to marry someone who is from a different culture and who speaks a different language.

get on your bike
for some internet magic

New York artist Yury Gitman is the creator of a bicycle that is also a wi-fi hub: a wireless bike that has access to Internet connectivity wherever it goes.

260

The bike has wi-fi antennas on the frame linked to a laptop in a bag behind the saddle. The Internet connection is received from nearby hotspots or the cellular network, borrowing bandwidth from open networks (a practice that is a grey area in law).

The idea was originally intended as an art project—a bit of fun—but more serious applications of the technology have since become apparent. In New York, the MagicBike (as Gitman calls his creation) is a cause célèbre in the art and cultural world, appearing at galleries and public demonstrations. At the leading edge of Internet connectivity, though, the bike could prove to be a genuine solution to problems of access. As Gitman says, his bike demonstrates that a grassroots bottom-up wireless infrastructure can be formed and pedaled to any place accessible by bicycle. As such, the idea is attracting attention from groups all over the world and many more MagicBikes, or similar versions of it, may soon be seen on the streets in countries across the globe.

→ **www.magicbike.net**

participate in peer-to-peer programs for medical research

261

A peer-to-peer project has linked hundreds of thousands of computers to use their unused resources to process data for medical research.

Anyone with a PC and an Internet connection can join in the venture, simply by downloading a program onto their computer. The program runs by using that individual's computer resources to process a small parcel of data, before sending the results back to a server. It then requests a new parcel of data to process and so on (the sending and receiving of data is done only when the individual is connected to the Internet).

The program does not affect the computer's performance, as it uses only processing power not being used. In this way, hundreds of thousands of computer owners can contribute to the fight against illness and disease, simply by using the Internet.

Peer-to-peer technology is best known as the basis for the music-swapping website Napster, but it simply refers to the sharing of resources (such as hard drives and processing cycles) among computers and other intelligent devices. In essence, the technology creates a huge virtual supercomputer by virtue of connecting lots of smaller ones together; the more personal computers that are connected, the bigger the supercomputer's power and reach. There are those who have concerns about privacy, security, and other issues with regard to peer-to-peer technology, but it has massive potential for doing good as well, as this project makes clear.

Other such projects could promote a whole new era of what might be termed techno-philanthropy: there are already peer-to-peer initiatives fighting Aids, researching nuclear waste disposal, looking for extra-terrestrial life, and supporting Alzheimer's research.

In 2004, IBM launched a charitable program intended to improve scientific research through coordinating such projects. The program, called the World Community Grid, was developed in collaboration with the National Institute of Health, the World Health Organization, the United Nations, and other organizations. The plan to combine computer resources and the shared knowledge of researchers will accelerate the pace of scientific discovery. The first area of exploration will be human gene calculations and genetic testing.

In addition to supporting philanthropic projects, peer-to-peer projects could have powerful positive effects in the business world as well. The technology's fast communication and collective power makes it suitable for large businesses to use for distributing information. Rather than having a large central server on the premises, a business can set up a system whereby an employee's PC simply downloads the file from the nearest computer that has that file. This speeds up the process and reduces the need for costly servers.

While much has been written about the security dangers of peer-to-peer, with its potential for unregulated, anonymous distribution of information, it is also worth noting that the technology could be used to improve computer security. It may not be long before anti-virus updates and patches to mend software problems are distributed in this way, ensuring a quicker tightening of loopholes for viruses and hackers. The possibilities for collaboration, instant messaging, document distribution, and anonymous storage are also massive, and could lead to a complete computing revolution.

→ **www.p2pwg.org**
→ **www.worldcommunitygrid.org**
→ **www.fightaidsathome.org**

revel in the revolution
of internet collaboration

262

Open source collaboration on the Internet began mainly in software development but it has major revolutionary potential across the board.

It is called *open source* because the process is open to everyone, as is the source code of the software. A piece of software can be improved upon by thousands of people worldwide. In essence, it uses dispersed networks of motivated programmers and coders to create better models and versions of software for free. In the software world, open source has challenged traditional ideas of who owns something, as well as determining the best method for fostering innovation. People are attracted by the ideals embodied in the open source process: openness, collaboration, low-cost, responsiveness, and independence.

The story began with Linux, a computer operating system developed by Finnish programmer Linus Torvalds. In the 1990s, he sent out an e-mail asking for feedback and suggestions to implement in his system. Thousands of programmers and developers replied; their input helped build Linux, widely regarded as the most stable operating system, second only to Microsoft in the world of servers and network computers.

People have always collaborated to develop new solutions or new ideas, because a diversity of voices helps ensure that nothing is missed. Similar concepts at work can be seen in the creation of the *Oxford English Dictionary* in the 19th century, in which philologists and etymologists sent in their definitions by mail. Now the Internet lets a huge network of people worldwide be instantly connected, to respond swiftly, to interact and edit online, and collaborate on a major scale.

Others have followed in Linux's footsteps. To go to the SourceForge website today is to see over 65,000 collaborative software projects in progress. Open source projects are spreading like wildfire across the net, relying on motivated people wishing to contribute their knowledge to create an impressive entity. There is Wikipedia, for example, an online encyclopedia created by contributors worldwide. Anyone is free to write an entry and, adhering to open source principles, anyone else can edit it. Revisions and changes are pored over by dedicated volunteers, and the encyclopedia continues to grow. Boasting more than 150,000 different entries, Wikipedia receives more web traffic than the online *Britannica*.

Other projects include the Massachusetts Institute of Technology's Open Courseware project, which has posted course materials for 500 classes online, all of which are freely downloadable. There is also Project Gutenberg, in which volunteers type in some of the world's famous classic literary texts: 6,000 are online. Delightfully, a related project called Distributed Proofreading uses volunteer copy editors to check the typed texts. There are open source cookbooks, open source films, open source crime solving, and open source music.

This openness, which carries proprietary issues of ownership, has often led to accusations of open source being anticorporate and anticapitalist, as proponents seem to be motivated by dislike of ownership and closed systems. However, the open source movement is more about being able to contribute and create than it is about being against anything. It is also not anticapitalist: companies providing bespoke Linux solutions (like Red Hat) have made a lot of money. Indeed, open source is in some ways the direct embodiment of free market ideals and the drive for efficiency and cost-effectiveness. What the open source movement is doing is encouraging people to question the way things are being done.

In answering these questions, the discussion begins to move away from technology-based solutions and ideas. Open source could provide a way of looking at how we do things in the real world as well as the virtual one. For example, we might apply open source principles and methods to democracy. On one level, politicians and campaigners could use open source more effectively to involve their audience in the process. Potential slogans could be run past the network, suggestions for improvements made on ad campaigns, policies posted and edited/improved by interested parties, all of which could decrease political apathy and disillusionment.

Douglas Rushkoff has suggested that open source democracy would require us to go back into the code of our processes and question everything that it is based on. This would involve stripping back the current system and collaboratively building it up from scratch to ensure that all have an understanding of how it works.

Open source can open our eyes to new possibilities: an open-source economy based on an open-source money model in which we are not at the whim of market speculation and a closed banking system; an open-source democracy created by the people for the people, in which participation occurs on all levels; an open-source world in which collaboration exists equally alongside competition.

These ideas might be seen as dreams, but open source is increasingly impacting our world and the way people think. Open source fosters a community of individuals who understand how involvement affects the whole, who understand self-education and participation, and who fully comprehend the effect of local individual actions in a global collaborative network.

➔ **www.sourceforge.net**
➔ **www.linux.org**

change the world from the inside with a blog

263

A web log—or *blog*—is a website where anyone can easily post daily thoughts about virtually any subject: an easily publishable online journal.

The term *blog*, which works as a noun and verb, originated in 1997, and the practice of blogging began. What began as a simple format for individuals to post ideas or personal concerns is beginning to change and affect society in different ways, many of which demonstrate what the Internet has been said to facilitate: empowering the individual, creating communities, and connecting like-minded people.

Blogs are being taken more seriously because bloggers can respond to events quickly and with great focus, and they have undeniable reach and audience. They are also able to break stories with great speed, and follow up links and leads that may have escaped the traditional press. It is also arguable that they have livened public debate in the US, at least among the web-savvy generation. As one *Time* magazine article on the phenomenon defined debating the issues online, "Blogs are America thinking out loud, talking to itself." The same is now happening across the globe in countries with substantial web populations.

This empowering of the people on the ground—the individual armed with only a computer, a web connection, and an engaged political mind—is one key to blogging's potential. Because of its interlinked nature, blog posts often rise up in search engines, so the realm of the bloggers (sometimes called Blogistan) has major online power.

Blogs have filled gaps in traditional media reporting and acted as a focused and powerful counter to reports relying on rumors and half-truths or misreporting in the media. Urban myths do not last long in this environment.

Some newspapers have taken an enlightened approach to blogger corrections, admitting that they do not have the manpower to check all facts. One paper, *The Philadelphia Inquirer*, invited the editors of one website (spinsanity.org) to provide weekly material evaluating the truthfulness of speeches and other media reports.

The blogging phenomenon affects not only media and politics, but also provides a platform for the specialist, the isolated, and the unacknowledged—voices that might not otherwise be heard.

→ **www.blogger.com**
→ **www.typepad.com**
→ **www.bloglines.com**
→ **www.globalideasblog.com**

chapter 12

economics
and business

boost your biceps for better business

264

Disputes between companies often result in lengthy court hearings and huge legal fees, with lawyers the only real winners. As an antidote, telecom companies Team Talk and MCS Global Digital in New Zealand decided on a new form of settlement: an arm-wrestling contest between their CEOs. At stake was access to a mobile radio network both companies wanted to use, worth £70,000 ($140,000), and the route to success was quite literally placed in their own hands.

After three rounds, Team Talk executive David Ware was defeated, claiming, "Sure, losing hurts, but not nearly as much as paying lawyers' bills." Ware's firm also promotes the unconventional use of leisure-related etiquette to provide solutions in other areas of business. For example, chatting around Team Talk's now legendary indoor barbecue, held every Friday, provides a desirable alternative to discussing work over formal drinks.

Whether arm wrestling will take off is questionable, but it does lead to a more general questioning of current business practices: more direct negotiation and fewer legal intermediaries could save a lot of time and money.

formulate a fat cat index for companies that are out of line

265

To identify quickly which company executives take most from their firms, you could define a measure for each company, calculated as the total remuneration package of the top-paid executive divided by the average number of employees working for that organization during the financial year. This idea could be called the Fat Cat Index.

This index should highlight those companies where each individual employee contributes unduly large amounts for the benefit of the precious few, and allow investors and potential investors to investigate where a company is out of line with other companies within a particular market sector.

Perhaps in being so visible to the public eye, the directors would be less able to hide behind the old barrier that the salaries are set by the remuneration committee.

Andrew Hobbs

contribute to community building to help humanity and heal the earth

266

An Egyptian firm, Sekem, is showing other companies the way to combine social, environmental, and monetary aims in a truly holistic package.

Sekem specializes in organic products and medicines and also funds schools, clinics, and other facilities in the community. As the company's website puts it: "We endeavor to build our economic, social, and cultural activities so that they invigorate each other."

Dr. Ibrahim Abouleish's thriving company pulls in $14 (£7) million annually; 15 to 20 percent goes to social developments and products. Products such as herbal medicines and teas are produced by Egyptian farmers, who pay $7 (£3.50) per cultivated acre. The farmers also donate a portion of salaries toward schools, clinics, and social developments. As a reward, workers enjoy a soccer field, recreation center, and theater.

"I had a vision of a three-fold social project that would allow me to contribute to community-building, humanity, and healing the earth," says Abouleish.

→ **www.sekem.com**

speed network for efficient supplier sourcing

267

Sales calls are the bane of all involved: it can be difficult for the caller to get through to the person they need to speak to, and the person called may find the call inconvenient.

However, sourcing good suppliers is vital; one way to do this is speed networking—it would work exactly like speed dating except that it would be a room full of potential customers and suppliers. Each customer would have ten minutes with each supplier, and if they think they might want to buy from or sell to the person, they make a note on their score pad. At the end of the evening, the organizers work out whose answers match and pass contact details on to those that do.

Chris Kemp-Salt

→ **www.networkingforprofessionals.com**
→ **www.contact25.com**

foster franchises
to perk up communities

268

As phone and Internet banking have increased, the closure of local branches of banks has become commonplace. The effect is twofold: loss of service to the community and a negative economic impact on local businesses, as people travel further away to bank and, therefore, to shop.

A bank in Australia has pioneered a new approach to this problem: the local community becomes a franchisee of the bank and takes ownership of the branch. This provides the community with the resources, technology, and expertise of a major bank, but also gives local residents and businesses a major incentive to use the branch's services, thus ensuring its viability. Moreover, the community bank initiative encourages the franchisee group to manage its capital better and to share in revenues (via dividends) from any profits from the branch. In this way, opening the branch of such a bank can also be part of a greater transformation of the community as a whole.

There are now well over 130 such franchises in Australia, with about 30 new branches opened each year. To establish a branch, communities form a local company or trust, which invests between £200,000 ($400,000) and £350,000 ($700,000) in purchasing the right to run the bank franchise.

Bendigo Bank, which started the initiative, performs all the banking functions, provides training and support, and retains some control over opening hours and credit decisions. The local community company provides the building, pays the staff, and covers all running costs. Whatever profit is left over is returned to Bendigo Bank, which distributes it as share dividends to investors.

The initiative has also proved to be a success for Bendigo, which has built up 250,000 new customers in just six years, and the demand has led to the creation of 50 new jobs at the bank (as well as 650 in the franchises).

The strength of the initiative is the way it ties in the local community. As shareholders and customers, the local user base will always be committed to using the branch. Bendigo Bank tries to help the communities get as high a return on their capital as possible, and encourages them to join together and use their collective power in other areas (e.g., recycling). Though the ultimate success of a branch relies on strong local leadership, skills development, and good governance, it is a model that could be implemented in other countries.

→ **www.bendigobank.com.au/public/
community_bank**

float your boat with interest-free bank loans

269

The JAK Members Bank is the first interest-free bank in Sweden. The bank is owned and managed by its 27,000 members, with its primary purpose being to provide members with interest-free loans. In essence, people trade in the right to earn interest on their savings for the right to be able to borrow without interest as well. JAK was formally recognized as a bank in 1997, having existed in various forms since 1965. This recognition meant that people's savings were officially covered and protected by the Swedish banking system's deposit guarantees.

The bank has initiated local enterprise banks, which allow members to earmark their savings to support local businesses. Two such Local Enterprise Bank accounts were opened in 2000, one by the administrators of an ecological slaughterhouse, the other by a village to support a Viking history replica project. Both projects had been turned down by other banks for loans, but were funded by JAK, as people moved their savings to the accounts. In the case of the slaughterhouse, many local farmers switched their bank accounts to the specific account, as it allowed them to conduct farming in a traditional and ecological manner. Local capital is used as a base to finance the local project, while JAK carries the credit risk.

JAK, which stands for Land, Labor, and Capital (*Jord, Arbete, Kapital* in Swedish), is renowned for campaigning to spread information about the potential for an interest-free monetary system. It disseminates examples of the damaging effects of the interest-bearing credit system while simultaneously providing an example of the possibilities.

C. Waite

→ **www.jak.se**

let happiness be a nation's measure of success

270

Led by King Jigme Singye Wangchuck, the kingdom of Bhutan is the only country in the world to measure well-being by Gross National Happiness (GNH) not Gross National Product (GNP). This unorthodox approach questions the values of unbridled economic progress and foregrounds the importance of maintaining a balance between tradition and modernization.

GNH is an official policy of the kingdom, passed in parliament. One example of its use is that the country limits the number of tourists allowed to visit, as the Bhutanese complained tourism was affecting the environment and spoiling sacred lands.

GNH also aims to put an end to spiritual hunger. Material and technological progress is not banned, but it must not be detrimental to the value of human life and humanity's soul. It puts Buddhist principles at the heart of life, replacing the conventional measure of a nation's economic performance, the GNP. Should a nation's success be judged by its ability to produce and consume or on the quality of life and the happiness of its people?

The Bhutanese approach is based on the belief that happiness is not determined by what we own, but by our knowledge, living skills, and imagination: by being, not by having.

The need to incorporate unquantifiable factors, such as emotional intelligence, in economics and to base development on more than production and consumption is becoming increasingly recognized. Amartya Sen, for example, defines economic development in terms of freedom of basic necessities like education and healthcare.

Steps in this direction include the World Bank's Wealth Index (which includes the concepts of human capital and environmental capital); the UN Human Development Index (which measures things like education provision and human-rights records); and the Calvert-Henderson Quality of Life Indicators, which include cultural values and activities of self-improvement and group participation.

But none of these incorporates the spiritual dimension, in which mind always comes over matter and material development is a means for people to achieve personal and spiritual development. This concept leads to a type of Buddhist economics, where material factors might be measured only for the amount of time they allow followers to develop their minds and inner selves.

→ **www.neweconomics.org**
→ **www.calvert-henderson.com**

make the small print
as large as the large print

Everyone complains that contracts and application forms use small print as escape clauses because people either do not notice or cannot be bothered to read through great swathes of written material, particularly when it is eye-wateringly tiny.

Why not enforce or lobby for a change so that all contractual material (including exclu-

271

sions, etc.) has to be the same size print as the rest of the text?

This would not only encourage (or perhaps force) companies to reduce their exclusions, but would also encourage these companies to make their documents as simple and as clear as possible.

George Rogers

start a procott
of ethical products

A procott movement is a positive way of promoting and endorsing earth-friendly and justice-friendly goods and services. A *procott* is the direct opposite of a *boycott* and would help support and raise the profile of those providing and producing ethical products and services.

The idea of a procott movement is to amass information in community groups about consumer choices, new products, and so on, and to spend a certain percentage each month on those ethical goods. Gradually, such mutual support and information sharing could help groups link into a network in which lists of retailers and service providers are swapped. A

272

procott catalogue and website may emerge, and collaborating groups would be a force to lobby businesses and retailers to produce and stock the products.

The citizen-consumer procott would organize people to buy ethical and educate them toward being more conscious consumers. Discussion groups with other members would begin a grassroots movement using a combination of cooperation and direct action to allow people to be non-violent activists for change.

Amy Coursen, Kathy Clark, Libby Friedrich, Gary McClelland, and Sox Sperry

→ **www.procott.org**

set up a tank
to test new ideas

273

Many people are unemployed, underemployed, or merely undervalued. These people, whether young graduates, retired workers, or those between jobs, can contribute much to developing ideas and products, but their expertise, enthusiasm, and experience are often not tapped into.

A local product tank could change this. For example, in the hub would be all the machinery, tools, and equipment needed to run a successful workshop. Retired electronic engineers could assist people with an interest in electronic engineering to work on projects sourced from business.

The tank would work as follows: a business may have a project to develop, but not enough time or money. The business would pay a small fee for the group to work on it. If they make a successful prototype, the business pays a success fee plus royalties. The outcome is employment opportunities and skill development for young graduates, a good retirement for engineers, and a low cost way of testing new ideas.

John Töns

play the fool for
corporate creativity

274

British Airways' employee Paul Birch was appointed as the company's official corporate jester for a term in the 1990s. Birch had approached the director of corporate strategy with his idea, proposing an official jester might play a useful part in the company, just as medieval precursors had in royal courts. His thinking was that the modern board of directors is like a medieval court, where no one questions the king or senior courtiers, because they have become far too important for anybody to challenge...as long as they can't possibly be wrong, they can continue doing the wrong things all the time and not know it.

A corporate jester is a means of counteracting tacit anxiety and conformity pervading management that inhibits open, creative thinking. The jester is not part of the reporting structure and can question management without fear of repercussions. He can therefore serve a serious role as the mouthpiece for unorthodox criticism, couched as harmless jest.

offer free eco-audits for firms that spread the word

The Eco-Lighthouse concept of free eco-audits has become one of Kristiansand's prime exports. It originated in 1996, when Kristiansand was selected along with six other municipalities to participate in Sustainable Communities, a Norwegian Local Agenda 21 pilot program.

275

The city authorities began by offering a deal to a diverse selection consisting of nine firms, ranging from a hotel and a housepainter to an ice-cream factory and a wood products company. The city paid a consultant to do an eco-audit of the firms and, in cooperation with workers and management, to draw up a three-year plan for reducing their resource consumption and environmental impact as well as improving the work environment.

In return, the firms undertook not only to carry out the plan but also to disseminate their experiences to other firms in the same sphere of business. Based on the audits, criteria for local environmental certification initiatives—specific to the kinds of businesses involved—were also worked out.

The original Lighthouse firms became eligible for certification once the first measures in the consultant's plans had been carried out. Other firms could apply for certification and receive a 50 percent subsidy for consultancy.

As a result of its success, the initiative was expanded to encompass 31 branches, and some 70 firms were certified in the Kristiansand region alone. Kristiansand was encouraged to sell its Eco-Lighthouse know-how to other municipalities. Many municipalities bought into the idea, and many firms outside Kristiansand became certified.

The Norwegian Ministry of Environment adapted the concept as a national program. The ministry granted money to run a national Eco-Lighthouse office in Kristiansand for a three-year test period and initiated a national board with representatives from industry and public organizations. The record is an impressive one: by March 2004, there were 58 different trade criteria, almost 600 certified firms, and over 180 municipalities in the project.

The project's success stems from two factors: 1) it has been kept cheap, simple, and practical; and 2) Lighthouse firms spread the concept to other colleagues in the same business. Most firms cut costs and environmental impact. Some of the most positive results come from improving the work environment—firms often report how having employees work together on a positive project is beneficial.

→ **www.eco-lighthouse.com**

make sustainability
pay for itself

A report from the UK's Royal Society suggests privatizing common areas of the world will improve conservation efforts.

276

The theory is that using market forces can give people a financial reason to conserve and thus help protect the world's environment and biodiversity. Furthermore, utilizing aspects of the capitalist system can cut the costs of conservation by making it more efficient. The study argues that traditional methods of government-led conservation have failed: protected zones, international aid and the like have all struggled to make any significant impact on the problem. This has led to economists calling for market forces to be introduced on a wider basis, in an effort to make sustainability pay for itself.

The model for the theory is the successful US market-based system for reducing acid rain. A market was created for permits to emit sulphur dioxide; trading in this way cut the expected costs of reducing emissions by 90 percent. Other examples of similar emissions trading of greenhouse gases were proposed under the Kyoto treaty. This report suggests going much further, though, with forest owners allowed to "sell" the carbon-absorbing capacity of their trees, thus allowing them to make money by not cutting them down. The economists envision this practice being extended to water markets where polluters could make money by cleaning up their own pollution, and to protecting soils by encouraging farmers not to plow (again via a market system).

The downside is that the people who trade in such markets would want ownership of the environment. Environmentalists fear this could be another way of stealing the planet's resources from poorer, developing countries. Millions live and rely on land and forest they do not own; a process of privatizing that habitat could well make them significantly worse off. And it will not ease those anxieties to know that the US is at the forefront of privatization suggestions and has yet to endorse the Kyoto Protocol.

There are problems with conventional conservation methods, but the concern is that introducing capitalist principles to the arena will only cause more. Ian Swingland, one of the authors of the report, disagrees, saying that, "Unless the enormous value of the biosphere and the services it provides can be made tangible to all through free markets and prices, we are all too likely to continue to squander them with disastrous consequences for biodiversity, and perhaps, for the human race itself." This is not a debate that is going to go away.

→ **www.pubs.royalsoc.ac.uk**

count on co-op to provide accounting for social sector

277

The social economy displays a lot of rhetoric about shared values and working together. Sometimes the rhetoric is more prevalent than the action.

The social sector needs to recognize, however, that it leaks money into the private sector all the time. Most commonly, this is for professional services including audit and accounting fees. Why can't professional services firms set up as membership co-ops be established to provide required corporate governance and audit/accountancy services?

Set up as a double bottom line social enterprise with a more than profit attitude, organizational needs would be met but profits would be retained in the co-op's membership. The advantages are not just financial: the co-op would display the values of the sector, and services could be designed to meet member needs not just compliance matters. In this way, charities and not-for-profit organizations could benefit from more targeted, more ethical and, potentially, cheaper accounting services.

Declan Jones

employ an internal activist to generate goodwill

278

Multinational corporations make many mistakes in their global dealings. They sometimes damage the environment, use child labor, or become involved with corrupt regimes. Occasionally, a group of activists strikes and successfully pulls off a boycott campaign. The company loses profit and decides to change its policy.

Why not bring activism inside the office walls? Employ an Internal Activist to collect due criticism and use the feedback loop to improve policy constantly. The activist would research potential points of criticism, such as unethical behavior or employee maltreatment. Then he or she stages a creative and humorous stunt to address these issues. Both management and staff are witness to the action, and even the press might be allowed a glimpse. Thus, the directors of the corporation acquire much goodwill and can make necessary changes in a supportive atmosphere.

Elena Simons

profile products to make environmentally intelligent choices

This proposal is for a plan whereby products that are mass-produced would come with a footprint or profile document, which describes in detail what raw materials, processing, and delivery mechanisms were used in its production.

This could be useful when making ethical choices between products with different environmental footprints. The following attributes of a footprint could be measured:

→ Fairness quotient: whether the goods have been produced and supplied with due concern for workers.

→ Environmental sustainability: what the lifecycle of the product is in the environment, whether it is recycled or recyclable, and what non-renewable resources are consumed in its production.

279

→ Health quotient: any known health issues for humanity or the environment arising from the product's properties.

Product profiles may be created in various ways:

→ Voluntarily: the company submits an independently verifiable footprint of the product.

→ Mandatory: governing bodies define the information that companies must provide.

→ Guerilla: a team profiles a product without the permission of the supplier.

The information should be accessible from a web browser, and the goods would be marked with a code that can be looked up online. A community of consumers could be empowered to change consumption habits in ways that are beneficial, or at least less detrimental, to the environment.

Kerry Channing

measure purchase-power parity with basket of burgers

280

The *Economist* uses an alternative method of comparing international currency rates: the Big Mac index. It is based on the theory of purchasing-power parity (PPP), which says that one dollar should buy the same amount in every country. The exchange rate between any two countries will move towards the rate that equalizes prices of goods and services in this way. To measure this price equalization, an identical basket of goods is needed for comparison, and the *Economist* uses a McDonald's Big Mac. The Big Mac PPP is the rate that would result in hamburgers costing the same abroad as in America. Economists compare this rate to the exchange rate to see whether a currency is under- or overvalued.

The index has become increasingly useful, mainly because McDonald's has become increasingly ubiquitous worldwide. While not everyone views this as a good thing, it has helped economists using this index, as they now have 120 countries to compare. In April 2002 the index showed that the cheapest burger ($0.78/39p) was in Argentina (following that country's massive financial troubles), and the most expensive burger ($3.81/£1.90) was in Switzerland. The Argentinian peso was the most undervalued currency at that time and the Swiss franc was the most overvalued.

The index contains some flaws, most notably that hamburgers cannot be traded between countries and national taxes can affect prices. However, it has been accurate in gauging the true level of a currency. When the Euro was introduced in 1999, many analysts said it would rise because it was undervalued. The Big Mac index disagreed, and was proved correct. The concept of PPP has been endorsed by several economic studies, which reveal it can be a particularly good guide to exchange-rate movements in the long term.

→ **www.economist.com/markets/Bigmac/Index.cfm**

share stock with directors as sole compensation

281

Albert Dunlap, who became chairman of the Philadelphia-based Scott Paper Company in April 1994, persuaded Scott's outside directors to accept company stock as their sole compensation (although out-of-pocket expenses continued to be reimbursed).

Dunlap said at the time that retainers and fees drain the directors' incentives to increase shareholder value and that bonuses such as guaranteed compensation prevented them from thinking like shareholders.

Sometimes, goes the contention, directors make decisions to protect their jobs instead of increasing share value. This situation is clearly ludicrous for company and shareholders. While an increasing number of companies are opting to give stock instead of more cash and perks to board directors, sole stock compensation is still rare.

Mr. Dunlap put it more simply still: "If you're in it just for the fee, then I don't think you ought to serve."

put a cap on employee interruptions

282

In a quirky corporate initiative, staff at the Leeds headquarters of the Asda supermarket chain were issued baseball caps that conferred on the wearer the privilege of not being spoken to for two hours.

If any of the 1,000 employees felt under pressure or unable to concentrate on a given task, he or she merely donned the bright red cap as a do not disturb signal. Colleagues had to refrain from speaking to the wearer, and were required to answer the phone and take all messages themselves in the meantime.

The initiative was the brainchild of the unconventional Archie Norman, then chief executive of Asda, the UK's fourth largest supermarket chain.

During his time at the helm, he launched weekly listening groups in each of his 200 stores (during which customers met staff to air complaints), as well as a monthly competition for all 65,000 staff (who were invited to select a product from the shelves and show how they would promote it). The winner enjoyed the use of a Jaguar car for four weeks.

put together your portfolio life one day at a time

283

Charles Handy, the social scientist and management expert, came up with the idea of a portfolio life while trying to evolve a lifestyle for himself. He resigned a full-time professorship and allocated the days of his year thus: 100 days a year for making money, 100 days for writing, 100 days for spending time with his wife, and 50 days for what he considered to be good works.

Handy went as far as to mark the specific days in his diary, so that when people asked him to do something, he could simply look it up and say, "Sorry, that's my day with my wife that week," or whatever the appropriate allocation turned out to be. He also claimed that the portfolio life frees a person in other ways, in that such strictly allocated time is often better used or, as he put it, "I find I do as much work in a hundred days as I used to in a year."

The idea of being a portfolio person is increasingly in vogue, as people seek to diversify their skills and to gain a more equitable balance of work and life. The concept of a job for life or even a career for life is becoming increasingly outmoded. In this new world of work, the portfolio life and, indeed, the portfolio career, will be the norm.

Organizing our lives as a portfolio of activities (some of which we do for money, some for interest, some for pleasure, some for a cause), may be the solution that brings an end to looking for the miraculous occupation that combines job satisfaction, financial gain, and time for friends and family in one neat package. It is also worth noting that if one part of a portfolio fails, the rest is not ruined.

Though this lifestyle might seem out of reach for some (not everyone can make enough money to live on by only working for a third of the year), it is certainly within the grasp of those who have retired. For more and more people, retirement can occupy almost as much time as their previous full-time career did. Under the portfolio lifestyle, retirement can set you free for a new, rewarding phase of life: disposable income increases, spending decreases, children have left home, the mortgage is low or paid off, and there are no worries from work. A perfect time, indeed, to start assembling the portfolio life.

fund the future
from a finite resource

284

The Alaska Permanent Fund was set up in 1976 to help create a sustainable economic future for all Alaskan generations to come. A percentage of all oil revenue is put into the fund, which can then be used for any lawful purpose that the state government wishes, including a dividend payout to every eligible Alaskan. The oil wealth of Alaska is thus saved for a future when there is no longer any oil. With the fund at almost $23 (£12.5) billion, there are upwards of approximately $1,400 (£700) in dividends each year. Some suggest that this could provide a model for a similar initiative in Iraq, in which the oil-richness of the country would be used to benefit all of the people, helping the poorest through a yearly dividend while also providing for social infrastructure and reform.

Through the dividend distribution program, the fund puts more new money into the state's economy than the total payroll of any industry in Alaska except the military, petroleum, and the civilian federal government. Compared to the wages paid to Alaskans by basic industry, dividends make a greater contribution than the seafood industry, construction, tourism, timber, mining, and agriculture. For a considerable percentage of Alaskans, the dividend adds more than 10 percent to the family income.

This is particularly true in rural regions of Alaska. However, there is still room for improvement on this exemplary initiative. The fund is managed in the same way as most investment procedures and such procedures pay no heed to ethical or moral concerns. However, the approach should be applied in other areas with natural resources. Eventually oil will run out, but if oil-rich states start planning now, the creation of funds like the Alaska Permanent Fund can soften the economic blows that will result when it does.

→ **www.apfc.org**

show CEOs when
to stand down

285

The biggest problem with unaccountable CEOs is that they do not know when to step down and let someone else run the company. In theory, the board of directors oversees the CEO, and can be sued by shareholders should they fail in that task. But in practice such failure is hard to prove; board members are often nominated by the CEO and they often nominate each other to their boards. In theory, shareholders can dump the board or top official at annual meetings, but a commons greatly reduces the incentives for any one shareholder to mount an expensive campaign to find and convince others.

This proposal is to create, for each stock, a separate market for trades that are called off if the CEO does not step down in the next year. The price in this market should indicate the market's expectation of the value of that company headed by a new person. If that price is consistently and significantly higher than the ordinary price, it is a clear market signal, from informed traders, for the individual to step down. (If there is no price because there is no trading, then there is no signal.)

Robin D. Hanson

→ **http://hanson.gmu.edu**

minimize overcompensation
with maximum wage legislation

286

Concerned about the amount CEOs and other public company officials are compensated for their efforts? Anyone believe this compensation, in comparison to the wages paid to company workers, is disproportionate? As controversial as minimum wage legislation is, perhaps it's time we consider a partner: maximum wage legislation.

Let's say the top official of a public company is ten times as productive (i.e., contributing to

the wealth generated by the company) as the front-line workers. Some would say the ten times figure is unreasonable, as people at the top would be nowhere without the people at the bottom. Using this level as a benchmark, however, governments could introduce a law restricting top officials to being paid a maximum of twenty times the average salary of all other workers in that company.

Martin Roberts

give ideas incentives and save thousands

287

When Martin Edelston mentioned to business colleague Peter Drucker that the meetings at his company were pretty bad, he added the caveat, "but meetings at all companies are." Drucker had a simple suggestion: ask everyone who comes to a meeting to bring two or three ideas for improving their department's productivity or for improving the company as a whole.

Edelston introduced the notion to subsequent meetings, putting the three ideas as item number one on the agenda. He added incentives to the process to encourage the wary, and arrived at these meetings with a gong, a horn, dollar bills, and sweets. An idea that struck the gong received a dollar, while the horn was sounded for weaker ideas, with the person receiving sweets instead. He soon ditched honking of the horn, and gave out a dollar for each idea.

Gradually, as Edelston put it, the sterility of the typical meeting format disappeared. More impressively, the accomplishments began to add up, and the company, Boardroom, began to save money because of the ideas that were implemented. Boardroom has since saved hundreds of thousands of dollars as a direct result of the ideas generated by its employees, as well as generating the potential for greater growth.

Edelston's recommendations are:
→ Take all ideas seriously, keep track of them, and ensure that other department heads do the same at their meetings. Add a central point where people can drop in suggestions as well (this is useful for ideas that employees might not wish to raise in front of others).
→ Every idea must fit on a Post-It note, which keeps the idea simple and focused. Edelston puts six of these on a page and photocopies it before taking the ideas home. They are then ranked with an A, B, or C. Each A idea earns $10 (£5), and the person with most A ideas per month receives a $50 (£25) bonus. Big money-saving ideas get a cash award.
→ As the candy and money show, feedback and reward are key features of any suggestion initiative. Part of this initiative is ensuring that everyone who submits an idea gets a response.

All of this takes time, of course, but the benefits have been immense and the initiative is so simple that it could be instituted by many different organizations. The idea for sharing ideas was Boardroom's greatest idea, and has since gone on to form the basis for a separate publishing and training business.

→ **www.i-power.com**

vote for a
view-sampling machine

288

Voting in a meeting is normally done by a show of hands, but this simple "yes" or "no" does not allow a person to express their opinion accurately or indicate a depth of feeling. Thus their opinion is devalued to an extent, or at best reduced to its minimum.

One idea to rectify this situation could be a view-sampling machine. Essentially, each person in a business or committee meeting would be equipped with a control knob showing positions 3, 2, 1, 0, -1, -2, and -3, signifying being wholly in favor of an idea (3) to abstention (0) to being totally opposed to an idea (-3).

The simple central computer display would then read out the vote, indicating the strength of the support for the motion.

A particular amount could even be set for the motion to be carried. This would represent value added to a decision at very little cost. Additionally the method would be quicker than counting hands, particularly at larger meetings or gatherings.

There are other uses that could also become commonplace. If members continuously adjusted their knobs, then the chairman could see instantaneously the existing degree of support and could cease discussion once the voters were already convinced. Where a chairperson felt that a contribution was irrelevant, he or she could obtain a snap decision and would then be in a far more assured position to end that particular speech.

Keith England

tackle corporate excess
in ten easy steps

289

1 **Three-strike corporate death penalty:** Just as criminals face a severe punishment if they are convicted three times in some countries, the same could be applied to corporations.

2 **Returning money obtained illegally:** Any judges considering sentences for executives of corporations should take into account the amount of money the individual has returned. A sliding scale of penalties and/or sentences could be introduced, where the penalty depends on the impact of the corporate wrongdoing (questionable accounting, insider trading, fraud) on pensioners, shareholders, and taxpayers, and on how much of the ill-gotten money has been returned.

3 **Incentives and benefits for local companies:** Central and local government can provide incentives for local enterprises serving local needs.

4 **Accessible information:** Transparency of a company to those with a stake in it should be enshrined in its charter or in law.

5 **Relating pay to performance:** Executives can ruin a company, bankrupt it, and make thousands of people redundant, then walk away with a golden handshake bonus. Ensuring that executive contracts contain clauses that relate pay directly to performance would help to rectify this situation.

6 **Tax on currency transactions:** This could calm volatile markets and generate revenue for global poverty elsewhere.

7 **Avoid political involvement:** While this may seem far-fetched considering the current state of political contributions from big business, it is a key factor in restoring faith in companies and, more fundamentally, in the present form of democratic government.

8 **No government contracts for lawbreakers:** Public money awarded to businesses should be more tightly regulated than any other allocations, and this should extend to the companies with which the public sector agrees to do business.

9 **Profit for the many, not the few:** The Code for Corporate Citizenship calls for a law preventing companies from making a profit at the expense of health and safety, the environment, human rights, or the welfare of the areas in which it does its business.

10 **Support ethical companies:** Individuals can buy fair-trade coffee, avoid certain oil producers, invest in ethical companies, put money with banks who have ethical principles, and buy local produce from small enterprises.

→ **www.citizenworks.org**
→ **www.waronwant.org**

chapter 13

transport

roll out car insurance by the mile for greater fairness

290

The car insurance system has been unfair for a long time. The occasional driver is charged as much as the daily commuter who journeys hundreds of miles. So insurance charged per mile is much fairer, and now possible. Some suggest global positioning systems be used to track mileage, thus ensuring odometer readings are not abused. Others prefer a piece of technology in the car to measure the amount of time the car is used. There could be a system under which a card is swiped for the ignition to be turned on and off. The card reader would then determine how long the car is used and this information could be used to decide a fairer rate of insurance.

In 2005, UK car insurer Norwich Union introduced a pay per mile car insurance for drivers aged between 18 and 21. Those taking part in the program pay £199 ($400) for a device to be installed that monitors usage of the vehicle. A monthly bill is then issued based on the mileage driven, with the cost per mile varying depending on the time of day (accidents are more likely late at night).

provide free public transport on poor-air days

291

On days when weather forecasters have predicted bad air quality, the city of Windsor, Ontario, Canada, provides free public transportation to get people out of their cars and onto the buses and trains. Public transportation use rose by 36 percent in the first trial. Transit Windsor was funded to provide this service by Windsor City Council and Environment Canada.

This idea is part of Ontario's Air Quality Initiative and Smog Alert Program, which has been running since 2000. This includes a three-day outlook air quality forecast, a website where smog day predictions are available, e-mail smog alerts for subscribers, and toll-free phone numbers for anyone wishing to have up-to-date air quality information. All are designed to make the public more aware of the state of air pollution, and of actions they can take to improve the situation.

→ **www.airqualityontario.com**

give the green light
to intelligent traffic signals

292

Scientists at an Italian institute have developed a set of traffic lights that adjust their red-green timings depending on the density and flow of the traffic.

The intelligent traffic light uses sensors to observe the traffic flow, and adds up the number of oncoming vehicles, and then alters the amount of time it spends on red or green accordingly. The aim of the idea is that the system adapts to the different traffic situations, so that lanes or roads with more traffic are allowed to flow more easily. In theory, the system should also prevent vehicles being unnecessarily stopped at junctions. This is particularly of interest in packed city centers where gridlock is an increasing problem.

This idea was also suggested to the Global Ideas Bank by a London lawyer, Ray Levy, who pointed out that having traffic lights programmed for fixed periods of time, regardless of the time of day or the traffic flow in any particular direction, is clearly not sensible. As congestion builds up in one lane, the opposite lane can have a green light for just a few vehicles to pass through. The lights such as those developed by the Antonio Ruberti Institute for Information and Systems Analysis may help introduce that solution permanently.

encourage use of public transport
with rail miles program

293

This suggestion is for an incentive program for tube (subway) and train passengers to rival that of the successful Air Miles one for regular flyers.

To be called Rail Miles, passengers would amass the points for traveling regularly by train or tube (subway). As with Air Miles, these points could then be used for purchases or for discounts on future tickets.

In a car-dominated country, such incentive programs could prove an effective foil to initiatives like congestion-charging and fuel tax rises; a carrot, as it were, to the stick of increased taxes and charges. To further persuade people to use public transportation, other similar programs could be introduced, such as Bus Miles or Tram Miles.

Marc Weeks

create a car-free city for cycles

294

In Groningen, the Netherlands' sixth largest city, the main form of transportation is the bicycle.

In the mid-1970s, heavy traffic congestion led planners to dig up the main roads through the city-center. Gradually, they introduced walkways, bus lanes, and, most crucially, cycle lanes. By the 1990s they were able to set about creating a completely car-free center. Within a year, the city had the highest level of bicycle usage in the western world, with 57 percent of its residents choosing to cycle, from a population of 170,000. In the UK, the average figure for cycle usage is about 4 percent.

Accompanying this change in transport usage has been an upturn in the business fortunes of the city. Rents in Groningen are among the highest in the country, while businesses have prospered. Those who have shops in streets that are yet to be "cyclized" clamor to be included.

There is also an influx of people to the city, attracted by its green credentials and its burgeoning economy. Indeed, one senior planner, Gerrit van Werven, stated that, "This is not an environmental program, it is an economic program. We are boosting jobs and business. It has been proved that planning for the bicycle is cheaper than planning for the car."

Through sheer weight of numbers, the bicycle lays down the rules, slowing the traffic. New houses are even built that can only be accessed by cycle, while out-of-town shopping centers have been outlawed. Everything is designed to compel the car driver to take long detours, but allow cycles to have easy access to the center. All new city center buildings have to provide cycle garages, and there are tens of thousands of parking spaces for cycles, either in "guarded" parks—the central railway station has room for over 3,000—or street racks.

→ **www.portalgroningen.medialab.nl**

restrict traffic through registration
license plate numbers

295

Many cities are becoming increasingly polluted and endangered by smog. These extreme situations have led to some radical solutions, notably the congestion charge in London, which has reduced traffic substantially.

Another radical proposal is to restrict access to the roads depending on the vehicle's registration license plate number. In Quito, in Ecuador, for example, the air pollution and traffic problems are very bad, and such a method would be an easy measure to introduce. No new technology is needed, and enforcement is simple, as the police would just need to check the car registration license plate to know instantly whether that person should be in the city center.

Such systems have been tried before: in October 1997, Paris restricted automobiles depending on whether their registration license plates ended in an odd or even number, an exercise which resulted in a 20 percent reduction in traffic. In 2002, in Northern Italy, the president of Lombardy introduced a similar program, which allowed drivers into city centers only on alternate days.

As well as the obvious benefits to air pollution, it is also worth noting that such a program would positively encourage car pooling and greater use of public transportation, as people's options would effectively be taken away from them on certain days.

Juan Esteban Romero and Agustin Acosta

switch on stop signal for
night-time traveling

296

A homeless man who became tired of being overlooked in the dark by buses has come up with a simple solution to the problem. Sean Westcott's bus stop signal light, by which a blue bulb is put at the top of the bus stop attached to a button on the pole, is now in trials in Oregon.

When the button is pushed, the bulb stays on for about a minute, and the light can be seen almost a mile away, even in dark and foggy conditions.

The light could also be helpful for people with hearing or sight problems, who are less able to know when a bus is coming.

follow the cycle path
for more sustainable transport

297

Sustrans ("Sustainable Transport") is a practical charity, designing and building traffic-free routes for cyclists, walkers, and disabled people all over Britain. Often the routes are on old railway lines, canal towpaths, or unused spaces. Sustrans focuses on major towns and cities, linking them with the countryside, and providing for commuter travel, cycling to schools, and family use. Road traffic is forecast by the Department of Transport to double by the year 2025. The Countryside Commission warns that traffic may treble in country areas. To Sustrans, this is unacceptable; they aim to build a traffic-free network (10,000 miles are in place thus far) for all those who will choose to cycle or walk for their shorter journeys, as long as the conditions are safe and attractive.

→ **www.sustrans.org.uk**

keep cars off the road
with negamiles allowance

298

The public and private sectors could work together to develop "Negamile" markets to help to keep cars off the road. This is the idea of green transportation expert Amory Lovins. He proposed that companies could charge employee to park in their parking lot. At the same time, employees would be paid a "commuting allowance" which, after tax, would offset the charge. If employees then decided to catch trains, ride bikes, or even walk to work, they could pocket the difference. If the program was carefully priced, the company could also make a profit, ensuring that everyone benefits.

Another example is the TravelBucks program of building developer, Intrawest, Canada. They hired Richard Drdul, a transport planner, to encourage their 500 workers to use cars less. His trip reduction program focused on public transportation use, use of bicycles, and of car-pooling, through TravelBucks. These were earned by employees at a rate of one for each time they chose to walk, cycle, car-pool, or take public transportation. These could then be redeemed for a lunch, transportation costs, or work on a car.

→ **www.drdul.com**

charge toll for empty car seats
to encourage car sharing

299

Toll booths exist in many countries, with governments using them to pay for new highways and the upkeep of roads. Historically, tolls are paid per car, no matter the number of people in the car. If a toll was instead paid on a sliding scale of how many empty seats remained in the car, this would provide an incentive for people to car-pool or use public transportation.

If using the car alone every day meant an extra hundred or even thousand dollars (£50/£500) a year, then people would want to pool on trips. For those who did not, the extra funds generated could be diverted into public transport improvements or environmental programs, without affecting the usual road upkeep and maintenance that the tolls were originally intended to pay for.

Alternatively, toll payments could generally be made cheaper, with the sliding scale ensuring the same amount of revenue was being brought in. This would enable those who were car-pooling to benefit financially every time they drive through (particularly as the toll payment would be shared two, three, or four ways).

If such a program were to be implemented, and much of the infrastructure is already in place (it would simply be changing the payment system slightly, and asking the attendants to count empty seats), then there might have to be some total or partial exemptions for those for whom driving is essential to their work or life (a disabled driver who has to store their wheelchair on an empty seat; a minibus going to pick up a youth group from an activity, etc.). Generally, though, the program could work as a preventative measure against unnecessary air pollution, and a push for people to car-pool or to use public transportation.

Motorway Highway lanes that are reserved for car-pooling vehicles, High Occupancy Vehicle lanes or HOV lanes, have proved to be a success in Australia and America, and the UK government is also testing the idea. Its High Occupancy Vehicle lane on the M1 near St Albans is off limits to solo drivers during rush hour. It is said that the number of cars on the roads could be cut by 5 percent if car-pooling were to be more widely adopted.

Geoff Cameron

dive into car-pooling for greener, friendlier driving

Mobility in Switzerland is Europe's largest car-pooling organization. At the end of 2003, it had nearly 60,000 members, who shared almost 1,700 vehicles located all over the country.

There are many benefits: no insurance or maintenance worries, no expense of buying a car. Car-pooling also brings considerable environmental benefits. Car owners who sell their vehicles on joining Mobility drive 70 percent less on average after doing so and travel more by public transport and by bike. On average, Mobility members use 55 percent less energy than Swiss who own cars.

In the US, Flexcar runs a system with a membership fee that covers all insurance, licensing, and maintenance costs, with members being charged a set rate per hour and per mile. Under their system, members of the program call a computerized system from a touch-tone phone. The driver can unlock the car with a master key; the same key opens a box containing the ignition key and a fuel credit card. It now operates hundreds of Flexcars, and claims that each one replaces six normal cars that would be on the road otherwise.

A popular online system in the UK, LiftShare, uses the web to connect people. A person can register their trip on the site and

300

be matched up with someone who is looking to get a ride for that trip (or part of it). The two e-mail each other and arrange a pick-up point, with the site recommending that the passenger pays the driver 10p (20 cents) per mile. With over 65,000 registered members, it is becoming a widely used tool.

→ **www.mobility.ch**
→ **www.carsharing.net**
→ **www.liftshare.org**

make buses run on
sewage and fish waste

301

The 12 buses in Trollhättan (a town of 50,000 inhabitants), north of Gothenburg, Norway, run on a mixture of the residents' own sewage and wastes from a nearby fish processing factory.

At the local sewage treatment plant, the waste is mixed in a reactor to produce a rich bio-gas (95 percent methane) which is then sent through a pipeline to the bus station in the town center. Here, a bus will have its tanks filled— the tanks are built in under the roof and run its full length. A full tank is enough for a normal full day's driving.

Compared to diesel oil, bio-gas is environmentally friendly, giving no net emissions of CO_2, less than half the emissions of NO_2 and minimal emissions of hydrocarbons, carbon monoxide and particulates. Participants in the bio-gas project, which began in 1996, include the municipality of Trollhättan, the largest Swedish energy company, Vattenfall, the local energy utility, the regional bus company, and the national Communications Research Committee.

→ **www.trollhattan.se**

auction the right
to have cars

302

Each quarter the Singapore government works out how many new cars it can permit in Singapore (based on the numbers of vehicles scrapped and the road-building progress) and allocates so many certificates to the four classes of private car, goods commercial vehicles, and motorcycles. Would-be owners get a form and make their bid for a Certificate of Entitlement to Purchase a new car.

In the first quarter, Singapore might permit 15,000 new vehicles. In the family car category, 9,000 citizens bid for 5,000 certificates. Officials then count from the top and the 5,000th best bid is noted. As the lowest successful bid, this sets the price for all certificates sold in this category.

In recent years, this has totalled as much as £9,000 ($18,000), as much as the cost of a car itself.

speed up train line with a whistle

303

The Midland Mainline company in the UK has come up with a novel way to improve its lamentable punctuality on-time record: loud whistles. Staff members have been given 500 Acme Thunderer whistles, which are renowned for their harsh sound, and have been using them when a train is about to leave to hurry up passengers. It is these small delays (passengers being slow in getting onto the train) that often cause larger delays further down the line. Thus the whistling helps reduce delays and, officials from the company maintain, keeps passengers and staff focused. In three months of using the whistles, the company's on-time record improved from 60 percent to 78 percent.

text times for better bus trips

304

In an innovative use of mobile phone and satellite technology, several bus services in the UK are letting customers know when their buses are due—by text.

The virgin service of this kind was offered by a Leicestershire company, Kinchbus. Instead of waiting in the rain, users of a 70-stop Loughborough to Shepsted bus route can text the six letters unique to their bus stop to a special number. After 30 seconds, travelers receive up-to-date bus arrival information, warnings, or service changes free to their cell phone, without even having to leave the house.

Aimed at retirees and students who make frequent use of the service, the "next bus" system uses satellite receivers on each bus to locate their whereabouts. With any variation to a bus timetable posing an annoying problem in more isolated and rural areas—where buses don't run every few minutes—the text messaging service is proving invaluable in Leicestershire and elsewhere.

Bus riders in Lancashire, for example, get the same assistance by texting "bus time, please" to a local number.

There is perhaps nothing more frustrating than waiting for public transportation for what seems like an eternity, and a simple text can reduce both passenger inconvenience and, in turn, passenger irritation levels.

use aeroplane food to form fuel

Los Angeles International Airport has teamed up with the city's Public Works department to introduce a program in which air passengers' uneaten food is transformed into fuel.

The leftover meals are pulverised, mixed with water, and heated; bacteria then break down the food, releasing methane gas to be

305

piped to a nearby power plant. The airport dumps over 8,000 tons of left-over scraps every year, so the potential use as renewable energy is substantial, as is the potential for doing the same around the world. It also makes a change for the airline business to be doing something positive for the environment, rather than polluting it.

drive a bargain to bridge the generation gap

Driving problems can often be caused by drivers at the ends of the age spectrum.

This idea confronts that reality head on. Under the proposal, when a high school student is old enough to get his or her license, they would have to register in the TeenSeen (for teenager and senior) program. For that year, each teen would be matched up with a senior, whom they would drive around one morning or afternoon a week. This could be in the older person's car, or in a car provided by the project. The intention would be for the teenager to learn how to drive safely within the speed limit, and also to learn from the wisdom and experience

306

of their elders. At the same time, the elderly person would be more active and get out and about more than might other-wise have been possible. There is also the possibility that the two will build up a friendly and mutually beneficial relationship.

The possibilities for such a program are many. An elderly group of golfers who can no longer drive to the course could get a lift, while ensuring the teenager drives sensibly. Teens and seniors could even be matched by profession and chosen career, allowing someone hoping to be, say, an architect to drive a retired architect and learn from them.

Anne Rosenberg

go on a city walkabout for surefire short-cuts

307

Amid complicated congestion charge programs, car-pooling, cycle lanes, and underground rail networks, it is sometimes easy to miss the simplest form of transport: our own two feet. Often in cities such as London or Paris, it is simpler and swifter to walk between two points rather than get lost in the rush for the bus or tube (subway). Using the knowledge of taxi drivers, short-cuts on foot could be printed as a booklet or on a website.

Myron Edwards

→ **www.quickmap.com**

reward people who live and work in the same city

308

The government could attribute an allowance to people who both live and work in the same city. Although life is much more expensive in big cities, residents do not get any refund for their transport though they contribute to the solution of traffic jams.

Such a program could prove to have more than financial benefits. A study funded by the Environmental Protection Agency in the US found that living near your workplace can benefit your health. The idea was first mooted by Gene Mullins, a Seattle transportation entrepreneur, who developed "proximate-commute" software to allow companies to measure the effects of such a change. Boeing let him put his theory into practice, with startling results.

Mr. Mullins was provided with funds to study 85,000 people between 1999 and 2000. He reported in December 2000 that half of the people working for Boeing could be doing similar work at Boeing plants nearer their homes, making apparent a massive potential reduction in expenditure, both financial, physical, and environmental. A sample selection of quotes by Boeing employees interviewed included: "To alleviate some of the 3–4 hours I spend in driving to and from work would cause a vast improvement in my stress levels" and "The work hours don't leave a whole lot of time for the family" and, more directly, "I dread getting up in the morning."

Greet Gosseye

remove ring road
for urban regeneration

The Belgian town of Hasselt is ostensibly like many others of its size. It has a population of about 70,000, and another 200,000 people commute in and out of it every day. What makes it different is what its mayor decided to do in the face of increasing traffic congestion and rising debt. He abandoned plans for a third ring road around the town and closed down one of the two that already existed. Having replaced it with trees, he laid pedestrian walkways and cycle routes. Then, having improved the frequency and quality of the local bus service, he announced that public transport would be free of charge.

309

A year later, the use of public transport had increased by 800 percent. Business in the center had increased markedly, as had social activity.

On the day that the mayor made the buses free, local taxes were also slashed, ensuring that the residents of Hasselt pay less local tax than a decade before. Along with the transport initiatives, this has attracted many more people to live in the town.

The city had been slowly losing population, but since the new measures were introduced, the population has been rising 25 times faster than the rate at which it was shrinking.

grant three-stage licenses for teenagers

310

Graduated licenses for teenagers create a three-tiered system of limited driver privileges that become increasingly generous as drivers gain more experience. Teenagers graduate through the stages by remaining accident-free. The mandatory learner's permit (three months to one year) requires a licensed adult passenger to accompany the teenage driver. The intermediate license requires an adult passenger but only during the (highest-risk) evening hours. After completing this stage a full license is given.

Sixteen and 17-year-olds constitute only about 2 percent of the driving population in America, but cause nearly 11 percent of crashes. Driver education classes seem to make little difference and raising the legal driving age would require parents often to act as chauffeurs. The statistics show a 5 to 16 per cent drop in teenage car crashes in states adopting the graduated licenses.

Over half the states in the US have now adopted the laws, as car crashes have become the leading cause of death for teenagers. This risk rises further when teenagers drive together, hence the clause about an adult passenger being present at certain hours of the day.

allow only golf buggies in inner cities

311

The following proposal may not be politically acceptable but it could solve urban transport problems in an instant. The idea is that all cars would be banned from the inner cities (with park and ride only for private vehicles). A fee would be charged for use of golf buggies. These would be run electrically so there would be no exhaust fumes. They can travel up to 20 miles per hour, which would be good enough for use within a city. Anyone wanting to get there faster would have to use the bus, which would be more likely to arrive on time due to the lack of other traffic to contend with. Parking would no longer be a problem as buggies are so much smaller.

The quality of life would be vastly improved for everyone. Road rage incidents would also probably decrease, as it is more difficult to rouse one's anger when sitting in a golf buggy.

Corinna Gallop

remove traffic lights and stop signs to improve safety

To improve safety on their streets, a small town in Holland has removed all traffic lights, stop signs, and road markings from one of its junctions.

The designers claim that such a system improves the flow of traffic and reduces accidents, and is based on their strong belief that people are capable of managing themselves effectively. The key to the way the junction works is fear, or danger; because people are uncertain and slightly fearful of the junction, they pay much more attention to all those around them and make a much more detailed assessment of when it is appropriate for them to move off. Traffic lights and stop signs take those decisions out of the hands of drivers, pedestrians, and cyclists, resulting in a more lackadaisical and less attentive attitude.

In the town of Drachten in Friesland (in the north of Holland), the junction is somewhat infamous, with cars, cyclists, and pedestrians negotiating their way across steadily and carefully. The speed limit is set at 18 mph, but those using the junction are forced to slow down in order to take in what is happening in front of them, and to then make a decision about the right time to move off. Much of the communication is between drivers and cyclists, by eye and hand contact, which is also a crucial aspect

312

to the program. This approach to traffic management, masterminded by Hans Monderman of the Friesland Regional Organisation for Traffic Safety, is rooted in the idea that the social nature of the town street should be emphasized above its highway nature; that people should be encouraged to interact with each other, rather than be aggressive or rail against those who have not obeyed the traffic laws. As Monderman says, the biggest mistake that we as traffic engineers can make is to give people the illusion of safety.

Although the idea seems to go against common sense, getting road users to re-engage with their environment can only help to reduce accidents and to encourage more careful driving. It is this reversal of commonly held wisdom that is the true innovation at the heart of the project, and will require a huge leap of faith and change of view if it is to be introduced in the UK and elsewhere. As Ben Hamilton-Baillie, a transport specialist from Bristol, points out, "In the Netherlands you often hear planners say 'If you want to make a junction safe, you want to make it dangerous'." Certainly, several local authorities in the UK are following the progress of the project, and are looking at introducing such dangerous junctions themselves.

customize cars with a happy horn for thanking

313

Cars should come equipped with two horn sounds. The current harsh tone would be appropriately complemented by a softer, mellower note that could be used in different situations. It could be employed when thanking someone for allowing you into a lane, or for apologizing for having cut somebody off by mistake. Similarly, it could be a way of communicating to someone that you are happy to wait for them to park or to go first across an intersection. It would be the honking equivalent of saying "Excuse me," rather than the current "HEY!"

Amy Rose Dobson

carry your own road signs

314

A portable orange sign, small enough to fit in your pocket, could be the answer to pedestrian-related accidents and deaths caused by cars that do not stop when they should.

Lester Goldstein, 79, retired biology professor, produced just such a thing in the American town of Wallingford, Washington. After joining the pedestrian advocacy group Feet First, Goldstein devised a foldout sign which he is trying to get patented.

His aim was to make pedestrian crossings safer, as well as to promote the rights of the pedestrian, who often comes second to the car driver and the cyclist. Although the law requires vehicles to stop for pedestrians on crossings, at crosswalks this is often ignored or forgotten, with occasionally disastrous results. Pedestrians usually have to step out into the street to get cars to notice and stop.

Goldstein's flag is designed to draw more attention to pedestrians, who can extend it out into the road before they step off the dangerous curb. He believes that this will stop the more than 80 deaths and 400 injuries that occur each year in his home state alone.

→ **www.feetfirst.info**

chapter 14

children and education

see blind actors perform
in darkness to enlighten audiences

315

An Argentinian acting company, consisting entirely of blind actors, performed in a theater set in complete darkness, in an effort to educate audiences on visual impairment. The play, called *The Desert Island*, was put on in an unlit basement that was so dark the audience members had to be led to their seats. The intention of the play was twofold: to raise awareness on the subject of blindness, and to challenge preconceptions people hold about who is able and who is disabled.

The idea works on a premise similar to that of the famous Blinde Kuh (Blind Cow) restaurant in Zurich, Switzerland, where diners eat in darkness.

The restaurant gives people an insight into what it means to be blind and provides employment for blind people: all the waiters are blind, and they memorize the orders, as well as leading diners to and from the table.

→ **www.blindekuh.ch**

partner children with
pooches for increased literacy

316

Children in some schools across the US are finding new reading partners a great help in improving their fluency. Their partners are dogs, supplied by the Reading Education Assistance Dogs (READ) project, and they have proved extremely helpful in encouraging children's fluency and confidence.

Therapy dogs have been going into nursing homes, hospices, and even prisons for a long time, to provide comfort and companionship, but the reading initiatives have shown that there may be other areas where

their talents can be used. Teachers have noted that the children read with much less hesitancy, and more motivation. With a dog as the listener, there is no threatening figure of authority (parent, teacher, older child) picking up on every tiny error.

A favorite technique of handlers is to tell the child that the dog needs to understand the story as well, encouraging them to slow down and fully understand it themselves.

→ **www.therapyanimals.org/read**

teach real-world lessons in virtual schools

Online schooling is emerging in the US and elsewhere as a viable alternative for pupils who find traditional schooling problematic.

These students may include victims of bullying, extremely shy children, those with mobility problems or learning needs, home-schooled children, or those who live in rural areas. There are well over 50 virtual charters in the US, ranging from small individual projects to statewide programs, such as Kansas's Electronic Charter School. Such programs can be seen as an extension of home-schooling or simply an exercise of educational choice, with students all across the US connecting with teachers, peers, and the biggest knowledge library in the history of the world, the Internet.

Though there are negatives to online schooling (no face-to-face interaction with pupils or staff being one, the problem of discipline being another), there are benefits: there is no back row in cyberspace to nod off in, and no troublemaker in class to distract or disrupt the learning process. Furthermore, technology today means that the online interaction between teacher and student(s) can potentially be as productive as in a classroom environment.

Danielle France, for example, is a teacher in a regional cyber charter school based in

317

Pittsburgh, Pennsylvania. With her seven students, all of whom have special needs, she can conduct real-time synchronized e-mail discussions and lessons at specified times using a whiteboard and audio-chat system that allows everyone to hear her speak and ask questions. She can also ask them to scan in their stories so that skills such as handwriting and spelling can still be checked. As Ms. France put it herself, "I have more contact with my online students than I ever could in my classroom."

The main hurdles to such initiatives are financial and technological. Clearly not all families can afford a personal computer, scanner, and fast Internet connection, so the financing has to come from somewhere, possibly central or state government funding. The technology, while improving all the time, is still susceptible to crashes, power outages, server upgrades, and the like, none of which traditionally create problems in the normal classroom.

Nonetheless, as ways and methods are found to overcome these obstacles, it seems that online schooling, adding real-time teaching and interactivity to the old home schooling premise, could be here to stay.

→ **www.palearnersonline.net**
→ **www.onlineecs.org**

recharge the student body
with power naps

318

High school students have become the latest section of society to explore the positive effects of a particular type of napping, one that is markedly different from the Sunday afternoon snooze. It is the fabled Power Nap. Power napping consists of a 20- to 30-minute period of controlled sleep that serves a dual purpose during the working day: to relax and recharge. As the lifestyle in educational establishments continues to become more pressured, as in business, so solutions used in business can be effectively transferred.

Every Monday, for example, high achievers at Greenwich High School in Connecticut shun badminton and drama clubs in favor of 20 minutes of intense snoozing. Thomas Murphy, spokesperson for the Connecticut Education Department, believes that (far from being a slovenly diversion) napping has become a sadly neglected diversion, and stated, "I believe naps have been very underrated in this world." It indeed seems that the prevalence of a so-called hyper-culture that employs Prozac as its emblem of choice begs for a counterbalance allowing people to effectively switch off and completely escape for a number of minutes during the working day.

The educationalists introducing napping in schools believe that, in school as in business, shutting down temporarily and then restarting makes the nap empowering, avoiding sluggish afternoon performance. That this method for improving student performance costs nothing to implement should not disguise its potential value. A refreshed and relaxed student is a more receptive student and is much less likely to be troublesome. Educational power-napping could even help take the notion of forty winks into a new era.

→ **www.napping.com**
→ **www.sleepfoundation.org**

give vouchers to students to finance creative projects

319

A reinvention of the long-debated school voucher idea could improve public education by allowing students to pursue their own educational goals. A new microvoucher program could be created to fund students who want to plan and carry out their own creative projects; the projects could be paid for by a tax break for the student's family.

The idea is for the students to plan and carry out as much of their individual projects as possible, thus becoming better acquainted with themselves, more knowledgeable about their talents, more mindful of their goals, and more engaged in the process of their own education.

Possible projects include: writing or producing a feature film or local cable TV show, designing a fashion line, starting and running an e-business on the web, creating visual art, volunteering in the community, restoring a local ecosystem, or any number of other possibilities. The key is for the project to be productive and constructive in the student's community.

Gregory Wright

grant young people the right to fund young people

320

YouthBank UK is a grant-making initiative run by young people for young people, in which local YouthBanks provide small grants to projects that benefit the community.

The young people themselves decide how the process is managed and run, and which projects are to receive grants. The nationwide network is also administered and run by a board of young people, with minimal outside assistance and support.

In this way, the program is not just about giving grants to community projects, but also about the development and training of those involved. The community benefits twice: once through the impact of the project itself, and again through the skills and experience its young people receive.

By February 2005, there were 28 YouthBanks established in the UK.

→ **www.youthbank.org.uk**

let laptops
lead the way

321

Every Year Seven student of Maine puts aside text books in favor of laptops as writing and research aids.

Governor Angus King has provided 18,000 twelve-year-olds with Apple laptops from Maine's educational budget since the program began in 2002. Such liberal provision of expensive equipment aims to break down socioeconomic inequalities, and to give every pupil the chance to improve their prospects when entering employment.

Information technology is not only a school subject but also an educational tool for learning and naturalizing computer literacy into the next generation. Providing students with laptops is a positive response to the digitization of information.

Trials across the US have shown a decrease in detentions and absenteeism resulting from the program.

→ **www.state.me.us/mlte**

bank on
father's brainchild

322

A New York father developed an innovative way of teaching his children about money management; he called it The First National Bank of Dad.

David Owen, to teach his children about finance, saving, and investing, opened his own bank. The bank started with rates of 5 percent per month (which works out to 77 percent a year), to teach his children both the bonuses of saving and the concept of compound interest (without having to wait as long as they would normally). As his two children (aged five and

ten when the project began) became more interested in saving than spending, he lowered the interest rate to 3 percent a month, to prevent himself losing out too much.

He started the Dad Stock Exchange when the children were older. In this venture, he allowed them to buy and sell shares of real companies, but priced them at exactly one-hundredth of their actual price. Before long, a money market mutual fund, a value stock fund, and a stock index fund were being demanded by his offspring.

give students real funds to invest in stocks and shares

323

Some universities offering courses in finance, investment, and portfolio management have been giving students real funds to invest.

The added fiduciary responsibility enables students to better understand the world of financial trading and investments, a world that inevitably includes learning from mistakes, answering to clients, and dealing with increased stress levels.

Making the exercise non-theoretical gives an extra incentive to students to research the field thoroughly and to think through every decision and choice they make. And while being entrusted with millions of dollars of the university's money might raise their stress levels if they make losses, they also get to celebrate gains with the knowledge that they have raised more money for their own educational institution.

There are well over a hundred US colleges and universities that give students school money to invest as they see fit. Of these, one of the most interesting is the University of Dayton, Ohio, where students have been given $2 (£1) million of the school's endowment to invest. In a classroom designed to simulate a Wall Street environment, the students decide as a team how they should invest, with each student required to research a particular area of business (they are graded on their research and effort, not their actual financial results). To add to the reality of the system, students sit down with the trustees (their clients) to talk through their portfolio and their decisions with them; this develops personal responsibility and professionalism that will stand the students in good stead in the future.

As with many of the other schools, the Dayton students have outperformed the average investor every year since the program started. Indeed, the trustees of the endowment plan to increase the amount they give student investors to $5 (£2.5) million. All of the profits from student investments go directly to the university, which gives staff an incentive to make sure their courses and teaching prior to the investment stage are up to the mark. The students benefit the most, though: the responsibility and pressure keeps them focused and concentrated, the entrustment of real cash gives them a sense of credibility and respect, and the decisions they make are excellent preparation for the real financial world.

→ **www.sba.udayton.edu/cfpm/default.htm**

give parents report cards to improve children's education

324

A school district in Philadelphia proposed the administration should give out report cards to students' parents. Parents would be graded on the extent of their involvement in their child's education, a key factor in the progress of children's performance.

Parental evaluations would be based on factors such as whether the student comes to school healthy and appropriately dressed, and whether parents attend parent–teacher meetings and evenings. The reports aim to encourage parents to keep abreast of their child's progress.

School authorities are keen to point out that the system will be voluntary and that each school will be allowed to develop its own version. They also prefer to call the evaluations "parent advisories" rather than report cards, as the intention is to foster good parenting, not to demand it or to criticize anyone. As schools' superintendent Marianne Bartley said, "We have a lot of parents who are involved and do a wonderful job, but we need to make sure that it's widespread."

→ **www.philsch.k12.pa.us**

see how kids can make child's play of technical reports

325

On writing a "care charter" for his patients at a hospital in England, Gordon Caldwell found that it was full of long words and incomprehensible jargon. Since the point of the charter was to clarify the relationship between the patients and the consultants, and how they might work together to improve their well-being, he decided that this document was not ideal. So, in keeping with the Plain English Campaign's view that such documents should be readable by eight-year-olds, he sent it to the local primary school for rewriting. The eleven-year-olds rewrote it so that the eight-year-olds could read and understand it. This process had two main results: a new, easily readable charter document for the hospital, and a lesson about communication, presentation, and health for the students.

→ **www.plainenglish.co.uk**

appoint a professor of heresy as an educational devil's advocate

326

Scientific progress is hindered by the preservation of reputation and the stigma of proposing ideas that travel outside the currently accepted dogma.

To counter this problem, the post of Professor of Heresy could be created. In each department of major universities, a professor would be appointed with this title. He or she would publish ideas that are unpopular (or unlikely to be investigated) yet have plausibility.

The professor could conduct research, publish papers, and give lectures without fear of reprisal, as their heretical views would be seen in the context of their role as educational devil's advocate. The professor could also express views and investigate areas that question current dogma, such as the efficacy of homeopathy, to encourage people to keep an open mind and to stimulate debate.

Charles Merriam

learn a language to break a record

327

At Birmingham's Learning Day in 2002 in the UK, the council encouraged people to learn five phrases in a new language as part of the biggest simultaneous learning activity ever.

Participants were able to choose from 22 languages spoken in Birmingham, including Somali, Vietnamese, and sign language, and learn how to say *hello, please, thank you, goodbye*, and *Birmingham is a great place to learn*. The idea was implemented to encourage learning at all levels, to showcase the city as a learning organism, and to foster understanding between the many different people who live in the city. This is of particular importance in a city such as Birmingham, where some schools have up to 39 languages spoken and 95 percent of the pupils speak English as a second language.

The record attempt took place at 10:10 A.M. and lasted for ten minutes. Each class in the city had to nominate a coordinator who recorded the event. In this way, the people of Birmingham created a new world record.

→ **www.bgfl.org**

ban junk food in schools

328

A London primary school introduced a ban on junk food brought in as part of children's packed lunches, and saw behavior improve markedly as a result.

New End Primary School's ban included sweets, crisps (chips), fizzy drinks (soda), chocolate, and even fruit juices. The only drink allowed in the school was water. In the school canteen, children could always choose a salad or fruit option.

The head teacher, Pam Fitzpatrick, reported that the children have been very positive about it and are much calmer in the afternoons, in the classroom and on the playground. As well as calming the children and playing a part in educating them about healthy eating, the ban resulted in a significant reduction in litter. Most parents backed the rules laid down by the school and hoped it would become a permanent move.

create a communiversity to learn locally

329

This proposal states that within every community there should be a *communiversity* that is supported by universities and that taps into local talent, skills, and knowledge.

Communiversities could be based in areas where the uptake of education is traditionally low, and could specifically encourage those who would not normally attend a traditional university to enroll.

To foster the sense of ownership and belonging, as well as to establish ties between the institution and the local area, the communiversity could be democratically owned by the local people. Such an establishment would seek not only to educate and inform, but also to address local needs by tying in elements of the curriculum to local issues.

Andrew Crummy

make parents truant officers
to avoid absenteeism

330

Instead of blaming parents for student absenteeism, some education systems are hiring hundreds of parents as truant officers, thus giving them the power to do something positive about growing truancy rates.

Philadelphia schools trained 250 moms and dads, whose experience and understanding of issues of childrearing, school, and parenting make them suited to visiting and advising the families of habitually truant students.

"Parents know the terrain, know the environment, understand the culture, and may even know some of the individual parents and kids," reports Paul Vallas, chief executive of the schooling system in Philadelphia, which has put $1.2 (£0.6) million into the program. In a previous Chicago-based incentive, the similar employment of 600 parents made a quantifiable difference in truancy statistics: the percentage of children playing truant fell from 5.7 to 3.9 percent.

Home visits made by truant officers are vital to uncovering the causes of a child's truancy and represent a more constructive exercise than condemning families from a distance. As parents, the officers are less likely to be judgmental. In some instances, the problem is money shortages, as parents cannot afford clothes or bus tickets. The visiting officer can inform parents of available options and resources. Conversely, some parents are oblivious to their child's absenteeism. Once enlightened, parents can play an effective role.

Thousands of contacts have been made between truant officers and parents since the program's inception. With absenteeism recognized as a real problem throughout the US and other countries, similar programs elsewhere could improve overall attendance figures in a logical usage of parents' natural resources.

→ **www.phila.k12.pa.us**

walk to school
and learn as you go

331

The aim of International Walk to School Day, held the first week of October, is to unite children in walking to school for one day to help make permanent changes to daily routines. The first was held in 2000 in Canada, Ireland, Cyprus, Gibraltar, Britain, and America. The next year, 21 countries took part, with an estimated three million walkers.

Walking helps reduce traffic congestion, encourages fitness for children, and can be coupled with teaching road safety rules. It can also help raise awareness of how walkable a community is, and where local people can lobby for improvements, thus encouraging a more permanent change in habits. It also brings environmental issues into children's lives; if the day succeeds only in provoking children to ask why they should walk, it has been a success. The concept need not be limited to one day: "Walking buses" are an alternative to the school run. The bus consists of children walking in a line, with a volunteer adult at the head (the driver) and at the tail (the conductor). There is a designated route with stops on the way to the school.

→ **www.iwalktoschool.org**
→ **www.walkingbus.org**

drive through
to drop off your kids

332

The often-difficult morning ritual of a parent finding a parking space in order to drop off their child at daycare may have found its solution.

In Stockport, UK, one nursery allows parents to drive through to a covered entrance where they can sign in their kids and go, all in two minutes. The parents are still able to go in and talk to their child's caregivers if they wish, but the potential is there for a much swifter morning routine than is presently the case. Indeed, the associated reduction in stress and irritation could prove to be a useful side effect of the program in the long term.

Whether or not this is the best idea for transporting children to school is debatable (see "walk to school," above), but it is certainly among the most pragmatic.

include money, courts, and taxation in modern education

333

At Gilman Middle School in Vermont in the late 1970s and early 1980s, things were a little out of the ordinary: pupils had jobs, paid taxes, spent their own currency, and enforced their own laws, as well as dealing with less-than-traditional educational problems: inflation, unemployment, and economic recession.

The innovative initiative, known as the Thaler System (thalers are the currency the system is based on), was introduced by a former principal of the school, Barry Grove. He believed that giving the students an understanding of the workings of economic and social systems was an integral part of a modern education. Therefore, the school had its own bank, payroll department, employment office, legal system, and post office. Students earned thalers by working in a variety of jobs, including library assistants, cafeteria (canteen) workers, or office staff, or by setting up private enterprises, such as a skateboard repair shop. Thalers could be used to buy real goods and services, ranging from snacks to equipment hire and even items from retail catalogues.

The school did not view the Thaler System as a game, but as a way of educating the pupils through the entire process: they accepted responsibility and were given control over their own environment. With inspiring challenges and novel incentives, most students responded in a positive way to life in the world of Thaler.

link a library with a school to aid self-education

334

An alternative to traditional educational institutions could be a hybrid between a library and a school.

These library–schools would be designed to aid self-study by anyone who wanted to improve their knowledge and expertise in a particular subject. A librarian-assistant, rather than a teacher, would provide general support, such as advice on assignments, project coordination, and research. Not only could such a place be a haven for those wishing to self-teach, but could also prove a low-cost and effective educational experience.

Eric Chen Yixiong

inculcate international sign language in every nation

335

A revolutionary proposition would be to introduce the learning of an internationally agreed Sign Language in every school in the world. This would teach all hearing children—or, pertinently, reintroduce to them—priceless communication skills and encourage their physical fluidity, expressiveness, and development. It would also help to eradicate prejudices toward the deaf or partially hearing, which are often centered around hearing adults' fears of being unable to engage in conversation without awkwardness. Furthermore, it could potentially end the disability status of deaf or partially hearing people, with all the inequalities that that involves.

Richard Sinnott

mentor new and young parents

336

Often new parents have neither good family support nor good parenting role models to assist them with the challenge and responsibility of raising children. Since children do not come with instruction manuals, a solution might be a linking of new parents with mature couples who have already raised a child or children to adulthood.

Even the small events of a child's normal development worry first-time parents. Mentors could reassure these parents. New parents could be linked with mentors through the hospital after the child's birth, or through their doctor early in the pregnancy. If things go well, lasting friendships might develop between the two families.

A similar idea was instituted in Dublin, Ireland, by the Community Mothers' program in the 1990s. An experienced mother volunteered to visit a new mother as a formal friend each month for the first year of the baby's life. An evaluation of the program at the end of the year found that babies on the program were more likely to be immunized, more likely to be appropriately fed, more likely to have mothers read to them, and more likely to play stimulating games than those who were not. In addition, the new mothers receiving this support were found to be less tired, more positive, and eating better.

Philip Averay

teach a class
to earn a pass

337

Final exams are renowned for making students nervous, as they apply a great deal of pressure in a short period of time. Students usually spend a few days cramming as much information into their short-term memory as possible and then forget it as soon as the test has been taken.

A better idea might be for each student to pick one theme from each of his or her classes, and then teach that theme to a class of local junior high school students. Many teachers will tell you that to teach someone else, you have to understand every element of the material yourself. The high school students would therefore be forced to look at materials in new and creative ways so they could teach them to others. They would have to break down the elements of each topic and understand how they fit together.

Teaching one theme from each course will make the students learn from their classes. It may not cover all the material as would a final exam, but it will allow the students to have a more complete and rounded understanding of a few topics that will stay with them much longer.

Grades could still be given based on how well a student presented the information; both the junior high teacher and the student's own teacher could provide input. The junior high students could even be included in the process, rating the teacher-student on clarity and information provided.

Not only would this allow high school students to leave a class feeling like they learned some information for life, but it might inspire more people to become teachers. While it may not totally replace the need for examinations, it could provide an additional form of assessment alongside traditional testing and coursework.

Kaleigh Gerity

appoint an advocate
for children's rights

338

Since 1981 Norway has employed an official called the Barneombudet —the Advocate for Children.

This person's job is to ensure that children are seen as people, with their own needs and their own rights—rights equal, but not identical, to those of adults. For instance, it successfully lobbied for a law to prohibit parental striking of children. As part-politician, part-activist, and part-adviser, the role is flexible and holistic : representing children, becoming actively involved in cases, and advising children, parents, and organizations on children's rights.

Trond Viggo Torgensen, Barneombudet 1989–95, set up a toll-free phone number children could call to leave messages about their concerns. This Children's Powerline remains in place, and staff members aim to give swift replies and information to callers. An Internet Parliament has been set up for students in secondary (high) school to empower young people through mini-referendums.

The European Network of Ombudsmen for Children (ENOC) was set up in 1997, linking independent offices for children from twelve countries. There are now network members based in 23 European countries.

→ **www.barneombudet.no**
→ **www.ombudsnet.org**

roll your sleeves up to learn a profession

339

A volunteer program could be created for potential students of law, medical, business, and other professional schools that would allow them to work in their chosen fields as non-professionals before they enter university or graduate school.

Universities may consider the work as seriously as they do grades, test scores, and references when selecting candidates for admission. A potential medical school student, for example, could spend time in a nursing home cleaning, caring for patients, and doing paperwork. The student would acquire a better understanding of patient needs, learn first-hand how they are treated, and how such organizations work. The same concept could be applied to almost any profession studied, making a more formalized work experience program a part of admissions procedures.

If someone is willing to roll their sleeves up and do some work in their potential profession, then an educator would probably be more ready to accept them into their program.

Linda Rallo

supervise classrooms to transform juvenile offenders

340

In a district in Washington State officials have experimented with an interesting alternative to juvenile detention: a supervised classroom.

The program involves eligible juvenile offenders reporting daily to a classroom that is run by a teacher and a detention officer. The project aims to free up more space in juvenile detention facilities by housing fewer teenagers there and to help young people get back on track through disciplined education.

The offenders are electronically monitored and must always be either at home or in school. The program helps youngsters turn their lives around. Every one of the participants who does not re-offend is a saving, financially (no detention costs, no future crime costs) and in social terms, as there is an immeasurable value in seeing individuals housed with their family and receiving a proper education.

→ **http://access.wa.gov**

pay for training with portable fellowships

341

In an interview, economist Paul Romer mentioned an idea that could help graduate and postgraduate students in their research. He suggested portable fellowships, which could be used to pay for training in any field of science or engineering at any institution of the student's choice. This would enable students to break free of what Romer calls the sometimes parochial research interests of university professors. In essence, it would help students to find courses and programs that are suited and shaped for their research and career interests, rather than having their research molded to fit with a particular professor's interest.

The students could choose supervisors and tutorials from all over the country, allowing them access to a range of expertise. Romer's idea extends to students in arts subjects, where some universities are known for particular viewpoints.

hop on the magic bus and cook with us

342

Obesity is one of the fastest-growing problems for children in the developed world, and it has led to initiatives to encourage healthy eating. What these solutions ignore is the dwindling numbers of children who are taught to cook and who therefore understand how to feed themselves and what goes into the food they are eating.

Focus on Food, an initiative of the Royal Society of Arts, confronts this problem by taking a cooking bus around the UK to encourage students to cook. The premise behind the project is that as more children enjoy cooking and know how enjoyable wholesome food is, fewer will succumb to a fast-food diet. The bus visited over 2,500 schools in four years, with celebrity chefs holding cooking lessons on board, including Sophie Grigson helping four-year-olds make bruschetta. She said: "Children can cook at a much younger age than anxious adults think [and we] have to encourage them whenever they show a spark of interest. If we don't, we'll end up with a generation who only eat bland junk food."

→ **www.rsa.org.uk**

sound out
rapid sensory learning

Rapid Sensory Learning (RSL) uses sensual stimuli in the form of color, music, and movement to incite advanced brain performance and increase learning potential. The UK-based ambassador of the technique, Kate Ginn, says the method helps participants retain far more information compared with other more conventional methods of learning.

One method of sensory learning involves reading new information through colored filters, which are said to speed up neural connections, thus allowing data to flow more readily. When a filter is attached to a computer screen, book, or report, the outcome is a sensory package more conducive to learning than traditional black on white. An orange filter, for example, reduces contrast, which makes text easier to read, and different colors work for different people.

The addition of soothing background music, preferably classical, aids the brain's transformation into a more fertile learning zone.

A further mental warm-up is gained through physically stretching and walking around prior to, or during, data consumption. According to Ginn, these mental and physical activities combine in increasing the overall receptivity of the brain to new data.

Ginn gives one-to-one and group tuition in RSL, claiming the method allows an individual

343

to retain a massive 80 percent of received information, compared with 20 percent if the method is not used. As well as enhanced data recall, those who regularly feed their grey matter via the technique can expect numerous beneficial side effects, including improvement in academic and work performance, reduction in computer-induced strain, and the bolder claim of increased IQ.

→ **www.mindlightlearning.com**
→ **www.thesoundlearningcentre.co.uk**

train technotots
in computer skills

344

A nursery in Dundee, Scotland, allows parents to watch over their children via webcam, while simultaneously teaching the toddlers computer skills.

Modeled on a similar techno-nursery in the US, the Technotots nursery allows parents to monitor their children via the Internet as part of its innovative approach. The other main aspect of its work is to teach the children (from three-year-olds upward) to become accustomed to computers and new technology. The nursery has a computer room with a bank of PCs that the children learn to play games on.

Parental access to the webcams is only allowed via a password-secured site. Any attempt by an outsider to access the virtual nursery immediately triggers a warning to the webcam operators (who themselves are not allowed to see footage, only streams of data). Parents who use the nursery are happy that the nursery is confident enough in its staff to allow parents to drop in and check on their children.

Those using the nursery believe it makes sense to teach children about new technology, and to make use of it themselves. Such places represent a tech-nursery revolution.

→ **www.the-technotots.com**
→ **www.cbabiesafe.com**

give kids a credit card
to beat bullies

345

A Kidscard is a type of credit card for children, which could have small amounts of money downloaded to it from their parents' computer.

The children would use it to cover the costs of school supplies, lunches, and other items, so that they did not have to carry cash. The system would have to be tightly regulated, with the card accepted only in particular outlets, as well as each child being given a password or code. This card could help eliminate the problem of some children bullying others for money as well: teachers and other school workers would instantly know if someone was using another person's card.

Kirk Haynes

sing science songs
to increase interest

Academics at the University of Liverpool believe new methods are required to interest more young people in science, particularly physics.

A method that makes connections between science and aspects of the students' lives outside the classroom would be useful, especially if these are embodied in the very mode of presentation and learning. In short, the academics propose physics karaoke.

Dominic Dickson and Laura Grant, who have written a paper outlining the method, give this simple and intuitive definition: Physics karaoke

346

is where the words to be sung to the well-known song are not the usual ones but are specifically written with a physics theme.

Physics karaoke can help students because, apart from the fun they derive from singing, the students' involvement in preparing and delivering a set of lyrics reinforces and embeds the relevant facts in their minds. It is necessary, when trying to fit words and concepts to a certain tune, to explore a range of possible ways of expression. This obliges students to translate the physics ideas into a familiar vocabulary. Rhyme and melody have long been used as mnemonic devices. One example is a reworked version of the classic Beatles' song, *Hey Jude*. Here is the opening to their version, *Hey Joule*:

> *Hey Joule, it makes me cool,*
> *When I do work adiabatically,*
> *But when some work is done upon me,*
> *That sure increases my internal energy.*

This is one of a number of examples written by Laura Grant and Emma Carrington and used in Science Roadshows in the UK in 2000 and 2001. There is no reason why this method could not be extended to cover other subjects and it needn't be restricted to the classroom.

→ **www.liv.ac.uk**

draw up a contract with your teenage children

347

It may seem a cold and radical move to draw up a written contract with a child, but such procedures can be effective in helping to solve disputes and improve relationships. When putting together a contract, the following points are important to consider:

→ The actions requested must be specific.

→ The actions chosen for both parties must be easily observed to determine their fulfillment.

→ There should be sanctions for failing to fulfill sections of the agreement and these penalties should be agreed in advance.

→ Any changes to the contract must be formally negotiated and agreed to by both sides.

Also recommended are a record book of achievements and the inclusion of inducements or bonuses for fulfilling the contract over a set period of time. An independent witness (a grandparent, perhaps) should settle any unresolved disputes; the witness can also be in charge of collecting penalties, such as fines to be given to charity. Once all of the tenets are set down, signed, and copies given to both sides, then the road to family harmony can begin.

take a class in national reality

348

If you believe education is fundamental to all people and that what we do as individuals in our society depends on the education we receive, then ensuring that education covers the main issues of importance is crucial.

In Ecuador, poverty is a major problem and the difference between social classes is huge. To change this, it is important for people in a more privileged position to learn and understand about the day-to-day reality of poor people. To understand this social reality, every school, by law, should have a new subject, in which students from seventh to twelfth grade learn about what might be termed "national reality." This subject would be graded and compulsory for graduation. Ideas of how to resolve problems in the country would be proposed and practical attempts at solving them made. In this way, students would leave school with a national conscience that would benefit everyone in the future.

Hector San Martin

retreat from the stress of exams

349

A school in South Yorkshire sent its pupils to a three-star hotel for short breaks before they took their GCSE (General Certificate of Secondary Education) exams (at age 16) and saw the number of pupils attaining grades from A* to C rise from 12 percent in 1997 to 36 percent in 2001.

The break at the hotel included motivational talks, revision workshops, and advice on controlling exam stress. It may well be the relaxation that was the key to success, for the UK education system is now a stressful place to learn, with over 105 exams possible between the ages of five and eighteen.

The head teacher of Wombwell High School, Irene Dalton, attributed the success of the breaks to two other reasons. "First, because the hotel is posh and the school is not, it lets [the children] know I think the world of them and, second, the pupils soak up the alluring atmosphere and are inspired to perform to a higher level." These factors made the breaks an appropriate and effective use of the school's resources.

contribute to community service to offset tuition

350

As the costs of providing education continue to rise, tuition fees have risen. Some feel that tuition increases unduly penalize lower-income families. One radical option could be to replace student tuition fees with student community service.

This would save the government money, as the students would contribute a great deal of social capital. It would also aid the social inclusion of students in the local area around their university and make them more aware of prob-lems prevalent in society. Students could be employed to manage the system so that they can learn management skills, while the costs of the organization are cut.

Community service could involve such work as visiting older members of the community or running youth programs. There would be the potential for students to relate community work to their subject of study, and their education in the ways of the world would be improved.

Alex Jacobs

study a real-world database for relevant research

351

Masters-level students dedicate up to a year to research their thesis. The choice of topic is usually up to the students, who base it on their field of interest or their interpretation of the need for such research. Often, their interpretation is wrong and the research is unread. At the same time, social and environmental organizations require research they are unable to conduct (due to lack of funds or professional knowledge). A win-win situation is possible in which students are involved in research on current, real-world issues, and their work used by organizations in the field. In practical terms, the ideal situation would be to create a research project coordination database that would accept research needs from national or international organizations (e.g., non-governmental organizations, or UN bodies) and that would be accessible to students worldwide. Service users would get masters-level research tailored to their needs while students would produce research that is relevant and worthwhile.

Avi Blau

use computers to build a bridge between the generations

352

Professor Edna Aphek started a program in Israel that sought to minimize the gap between generations, and bridge the divide in technological literacy between age groups.

Children between the ages of seven and thirteen tutored senior citizens in computer and Internet skills, while at the same time writing an e-book based on a section of the elderly person's history.

The rationale behind this unique program was based upon the following three assumptions:

→ New technologies have created a new situation, hitherto unknown in human history, wherein young children master a skill much needed by adults in general and senior citizens in particular.

→ In today's hi-tech world, in which children speak the language of information technology just as well as their mother tongue, it is indeed fitting to put their mastery to good use and to train them to teach this language to adults, especially those unacquainted with the language of the computer and the Internet, and the elderly in particular.

→ There is a dire need for preserving knowledge at risk of disappearance: precious wisdom is stored in the minds of senior citizens. Many seniors could be seen as walking treasures of history, folk art, and music that are about to disappear.

A similar project took place in Maryland. Senior residents of the Hebrew Home in Rockville learned how to use the Internet with the help of two fifteen-year-old girls.

The effort began when the two high-school sophomores, Rachel Gopenko and Allison Lewis, decided they wanted to fulfill Maryland's community service requirements by using computer technology in order to help the elderly.

Through donations, the girls received laptops and some of the latest computer software to begin helping the elderly residents of the Hebrew Home.

After an initial response of both disinterest and confusion, the residents began to understand and enjoy being able to communicate with members of their families through the Internet.

Resident Beatrice Litman said it brought her closer to her granddaughters and began a whole new relationship. "What separated us was that they were computer kids and I was not," she said. A gap was bridged as the young tutored the old, and all learned valuable lessons in the process.

subtitle songs to support mass literacy

Literacy levels among portions of the Indian population have been exceptionally low for many years, and it is a problem that many plans and initiatives have attempted to alleviate, with varying levels of success.

One of the simplest and most cost-effective ideas is that of Same Language Subtitling. Capitalizing on the popularity of films on television, Same Language Subtitling simply shows the lyrics of film songs as subtitles in the same language as the audio.

The concept was put into place in the late 1990s in the state of Gujarat. The weekly broadcasts of *Chitrageet*, a program of Gujurati film songs, were subtitled with words that changed color in exact coordination with the audio. Several thousand postcards were sent in from people who thought the idea was worthwhile. Most people enjoyed it because it allowed them to sing along, to understand the lyrics, and to write songs down. The idea is powerful because it is covertly, rather than overtly, educational.

Indications of the enormous potential of Same Language Subtitling for promoting state and national reading skills improvement were obtained from an extensive three-month trial involving children in an Ahmedabad primary school. The children's reading improvement was measured and found to have been greater among those who had watched the program with subtitles than without.

The concept is particularly cost-effective. State expenditure in Gujarat in 1999 on literacy amounted to about two dollars (£1) per neoliterate each year. The annual cost of Same Language Subtitling in the state was the equivalent of less than a cent (half a penny). Another major advantage is that it encourages reading without any dependence on formal education provision or on individual motivation.

→ **http://.sls4literacy.tripod.com/ frameset.htm**

teach yourself computer literacy to enhance self-esteem

Sugata Mitra, who headed the research and development wing of India's primary software company, started an innovative project that he put under the umbrella of minimally invasive education. He placed a high-powered computer with a high-speed connection into the back wall of the company's grounds, which backed up to a slum. He left it both on and connected to the Internet and allowed anyone who was passing by to play with it, meanwhile monitoring all activity via a video camera in an adjacent tree.

He found within days that slum children were able to teach themselves to use the machine: not only to use the mouse, to copy and paste, and to use software such as Microsoft Paint, but also to surf the net and obtain information from websites. After playing a music file for them, Mitra watched as the children learned how to download MP3 files and play them on the computer within the space of a week.

Mitra theorizes that by simply providing computer equipment and a minimum of training, children can achieve basic computer literacy through self-education. He believes that huge numbers of children could be brought up to this basic level with a relatively low investment of capital and in a comparatively short period. Curious children, working as groups,

354

attained basic computer literacy without outside assistance, which means no formal infrastructure is needed to teach them.

Children also invented their own terminology for the different parts of the computer. Thus, the mouse pointer (arrow cursor) was named *sui*, the Hindu word for "needle," while the egg timer symbol that appears when something is loading was called *damru*, after the hourglass-shaped drum that the god Shiva holds in his hand. The children soon learned that the sui became a damru when the computer was doing something, which showed that the technology could be used regardless of how different aspects of its use were identified.

Based on this and other experiments, Mitra has asserted that if he were given the resources and funding to conduct this experiment for five years, with 100,000 kiosks, then 500 million Indian children could become computer literate.

He believes that it would cost about $2 (£1) billion, but that using traditional methods of teaching children computer technology would cost more than twice as much. Mitra maintains that this system is the way to truly open up opportunities to all.

→ **www.niitholeinthewall.com**

train teenagers
to tackle emergencies

355

Since 1970, secondary school children in Darien, Connecticut, have run an ambulance service for the town. Boy Scout Explorer Post 53 runs three ambulances for the 20,000 locals, and has a squad of sixty children. John Doble and his son came up with the idea that such a project could contribute to the community and educate youngsters about the dangers of drugs, alcohol, and the accidents they can create. The service deals with about a thousand calls each year and, though an adult supervisor is always present, the teenagers take the lead. In the first two years, students put in 150 hours of training to become an Emergency Medical Technician. Training includes how to treat conditions such as broken bones, wounds, and burns.

In a similar project at Atlantic College, Wales, students help run the inshore lifeboat service in the Bristol Channel. They learn basic seamanship skills and first aid.

→ **www.post53.org**
→ **www.atlanticcollege.org/ilb.htm**

perform poetry
challenge for charity

356

The Poetry Challenge, conceived by Nicholas Albery, the prolific social inventor, is an event in which members of the public are sponsored to learn poems by heart and recite them. He hoped it would encourage love of poetry and self-confidence, as well as raise money for charity.

From the 1990s, he held annual London events for friends and family. Gradually, the net widened as the public became aware through press coverage. He realized the combination of encouraging a love of literature and a fundraising event was perfect for schools. He mailed them with information and template certificates, sponsorship forms, and posters (now downloadable from the website). He also edited an anthology of poetry perfect for learning by heart: *Poem for the Day* has since become one of the most popular poetry anthologies in the UK.

→ **www.poetrychallenge.org.uk**

surround children with circletime support

Murray White, formerly a head teacher in Cambridgeshire, UK, had a strong belief in the link between a child's self-esteem and level of academic success.

He instituted Circletime for every class in the school. This involves the children sitting in a circle with the teacher and completing, in turn, an incomplete sentence. Some examples include, "Today, I'm feeling…" or "I wish I was…" or "What makes me laugh is…." The purposes of the exercise are to establish the group (a joining together in the class), to provide a chance for children to express themselves,

357

and to create the opportunity for staff to become aware of children's feelings, problems, and other issues. The key is that the children recognize Circletime as a safe environment, which frees them to open up and use it as a chance to be both creative and direct. This, in turn, aids their development both individually and collectively as a class.

Another element is to select a Special Child for the day. This involves a fun selection process, and the Special Child receiving a badge before being asked to leave the room while the others discuss nice things that can be said about them. The Special Child then receives a barrage of compliments, all of which are written down by the teacher as a keepsake.

The only rules of Circletime are that only one person may speak at a time, that everyone can have fun, and that no one should spoil another's fun. As White says, "It is a time when the children find out a bit more about themselves and what they are capable of, and how they relate to each other… If the children have an inner sense of well-being—a core of self-esteem that allows them to make the best use of their abilities—they will be better able to respond to the trials of daily life."

→ **www.esteem-workshops.co.uk**

discover your dream job through emulation

358

When school students are starting to think about their future career, or what sector they may want to work in, the emphasis is usually on picking the job from a list of job titles. Sometimes, this list emerges from a piece of computer software that asks the student questions, and produces a list of possible suitable jobs at the end of the process.

A different approach to help finding the ideal career would be by "emulation": by choosing someone and considering what particular steps would be needed to emulate this person exactly.

The student could even consider what steps would be need to be taken to become an "imposter" of this person. This would make the process much more creative, and make the student's role an active (and interactive) one, rather than that of a passive receiver of information and advice.

Each student could draw up a list of people (or select one from a pre-prepared list), and then decide which person they are going to study in terms of emulation.

This method could provide inspiration in several ways:

→ The student may find that they would like to emulate this person as much as possible and thus the career of this person is the ideal career choice for them.

→ They may find that one of the steps needed to complete the emulation would be so interesting that this is an area that would suit them as a career.

→ The process of analysing someone else's career may give them a greater insight into the possibilities and opportunities available (in switching between sectors, different jobs, taking sabbaticals and so on).

→ The person chosen may prove to be an inspiration in a more general way because they match some characteristics or experiences of the student, such as not being strong academically, being told they would not achieve anything, or coming from a difficult background.

The emulation–career process would prove a valuable educational tool for students, as it would require them to look at the way in which the real world works, how people strive to achieve things, make connections, make decisions and get on in their lives. This is something rarely covered in school courses, even in business studies or economics, and would help prepare students for the world at large.

John Tunney

chapter 15

neighborhood

slow down cities for high-quality local life

359

The slow movement that started with Slow Food (see page 42) has diversified into a new network of slow cities—towns that value their heritage, gastronomy, environment, and a local way of doing things.

It is part of the continuing backlash against the so-called Global Village in which all parts of the world start to look the same, and in which all are dictated to move at the same pace with fast food, fast cars, and 24-hour life. The Slow Cities movement (CittaSlow) says that living in a slow city means treating humans, the environment, and local history with respect. The network in 2004 encompassed 35 Italian towns and cities, and towns in ten other countries (Ludlow was the first UK town to receive certification). The movement campaigns for bicycle lanes, environmental policies, and local festivals, and against car alarms, advertising billboards, and neon advertising.

→ **www.cittaslow.net**

make a mutual aid fund for friends in need

360

Rather than dealing with faceless insurance companies who don't attend to the individual and their challenges, Charles Gray and friends decided on a more personal approach: they set up a mutual aid fund.

Each member would deposit an initial lump sum and contribute a small amount each month. The fund was called FIN (Friend In Need) and allowed its members to request money when an emergency arose. With this simple method, they combined financial security with community spirit in an easily replicable solution.

At monthly meetings, large amounts of money could be requested for more serious problems, but the fund provided more than just cash. The meetings were also a forum for creative solutions to the problems the members faced. Gray highlights how when his bicycle was stolen, the members were able to contribute spare parts and start bicycle assembly workshops. In this way the FIN program helped to create a small community support network that was highly responsive to its members' needs.

request utilities plant trees
when they dig holes

361

The UK news anchor Jon Snow has suggested an innovative way for towns and cities to increase their greenery.

Quite simply, the proposal is that when utility companies dig up the streets to carry out work, if they dig up more than a certain distance (say, 30 meters [150 feet]), they should have to plant trees in the holes they create. Because they would already have had to map the position of the street's underground workings to carry out maintenance, they can avoid any pipes and cables when planting. Trees are cheap, as are the soil and fertilizer needed for them. These supplies could therefore be bought by the local government, so the only cost to the utility company would be either the cost in labor of planting or the cost of hiring someone else to do so.

The plan could extend the impact of such tree-planting initiatives as Trees for London. .

→ **www.treesforlondon.org.uk**

keep chickens
in a city setting

362

For city-dwellers pining for the country life and wishing to be more self-sufficient, there is an invention that may help.

The Eglu is an urban chicken coop for two chickens (or three bantams) that promises to make keeping chickens fun and rewarding. It is made by a UK company from 100 percent recyclable materials. Two chickens should deliver half a dozen eggs a week, which can be collected from the coop's egg-port and should be enough for most urban households. The Eglu has been insulated to stay warm in winter and cool in summer, and claims to offer a standard of living not seen before in chicken-house design.

While the group behind the invention clearly has a light-hearted approach to it (they are called Omlet), it could prove a viable and worthwhile option. If even 1 percent of a city's households were to keep chickens rather than buy eggs, the effect in reducing packaging, transportation, and so on could be substantial.

→ **www.omlet.co.uk**

participate in people planting to strengthen community

A neighborhood initiative, dubbed "People Planting," offers children and community-based groups the means to develop their own areas of woodland, thus providing a practical and symbolic way for communities to tend to an earth in crisis.

363

Developed by the Green Light Trust in association with UK home improvement retailer B&Q, the People Planting initiative gives toolkits to interested groups; the kits contain practical woodland management information and ideas for creative fundraising. While physically cultivating the earth alleviates a sense of help- lessness in the face of worldwide environmental horror stories, the subtext of the initiative is to instill community spirit and pride through maintaining woodlands and engaging in related activities. Thus, the basic tools for kick-starting woodland projects are accompanied by resources that promote storytelling and other community-inspiring events incorporating song, dance, and traditional crafts. The idea is simple enough that it could easily be extended to other countries.

→ **www.greenlighttrust.org**

connect and communicate
with a community directory

364

A telephone booklet containing the numbers of one's immediate neighbors would be a useful tool in many emergency situations such as power outages, fuel shortages, wildfire, floods, or suspicious noises at night. By making calls, individuals could request help, alert their neighbors, and talk over possible strategies to deal with the problem at hand.

We are rarely close friends with our close neighbors; in fact, we often do not know their last names, even though we occasionally speak to them. It is often impossible to call them when a community crisis arises. One solution would be for the government or local authorities to declare neighborhood booklets as being in the public interest and encourage phone companies to distribute them.

The many benefits of this proposal, including more potential for community organization and support, would also give a new perspective on how to view citizens in need. Individuals could be empowered to help each other and themselves, rather than responding as isolated victims in need of public services.

Roger Knights

→ **www.franis.org/868**

put on a potluck picnic
to encourage public spirit

365

In an increasingly urbanized world, it is often difficult to get a sense of community, or to meet people who live in a particular area. So here's a suggestion to remedy that: pick a date for a potluck picnic in a local park, then invite everyone whose phone number happens to have the same last four digits as yours—3986 or whatever. Publicize the lunch through the mayor's office, posters, and local media. On the day of the picnic, bring something good to eat and meet people of all demographic categories you might not otherwise have come across in a social situation. Each person will get a better picture of others who live in their area and in their city. The experiment could be interesting and fun, and is likely to attract other open-minded people.

Paul Spinrad

garden to grow
health, happiness, and hope

366

Dan Barker, a poet and novelist, gave away vegetable gardens in Portland, Oregon, for almost twenty years. Funded by private foundations and trusts, his Home Gardening Project built gardens in the back yards of recipients, free of charge.

Each resident received soil frames, a trellis, seeds, fertilizer, tomato cages, pest controls, instructions, advice, and tips. Barker deliberately carried out the work in the more downtrodden neighborhoods, where the work's impact—material, psychological, and spiritual—could make the greatest difference.

The project has been responsible for over 1,400 gardens in Portland, at an average cost of $400 (£200) per garden. Each garden can produce over $500 (£250) worth of food each summer.

It is not just about economics and food, though; it is about pride in accomplishments, self-esteem and self-sufficiency, a reconnection with nature, and a gratitude that, with the garden, people can do something for themselves rather than ask for handouts.

→ **http://home.teleport.com/~hgpf/**

recycle large items
on your doorstep

367

In Germany and Austria as well as in some French cities, there is a regular time each month when everybody puts outside their front door large items that they no longer want or need. These can range from lamps, beds, tables, and chairs to fridges, computers, and vacuum cleaners. Before the garbage men arrive, students, newlyweds, bargain hunters, and people who simply enjoy browsing are allowed to help themselves to anything that takes their fancy.

This is a simple and effective way of recycling goods, as long as rules are applied to keep out commercial dealers. It might even help the local authorities, who could hire vehicles and extra staff that day, knowing that there will be such items left out. This could then become a more coordinated process, potentially cutting down on illegal refuse dumping, which is a growing problem in areas where people do not have their own transportation.

Hugh Barnard / Carola Zentner

share a shop to save
social heart of village

V illagers in Wiltshire, UK, reacted to the closing of a local shop by deciding to buy it themselves.

368

The inhabitants of Maiden Bradley raised £21,000 ($42,000) from the government's countryside agency, and over 60 percent of the village adults contributed sums of between £5 ($10) and £500 ($1,000) in return for shares in the store. The shop's future has been assured, and the village now leases it out, with all proceeds going back into the community. More than just preserving a local store, this piece of direct action has strengthened the commu-

nity as a whole. People have an interest in the shop, use it themselves, and it provides a center for the residents of the village to chat or make contact each day.

The village also refurbished the store itself, with locals volunteering to strip, clean, and repair the property. The strong reaction of the village came about because it had already lost its local school, dentist, and police station, and has poor transport links. At least in Maiden Bradley, the breakdown of another rural community has been halted, with the shop maintained as the social heart of the village.

create your own
quality of life

T he world is preoccupied with developing material wealth and has achieved it in much of the western world. Many countries in Asia, particularly China and India, are quickly catching up, as are parts of all the other countries of the world. It is an appropriate time to develop our psychological and mental wealth as well—to focus on quality of life.

369

A group of interested consultants and community workers in each village, town, and city could work with politicians and citizens in work-

shops to create a quality of life measurement for locality. The consultants/ community workers would receive a booklet with suggestions on programs that could be used. A group with website expertise and public relations competence could publish the results.

A contest could be held annually to see which entity best lived up to its own measurements. Public relations people would disseminate the results worlwide.

Natalie Dian

create community consciousness and safer streets with home zones

370

Home Zones are an attempt to reclaim the streets from cars and return them to the people who live on them, thus making the streets safer and improving community cohesion.

A Home Zone is defined as a residential street where the living environment clearly predominates over any provision for traffic: essentially, the traditional domination of cars over pedestrians is challenged. Strategies for creating such a zone include traffic slowing measures, tree planting, and the introduction of benches and play equipment. In effect, the car passing through becomes a guest of the neighborhood, rather than the road owner. Such zones reduce traffic accidents, encourage children to play outside, create a greater sense of community, and help foster a sense of community ownership.

The concept, called *woonerf*, originated in the 1970s in the Netherlands, where there are currently over 6,500 zones. They have also been introduced in Germany, Denmark, and Sweden.

→ **www.homezones.org**

set up a living-room in your street

371

Some inner city residents in Stavanger, Norway, took a novel approach to fostering a sense of community spirit in the late 1990s. They transformed a whole street into a permanent living room (or social space) by fitting it with benches, tables, potted plants, a bulletin board, an Internet connection, and a flagpole. The pole is used regularly, as a flag is hoisted on it to celebrate any resident's birthday.

The idea originated when Trond Sigvaldsen moved his father's bench into the street to polish it. People congregated around it and someone suggested making Vikesdalsgata Street into a living room. They got residents' agreements and negotiated with the local government to furnish the space. It was launched in 1999 to much success.

→ **www.stavanger.kommune.no**

guide villages
toward regeneration

372

In 1976, Lauri Hautamaki, then Assistant Professor of Geography at the University of Helsinki, had studied the theories of participatory action research with particular emphasis on village-led rural revival.

With colleagues, Hautamaki identified 51 villages in Finland that had tried to preserve or defend their way of life through the use of their village committees. The researchers traveled through the Finnish countryside and disseminated the work of these activist villages, and how their many and varied activities had helped save local services and win resources for the community. Other villages began to follow their lead.

In 1978, the Village Alive Campaign was launched, and a relay baton was passed from village to village to symbolize the regeneration of village life. This involved distributing a guide that the researchers had compiled, emphasizing the central role of the school in village life and organizing events with Adult Education Institutes. Within ten years, there were more than 2,000 village committees in place, all democratically elected each year, which covered almost every rural community in Finland.

create a community space
to get to know your neighbors

373

In many urban settings, apartment building residents hardly know who their immediate neighbors are, much less the others who live in their building.

This idea could help bring people together in an unforced way. Find an unoccupied or underused space in your immediate vicinity. With help from your neighbors, renovate it into a public living room and use it as a gathering space for holidays, events, hobbies, politics, or relaxing. This would create a more integrated environment in the urban setting, working against the feelings of alienation and isolation that city-dwellers often feel.

To get this project off the ground, engage others in your apartment building, condo, or other multi-unit housing system. Talking to them in person is usually best, but you could leave flyers under doors to explain the project.

Chris Thomas

join church with state
to provide postal services

374

As post offices in rural areas of the UK continue to be closed down, merged together, or moved to bigger towns, an unusual alternative has recently emerged.

Residents in the Leicestershire village of Sheepy Magna were given the option to drop off mail or collect their benefits at the local church. After it was announced that the local post office was to close, the church applied to take over the role.

The church council then gave its go-ahead to the plan, and All Saints Church may be the post office in the community for some years to come. As well as fulfilling an important local need, the idea could signal a willingness of the church to find new ways of retaining its place at the heart of the community. If people aren't coming to services on Sunday, at least they'll be using postal services during the week.

There were some minor objections in the community to the move, but most were delighted to have a satellite post office in the village. The elderly members of the community, in particular, no longer had to find transportation to get their pensions from the nearest post office. The church makes no profit from running the post office.

tool up libraries
to equip the community

375

While the concept of lending books out is firmly established, some communities have taken the idea further. In the 1990s, libraries in California started lending tools as well as books. There are now over 20 such libraries in the US; the most active are the original few (Berkeley, Oakland and San Francisco). They typically lend a mix of basic hand tools and more advanced landscaping, construction and gardening tools. The more unusual tools are often borrowed most, including the jackhammer, the "drain snake" (for clearing blockages), and the belt sander. They can be loaned out to anyone with a local library card. Costs are relatively small, with insurance the only major expense.

→ **www.berkeleypubliclibrary.org/tool**

place local communities
at the heart of policy-making

Placing the community at the heart of policy-making is a wise move, not only from an ethical and moral standpoint, but also from an economic and political one, for it is not just local markets that are threatened by globalization, free trade, and mobile capital, it is local democracy and community feeling. So how can the seemingly inexorable march of globalization, urban sprawl, and social and fiscal mobility be challenged? Through a range of innovative place-based solutions.

376

Take urban sprawl, in which rich citizens leave the city center and create isolated spaces which enforce divides. Some solutions may be:
➜ Impact fees in which private developers have to pay public costs of a suburban development.
➜ The establishment of an enforced growth boundary around a city or town.
➜ Reverse commuting, in which transport for city center residents to the suburbs is subsidized, so employment opportunities are open to all.
➜ Reconversion of military bases: As military bases close, the impact on local communities can be substantial and damaging. A program of focused investment targeted at redeveloping the bases has proved a success in the US, with a quarter of ex-bases creating more civilian jobs in the years after closure (as airports, call centers, and so on).

➜ Clawback laws: Several states have introduced clawback laws to ensure that corporations do not irreparably damage communities. In Vermont, incoming businesses receive subsidies as an incentive, but if employment falls by 35 percent within two years the state receives the full amount back.
➜ Community land trusts: Placing land under the control of the local community is an effective way of ensuring development is done for the community's benefit. They are structured to distribute benefits of development more equally, so the whole community, not a private developer, benefits from any wealth influx.

fashion tools to build communities for the future

377

A project run by the Institute for Local Self-Reliance hopes to create a storehouse of rules to help build local communities. The New Rules Project proposes rules that build community by supporting human-scale politics and economics. The rules call for:

→ Decisions to be made by those who will feel the impact of those decisions.

→ Communities to possess or own sufficient productive capacity to generate real wealth.

→ Communities to be responsible for the welfare of their members and the next generation's.

The rules are divided into nine sections: agriculture, energy, environment, equity, finance, governance, information, retail, and taxation.

Each section on the website contains rules relating to that topic, rules that honor a sense of place and prize rootedness, continuity, and stability as well as innovation and enterprise. Each topic sector also contains a list of policy tools for that particular area.

The Institute for Local Self-Reliance is a non-profit organization devoted to the case of what they call New Localism. The Institute believes that localism, not globalism, is progressive, and that localism and smallness are not only more environmentally friendly and more democratic, but also more cost-effective and more profitable.

→ **www.newrules.org**

throw people, ideas, and food into the mix

378

An idea for bringing people together in the community is through sharing food. This project could be called The Mixing Bowl and would involve asking people who have an interest in cooking to come together to taste new foods and share a meal. Once per month each person (or family) would bring one uncooked food item to be part of the menu for a meal. Upon arriving and discovering what food people have selected and brought with them, the group will decide what dishes to prepare, then cook and eat them.

The Mixing Bowl would combine the quirkiness of a cookery TV program format with a social purpose.

Shawn Woodin

question your neighbors for help and support

379

Think how much money, trouble, inconvenience, and frustration could be saved if only people knew their neighbors.

For example, the working parent who has trouble affording or finding childcare could be unaware that a few doors away lives a stay-at-home parent who would be happy to look after another child now and then; or, to take the most extreme case, someone in an accident in their home may not know that their neighbor is a qualified first aid provider..

Why not have a system whereby a questionnaire is sent around to all households on a street? This would allow people to choose from a list of skills/services/help they need or can offer, and when they are willing to share these skills. Options might include minding children, small electrical repairs, car mechanics, or grocery shopping. The questionnaires would then be collected and details of need matched with those of supply, so everyone could have a list of people they could call on for whatever they might need.

If this worked it could really improve people's quality of life, as well as helping them to get to know each other again. Everyone complains about lack of time to sort things out, but so often the answer may really be on your doorstep.

Claudia Conway

give gardening gifts to regenerate neighborhoods

380

The concept behind the contest is to regenerate neighborhoods that have been particularly neglected. An announcement is made in the neighborhoods that a spring planting contest will be held, with prizes given each week and signs to be placed in the yards of the winners. After several weeks, the places come alive. People who have never won anything begin to realize they can win. This helps build the family's self-esteem and pride in its property.

Clif Judy runs such contests in Columbia, South Carolina, paying the costs of prizes and signs out of his own pocket.

→ **www.yardoftheweek.org**

take steps to instigate a walkability index

Walkability is pretty close to livability, to healthy communities, and to sustainability, but it's not as abstract. We can all relate to it. And it relates to quality of life: health, community, social equity, enjoyment, attachment to place, environment, fitness, and low stress.

The creation of a walkability index would be a good way of measuring desirability of a community and for providing a motivation for action.

Walkability has four basic characteristics:
1 A foot-friendly, man-made, physical microenvironment: wide, level sidewalks, small intersections, narrow streets, litter containers, good lighting, and an absence of obstructions.
2 A full range of useful, active destinations within walking distance: shops, services, employment, recreation, libraries, and so on.
3 A natural environment that moderates the extremes of weather (wind, rain, sunlight) while there is an absence of man's overuse (no excessive noise or air pollution).
4 A local culture that is social and diverse. This increases contact between people and conditions for social and economic commerce.

The index could measure:
→ Density
→ Parking places per household

381

→ Number of sitting spots on benches per household (include in front yards)
→ Chances of meeting someone you know while walking (survey)
→ Age at which a child is allowed to walk alone (survey)
→ Women's rating of neighborhood safety (survey)
→ Responsiveness of public transportation.
→ The number of neighborhood places of any significance
→ Park land (measurement)
→ Sidewalks

Chris Bradshaw

watch the global neighborhood
via the internet

382

People from the other side of the world could watch your street for crime during the night by using video cameras and the Internet.

Such a system would allow people working on their computers in other countries to alert that particular neighborhood of any ongoing crime. By using video cameras with motion detectors, the cameras would be set up to only transmit digitized output when something is happening. Then the video could be put online, once the neighborhood's computers are linked to the Internet. Meanwhile, in the UK or Australia, while the crime-ridden neighborhood in America sleeps, the computer user could be alerted when something is moving on-screen. If the movement is innocent, a green button could be clicked; if a crime is in progress, a red button could be clicked to sound an alarm on the American's computer. The reverse could happen during nighttime in Australia or the UK.

Despite flaws, if enough people in enough countries are interested, a Global Neighborhood Watch could become a reality.

take your tribal
vitamin daily

383

It is an important idea in the age of urban isolation to help people take note of the extent to which they are detribalized and rootless, and whether or not they are getting their Recommended Daily Allowance (RDA) of what we term Vitamin T, the tribal vitamin.

Vitamin T is made up of contact with local people, a sense of belonging locally, and a connection to the people and place where you live. To work toward your RDA of Vitamin T, chat with local people, greet people in the street, think how many locals would notice if you left or how many would help if you were ill, ponder about how many local places you could drop in for a chat or even a meal on impulse, count up how many rituals (religious service, drink in a tavern) you engage in.

Nicholas Albery

→ **www.globalideasbank.org**

participate in city budgets
to improve democracy

384

The Brazilian city of Porto Alegre adopted in 1989 a radical solution to its major problems of poverty and unaccountability: a participative budget.

Since then the city's residents have decided how the budget for public works should be divided and allocated. Smaller neighborhood groups put forward projects, then delegates from community groups and non-profit organizations (themselves elected by their neighbors) decide which projects are to be implemented. Sometimes, the community delegates themselves to oversee a project that is going ahead. The introduction of this budgetary system has had a threefold impact: a massive increase in democratic participation, improving specific problems on the ground, and largely eradicating the mishandling of funds.

The system is not only viewed as a success by the citizens (who recently gave it an 85 percent approval rating in a poll), but also by other cities in South America.

→ **www.portoalegre.rs.gov.br**

relax rules for
social innovations

385

To foster social innovation and entrepreneurship, allowing innovative arrangements to be tried out in specific communities could be an attractive option.

Relaxing regulations to allow the testing of economic, social, and political innovations could allow a forward-thinking community to help itself at no cost, while also providing useful information for those in power. The community in question could even choose to put itself forward: a referendum could be held in which, if a set majority (two-thirds or three-quarters, perhaps) agreed, the district could become a place for social and political experimentation. Each proposed initiative could be voted on by the local people in the same way. The locality might not only prove to be attractive to incoming people (particularly if the area was given tax relief in recognition of its pioneering role), but also to give a sense of pride and power to those already in the community.

David Robinson / Gregory Wright

chapter 16

health

subtitle smoking
to discourage the young

386

The Italian health minister proposed a novel way to discourage young people from smoking: a subtitled warning under scenes in which cigarettes are featured. Girolamo Sirchia suggested the message could read: "Warning, this is pro-smoking propaganda," and could combat the influence of tobacco companies on the young. The minister, who was previously a surgeon, proposed the idea after reading research estimating that a cigarette appears on TV every seven minutes during programming aimed at the young.

The controversial proposal, which could change the way TV programs and films are viewed across Italy, would follow a raft of other new anti-smoking legislation. As of December 2002, smoking in most public places was banned, with the exception of specially designated smoking areas.

These measures are aimed at cutting the number of smokers in Italy, and thus the number of deaths due to smoking-induced cancer; a quarter of Italy's 58 million citizens are smokers.

vent your frustration
in a screaming booth

387

Rage, stress, anger, frustration, and irritation (and the discomfort, dangerous acts, and illnesses that they precipitate) are unfortunate but real and dangerous side effects of the way we live today. Ideally we should recognize these problems and reshape society to minimize them, but for now they are real problems that deserve immediate attention.

One way to rectify this problem would be to provide soundproof booths, which need be no larger than telephone booths, at various loca-

tions throughout urban areas, particularly in places where stress is more likely, such as busy shopping centers and stations.

The idea is simple. When in need of emotional release, the irate citizen finds a local booth, enters it, closes the door, and lets out any sound that needs to come out. People can scream, shout, cry, or sing in complete privacy, experience the release, calm down, and carry on with the day as a far less dangerous animal.

Louisa de Prey

take up the tools to be truly happy

388

Psychologist Dan Baker believes that there are six key tools to achieving happiness—tools that can help us avoid "the four happiness traps:" the "Trying-to-Buy-Happiness Trap," the "Trying-to-Find-Happiness-Through-Pleasure Trap," the "Trying-to-Find-Happiness-by-Overcoming Weaknesses Trap," and the "Trying-to-Force-Happiness Trap." Each is self-explanatory, and, while they are interesting in terms of patterns to avoid, more interesting are the six tools that Baker offers:

→ Appreciation: The outward-bound kind of love that gives everything and asks for nothing, making it pure and strong.

→ Choice: Anyone can choose the course of their lives, but only happy people do it.

→ Personal Power: A proactive force that gives individuals power over their feelings and their fate. It is made up of two constituent parts: taking action and taking responsibility.

→ Leading with your strengths: Focusing on strengths, rather than focusing on weaknesses, enables a swifter resolving of situations.

→ The power of language: Language can be used in a healthy or horrible way, and words have immense power to constrain or liberate.

→ Multidimensional Living: Putting energy into the three main components of life (relationships, health, and purpose) is the final key.

Martin Seligman, another American psychologist, suggested three additional ways to be optimistic and happier in life, particularly in the key three areas of love, work, and children. His three suggestions are to:

→ Keep your illusions: Research shows the happiest couples are those who sustain romantic illusions about each other, rather than being realistic, avoiding false expectations. This is because people who idealize their partners are more likely to forgive small transgressions swiftly, while the idolized partner is more likely to try and please their partner.

→ Turn work into play: The key to happiness at work is not to find the perfect job but to find the job that can be made perfect (or at least better) by the individual. People who are engrossed in their work or who feel it is their calling are consistently happier than those in jobs or, more generally, careers. Find an activity in which the challenges mesh perfectly with the person's abilities.

→ Teach children to thrive: Give children safe and welcoming spaces to ensure that they know their actions count, and that they experience positive emotions through having some measure of personal mastery.

→ **www.AuthenticHappiness.org**

picture the damage that smoking does

389

Photographic health warnings have appeared on Canadian cigarette packets since 2000 with the aim of convincing smokers to give up. Studies have shown that written warnings are 60 times more persuasive when accompanied by photographs.

Regulations allow for a variety of photographs, including images of lung cancer, bleeding gums, and damaged brains, in addition to the written health warnings required by Canadian law (including "Don't poison us" and "Tobacco smoke hurts babies").

Beyond the shock value of the graphic warnings, this method could be used in developing countries, where lack of literacy is an obstacle to communicating health messages.

In 2004, the European Union announced that it would encourage its members to follow suit, based on research from the Canadian experiment, which found that 44 percent of Canadian smokers felt more compelled to quit following the introduction of the photographic warnings.

float the idea of dolphin midwives

390

Igor Charkovsky is renowned, not for having been a male midwife, but because he helped women give birth with the aid and assistance of dolphins. He began experimenting with dolphins in 1979 at a research station and discovered that they were extremely sensitive and gentle when brought into contact with children. He was amazed by the care and understanding that was apparent in their treatment of the children, even when the children were riding on the dolphin's backs.

At the same time, he noted the peaceful effect of the dolphins on newborn babies, who he observed sleeping quietly in the sea while dolphins swam around them. He concluded that dolphins could reduce the stress of the mother and baby during birth and immediately afterward. So he started to help pregnant women give birth in the Black Sea surrounded by dolphins, whose caring and kind natures were seen to give the mother and child a sense of security and relaxation.

organize citizens to decide on organ donation

There are not enough organ donors to satisfy every transplant patient, thus there are long waiting lists and people often die while they are waiting. A solution that many people have suggested is to introduce two measures: compel every citizen to decide whether or not they want to be an organ donor and then give priority to those who are prepared to donate. If one day a potential organ donor needed an organ transplant, he or she would then move ahead of those who chose not to donate. Organ donors would, in brief, be given priority over non-organ donors.

Other factors would have to be taken into consideration, of course, such as greater need or urgency, but in cases that are similar (both patients are on dialysis and need a new kidney), organ donor status would be the deciding factor.

This plan would have two effects: it would create an incentive for people to become potential organ donors and it would add a sense of fairness to the system. There would have to be a legally binding nature to the decision, otherwise those who said they would not donate would simply change their mind when a personal need became apparent. A simple time delay system that did not recognize those who had changed their minds within the last five years might solve this.

391

In the future, after this exercise is done for the first time, every citizen could be asked the organ donor question when they turn eighteen. The shortage of organ donors would then be reduced significantly, not only in the short term, but in the long term as well.

David Janowick

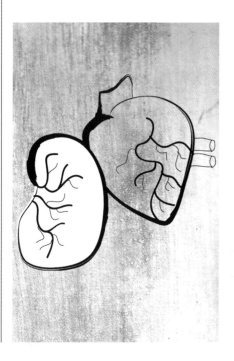

sit on the floor
for health and humility

392

In a western world increasingly filled with bad backs, poor posture, and arrogance, it may be time to look to a simple idea from the east: using the floor.

Sitting on the floor results in better posture and also makes one feel more humble: it is difficult to look down on people metaphorically if you are looking up to them literally. There is also the environmental angle: imagine if even 10 percent of the US or UK population decided they could do without their plastic chair at work or home, and how much that would save in terms of raw materials.

The best reason for sitting on the floor is health. We used to live without chairs, sofas, or beds off the ground, and had to stretch many times a day getting up and down. Nowadays, people are often on the same level (from bed to chair to sofa to bed) and do not exercise their muscles as much.

listen to crazy radio
to stop stigma

393

Radio La Colifata ("crazy radio") in Buenos Aires, Argentina, broadcasts live from a psychiatric hospital, with patients presenting their poems, songs, and thoughts. It started with a session led by Alfredo Olivera, who invited patients to speak about whatever they wanted into a Dictaphone. These tapes were picked up by community radio stations and then by network radio shows; now the hospital's radio segments reach an estimated 12 million listeners. Not only do the patients feel valued and listened to, but also barriers between society and the institution are broken down. The broadcasts have shattered people's preconceptions about mental illness. Indeed, many listeners tune in for insights or stimulating thoughts that they would not hear elsewhere. It has also been effective at reuniting patients with their families and homes.

Thirty percent of patients who have participated in the program go on to be discharged and, of those who continue outpatient therapy with the radio, none has been readmitted (compared with two-thirds of those who do not).

→ **http://lacolifata.openware.biz/index.cgi**

donate blood during visiting hours

394

When we lived in Kuwait my husband had to have an operation. Beforehand, he was asked if he could find three volunteers to give blood, of any blood type. For Kuwaitis, most of whom have large extended families, this standard request would have presented no difficulty, but we were unable to supply the blood required. Nevertheless, the operation went ahead as scheduled.

Afterward my husband received many visitors in hospital; he was later told by doctors that eighteen of them had given blood, slipping off to do so during the visiting hours. He asked for their names, but was told that it was not hospital policy to reveal them. We also discovered that donors received payment and that those who didn't want it or need it could give it to the poor, thus increasing the good effect of their actions.

It seems to me that this policy could be adopted in other countries to great advantage and at little extra cost, by having donor units operating in hospitals during visiting hours.

Joyce Sadek

put daily choices in perspective with a richter scale for risks

395

Professor John Paling, a former Oxford University biologist who previously worked as a risk analyst in the US, believes that half-understood health scares will periodically dominate the media until we develop an accessible means of quantifying relative risks.

He therefore formulated a Richter Scale For Risks to put anxieties into perspective. He believes that for the public to understand the relative levels of risk, there must be some way of comparing new levels of risk in daily life and those we are already familiar with. He got the idea when he saw a woman smoking a cigarette while trying to determine the benefits of buying a water-purification kit.

The Richter Scale for Risks goes from -6 (1 in 1 trillion chance) to +6 (a certainty, such as dying). Zero is a 1 in 1 million chance. Thus, for the US, the risk of being killed by lightning rates about -0.4 and the risk of becoming a murder victim rates in the region of +1.9.

enhance health and wellness
with patient-centered hospitals

396

Planetree has developed more than twenty hospital affiliates in the US and two in Europe since its founding in 1978, all committed to providing healing environments and patient empowerment in their care.

The person behind Planetree's approach is Angelica Thieriot, who was hospitalized in San Francisco for a mysterious viral ailment in the 1970s. She was relegated to a room that was completely bare except for a bed and a metal chair; her only view was of a cement wall. She was ignored by the staff, apart from when they needed to take a blood sample and even then it was rarely the same person. Following her recovery, Thieriot set about looking for ways to change the hospital experience, a search that ultimately gave birth to the Planetree organization.

Planetree's aim is to create healthcare environments that support and nurture healing on all levels—physical, mental, emotional, and spiritual. Planetree therefore encourages consumers to become active participants in decisions relating to their treatment and care.

Specific programs that have been implemented include care partner projects, in-depth information pamphlets, healing-centered architecture, and massage, as well as healing gardens.

Planetree hospital affiliates report increased patient, nurse, and doctor satisfaction, decreased nurse turnover rates, decreased post-operative infections, and an increase in the number of patients making lifestyle changes conducive to health and wellness.

Planetree programs both encourage and support:
→ a healthcare environment that optimizes wellness through nutrition and stress management, and that also integrates a wide range of healing options for the body, mind, and spirit;
→ an environment that allows medical facility staff members to be nurturers as well as caretakers, educators, and human beings;
→ community-based Health Resource Centers that provide consumers with access to books, articles, videotapes, support networks, research services, and educational programs on a wide range of health and medical topics.

The patient-centered Planetree approach is now featured or utilized in over 80 different healthcare environments throughout the US and Canada.

→ **www.planetree.org**

pogo punk-style
at anarchic aerobics

An explosive union of punk music and the desire to keep fit resulted in Punk Rock Aerobics (PRA), part satire and part high-energy alternative to the traditional workout.

Hilken Mancini and Maura Jasper devised anarchic cardio-exercise as an antidote to the clean-cut Lycra-clad world of aerobics set to a perky pop beat, an exercise regime that simply didn't appeal to their personal music tastes.

Their innovative approach remolds the fitness workout for an alternative audience who dislikes the current image of gym exercise. "We decided to make a class that we would go to," said

397

the punk rockers, who run regular workout sessions at the Middle East Club in their native Boston, US, and the legendary New York punk hangout, CBGBs. The classes offer serious cardiovascular and strengthening exercise alongside the social commentary.

Moves named the Teenage Kix and the Skanks, for example, replace high kicks and stomach crunches. The sessions incorporate classic punk moves such as pogo-dancing and moshing, which have always raised the pulse.

→ **www.PunkRockAerobics.com**

rate restaurants
to enhance health

398

A rating system for the cleanliness of restaurants has dramatically improved health standards in Los Angeles. The rating is issued by Public Health inspectors making surprise visits. A perfect score is 100 points, and restaurants are awarded a grade of A (90–100 points), B (80–89) points, and C (70–79). Points are deducted for such things as hair in food (one point) and a sneezing cook failing to wash their hands (six points). The rating system has had a real effect on the way consumers choose where they eat, because the grade given must be displayed on the restaurant building.

→ **www.lapublichealth.org**

salvage excess medicines
to save lives

399

Millions of people worldwide are prescribed medicines by their doctors. Nearly a third of these medicines are changed before the original prescription is consumed. The result is a lot of unused prescription medication, which expires and is binned.

If places of religious worship (churches, mosques, temples) could serve as collection centers for these medicines, they need not be wasted. They could instead be channeled for the use of charitable medical organizations like Red Cross, Red Crescent, where trained physicians will know how to process them for the benefit of the less fortunate in society. All it would take is an aggressive information campaign launched at the level of the religious places of worship. The religious leaders must specify that medicines requiring prescription are the real target of this effort, rather than cheaper over-the-counter medicines.

The donors would benefit by being safer: it is never wise to take medicines without the guidance of medical professionals. On the part of the religious leaders, this would not contravene their teaching, and could even help promote social responsibility among congregation members. The collected medicines would be a great help to charitable medical institutions, without incurring added cost to society.

Ed Joaquin

cycle on bumpy terrain to improve bone density

400

Cycling on bumpier terrain improves the bone density of the cyclist. Scientists at the University of Utah measured the bone density of a group of mountain bikers and compared it to that of road-racing cyclists. Those who cycled off-road had denser bones, which are less prone to breaking and fracturing. Janet Shaw, who led the research team, said the results could be explained by the fact that the skeleton responds to things out of the ordinary, meaning the off-road spills and thrills of the mountain bikers had helped improve their bones, contrary to what you might have thought.

perform arts to speed recovery

401

The view that a sick or an old person sees from a hospital bed is often only a white ceiling or empty rafters. This can hardly inspire positive thinking, bravery, or hopes of becoming well again.

What if there were projected pictures and texts on the ceiling? They could help activate an individual's hopes for healing. Doctors, therapists, and psychologists could help in finding appropriate pictures and messages. It is true that hoping and believing can help one get well: these images could help place new thoughts and images in people's minds to begin or hasten the healing process. The method is inexpensive: the technology already exists and could be introduced to hospitals in all countries simply and quickly, with potentially revelatory effects.

One UK doctor, Malcolm Rigler, introduced art to his work as a community doctor. He employed local visual artists to work with his community and devise health education posters, and a celebratory lantern procession. The doctor went on to employ a poet who offered advice in the surgery to anyone interested in writing, with a particular focus on enabling people to articulate their experiences of being ill, being cared for, and of getting well. The focus throughout was on shared artistic endeavor and a holistic approach to the well-being of the community.

Veikko Varjus

keep a journal to show the pen is mightier than the pain

Keeping a journal can have a profoundly positive effect on our mental and physical well-being, according to a report of a study in the *Journal of the American Medical Association*.

402

In the study, led by Joshua M. Smyth, professor of psychology at North Dakota State University, 112 men and women with asthma or rheumatoid arthritis were split into two groups. One group was asked to write about the most stressful event in their lives, while the control group was asked to write about emotionally neutral topics. Group members wrote for 20 minutes on three consecutive days. Overall, 47 percent of the experimental patients had clinically relevant improvement in symptoms. No one is sure why, but writing about such events may help patients deal with tragedy, thus improving stress and sleeplessness and so general health.

People may also gain a sense of empowerment from finding their own answers to their problems through writing, rather than relying on outside help.

distribute nearly expired health products to the needy

Many hospitals have to destroy or dispose of thousands of pounds' (dollars') worth of medications because they are approaching the manufacturer's expiration date. This is a massive waste, but there could be a solution to the problem. A website could be created on which health facilities can post their inventories which are approaching expiration and receive requests for donations from charities, patient groups, and other organizations.

Dale Frier / Paul Christy

tax pharmaceutical and food giants to fund independent truth

To counter the advertising impact of pharmaceutical companies and fast-food giants, the economist Norman Solomon proposes taxing their advertisements to fund alternative, independently researched truth advertisements dispensing health information.

The problem in the US and elsewhere is that the public is bombarded by advertising telling us what to put in our mouths, both to feed us and cure us. This advertising is never balanced by equal airtime of objective, scientific information. Taxing food and drug advertisements would provide money to pay for advertisements by an independent truth commission to inform the public about the latest research on the risks and benefits.

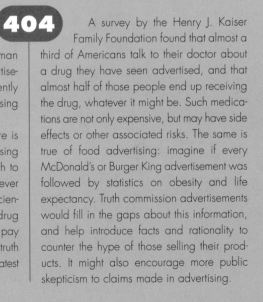

A survey by the Henry J. Kaiser Family Foundation found that almost a third of Americans talk to their doctor about a drug they have seen advertised, and that almost half of those people end up receiving the drug, whatever it might be. Such medications are not only expensive, but may have side effects or other associated risks. The same is true of food advertising: imagine if every McDonald's or Burger King advertisement was followed by statistics on obesity and life expectancy. Truth commission advertisements would fill in the gaps about this information, and help introduce facts and rationality to counter the hype of those selling their products. It might also encourage more public skepticism to claims made in advertising.

stop smoking throughout the land

405

Bhutan, the Buddhist country perched between China and India, is aiming to become the first nation to be free of cigarettes and tobacco. Nineteen of its twenty districts had banned smoking and the selling of tobacco products by 2003, and the capital Thimphu followed suit in 2004. Many of the districts have banned smoking on religious grounds, as Bhutanese Buddhists view it as a sin. The Ministry of Health is providing support services for those giving up. The ban is part of Bhutan's move toward democracy: the country's first constitution is being drawn up. Democracy brought TV with it in 1999, and many Bhutanese teenagers took up smoking after seeing TV actors doing it. The attempt to make the country the first tobacco-free nation is a response to that development.

→ **www.kingdomofbhutan.com**

publish the good, the bad, and the side effects

406

Pharmaceutical companies in Spain are requested to publish both positive and negative test results in scientific journals following legislation passed in 2004.

The new law stipulates that when research is published on the effectiveness of new drugs, it must be accompanied by information on the funds obtained by the authors for performing the research. As the guidelines are initially voluntary, it might seem that drug companies would have little incentive to agree to them, especially if they threaten their sales by revealing unfavorable test results. However, consumers could soon find out who agrees to be open and who does not; those who decide against transparency could soon undermine consumer trust in their products.

A similar initiative is being undertaken in the US by means of a database including both positive and negative results from pharmaceutical trials. These results will not be made public, but will be accessible by doctors and physicians. The objective of this initiative is to allow doctors a full picture of the effects of any particular drug, especially when that drug has only recently been released into the market.

use personal logbooks for patients' peace of mind

407

Patients feel better if they keep a logbook recording the medical treatment they have received, according to Dr. Harry Howell, of the Candida and Colon Clinic in Dorset, UK, who started a program with this aim in mind. The logbooks not only contain a comprehensive record of the treatment given, but also include details of the particular patient's medical history. There is even a page dedicated to good dietary advice.

Dr. Howell took to filling in the patients' logbooks himself and, although it created extra work for him, the benefits to the patients were always uppermost in his mind.

As he explained, "Patients have a right to know the truth about their condition, and having a logbook to keep with them certainly helps them to feel more relaxed and involved with their treatment."

count your calories and your change at the same time

408

Obesity is becoming the most significant threat to people's health in the western world, particularly in the US and Europe. This trend is leading to a whole range of related illnesses, from increased likelihood of heart disease to increased incidence of diabetes. Many think that education has to be a central part of any solution: letting people know which foods are good or bad and about the calorific value of certain foods.

One idea is for the calorific value of a meal to be printed on the receipt or bill when the person buys their food. So next to the price of the meal, the receipt also shows the calories the food contains. This system might encourage people to eat less fast food and to eat more healthily as it educates people on how well or poorly they are eating.

In 2004, it was reported that McDonald's was considering introducing such an initiative in their fast-food outlets. Others have suggested that the same measures could be taken at supermarkets with a fat tally appearing as a graph or chart at the bottom of the receipt that relates directly to the food the person has just bought.

Ari Opitz

fight discrimination against addicts

409

The National Association for the Advancement and Advocacy of Addicts (NAAAA) in the US is a not-for-profit organization formed to fight discrimination against addicts and to promote the hypoism paradigm of addictions and its principles.

Hypoism is the name of the disease hypothesized for the purpose of developing a global concept of addictions as a real disease. That is to say, hypoism, which is a chronic, progressive, and frequently fatal (albeit reversible) thinking and decision-making disorder, is the disease that addicts of all types suffer from.

The purposes of the Association include:
→ To provide a rational context into which all addicts are perceived and placed by themselves and society.
→ To provide advocacy free of charge on all levels (social, legal, political, medical, financial, occupational, criminal justice, and various local, state, and federal administrative boards) to legally confront discrimination of addicts in these areas.
→ To educate the public, including addicts, on the true nature of addictions, based on the hypoism paradigm, to end stigmatization and denial and to improve recovery.

The National Association for the Advancement and Advocacy of Addicts does not advocate the use of addictions, but is realistic about non-recovering addicts using addictions. It makes no judgments about the use of addictions, but supports addicts, using or not. It believes that addicts will always use their addictions until and unless in recovery.

The Association supports recovery and all means to allow addicts to enter recovery, including destigmatization, decriminalization, and preventing the abuse and de facto punishment of active addicts. In no way does the Association support or condone hurtful interpersonal actions or crime by addicts, but does believe that the rational and realistic attitude we have about addictions and addicts will lead to significant reduction of addiction-based crime.

The organization's goal is to ensure that addicts get fair and equal treatment under the law and that unconstitutional and prohibitionist-type statutes are repealed and replaced with realistic laws which will benefit society and put an end to the war on drugs and addicts. Addicts need to perceive themselves as a discriminated-against minority, and to take responsibility for confronting and resolving their own legal, political, medical, and social issues.

Dan F. Umanoff, M.D.

→ **www.hypoism.com**

lower pain
with poetry

410

Dental patients in the UK have been given the chance to distract themselves from the drill by reading poetry. Relevant lines of verse, such as Kevin Crossley-Holland's "Mouth shapely, concealing a canine capped and painted in subtle tinges," were made into posters for display in dental offices around the UK.

Poetry on the Ceiling was a joint initiative by Enitharmon Press, The Arts Council, and Barnado's, and was conceived in part as a fund-raising campaign. Most of all, though, the posters worked as a distraction technique: pinned to the ceiling above the dreaded chair, the posters aimed to lower pain awareness and heighten poetry awareness.

put patient feedback
with medical records

411

A triangular correspondence could be set up between patients, doctors, and specialists to promote the involvement of patients in their own care. It could work as follows:

→ The general practitioner or doctor writes a referral letter to the specialist (or consultant), which the patient may see.

→ The consultant reports back to the doctor, and sends the patient a copy of the letter. At the same time, the patient writes to the consultant about her/his experience of the illness and its management, sending a copy to the doctor.

→ The consultant may reply to some points raised by the patient in their letter.

This triangular correspondence would become part of the medical records, wherever they are held.

The feedback on the patient's experience of the consultation and/or operation could prove helpful to the consultant, the doctor, and ultimately to the patient.

In an effort to give patients greater information about the treatment being planned for them, the UK government's National Health Service includes the measure that patients will automatically receive copies of letters between health professionals about their care.

→ **www.dh.gov.uk/Home/fs/en**

offer a listening ear and laughter to deal with disease

Dr. Patch Adams founded the Gesundheit Institute in Northern Virginia in 1971 to offer free healthcare and rediscover the joy to be found in medicine. Part of this is to encourage people to have fun: laugh, do something crazy, try a new way of living. He also urges people to learn how to play, have fun, and try new ways of living. The institute emphasizes understanding the person as much as their condition; as Adams puts it, "I'm there to be a good listener first and to be a good friend, and then to do what intuitively and scientifically both come to mind."

Adams charged nothing and lived with patients on a 320-acre (130-hectare) farm. The Institute survives through donations and fees from talks and workshops. His medical approach means nutrition, exercise, curiosity, and wonder are as important as any drug. He views health as a "happy, vibrant, exuberant life." Anything less is, to some extent, a sign of disease.

These efforts address the boredom, loneliness, and fear that can affect patients as much as a medical ailment. It is an alternative methodology in which cooperation and compromise are key words: patients and healthcare workers at the hospital are interdependent. And, in building friendships and trust, Adams has shown that there are different solutions to problems that health providers face the world over: the relationships between patients and staff, and the cost of care.

There are now caregivers and ambassadors for the Gesundheit principles throughout the world. Adams continues to travel to war-torn areas with his clown-diplomats, preaching the need for peace, interdependence, and love, and practicing his own brand of medicine.

→ **www.patchadams.org**

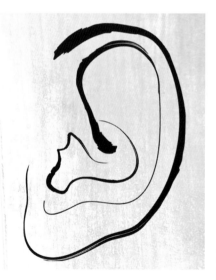

412

join the comedy club
for hilarious healing

413

Endorsement of the proverbial wisdom about laughter's health-giving properties recently came from Bombay, where a local doctor instigated a trend for medicinal laughing clubs. Dr. Madan Kataria, who propounds a mirth-inducing posture technique derived from yoga, set up the Priydarshini Park Laughing Club in 1995. Since then, more than 100 laughing clubs based on his model have been rapidly established across India.

Members of the clubs meet in groups of up to 50, where after limbering up and breathing exercises, they egg each other on into extended bouts of hilarity.

Practiced gigglers learn how to produce a repertoire of different styles of laughing, and the health benefits claimed are numerous. As well as loosening inhibitions and boosting self-confidence, Dr. Kataria says it is also good for breathing, as an aid to giving up smoking, and as a means to alleviate hypertension, arthritis, and migraine.

In 1998 Kataria organized a World Laughter Day at the Bombay Racetrack and 10,000 people turned up. "We all had a jolly good laugh," he said. There have been several such events since, including one in Copenhagen. While his laughter work has focused on the provision of practical benefits,

scientific research has shown that laughing lowers blood pressure, reduces stress hormones, and boosts immune functions. It also triggers the release of endorphins, the body's natural painkillers, and fosters spiritual sunniness.

Robert Holden, who founded the Happiness Project in Oxford believes that the physical act of laughing is akin to stationary jogging or internal aerobics. After years of running UK workshops and forums devoted to all aspects of happiness and joy, Robert Holden has stated that a ten-minute bout of laughing can have the following effects:

➜ As the person laughs, carbon dioxide is driven out of the body to be replaced by oxygen-rich air, providing physical and mental freshness.

➜ It can produce anti-inflammatory agents which can aid back pain or arthritis.

➜ It encourages muscles to relax, and exercises muscles all over the body, from the scalp to the legs.

➜ It reduces levels of cortisol (stress hormone).

➜ It may aid immune system responses.

➜ It exercises facial muscles.

➜ **www.laughteryoga.org**
➜ **www.happiness.co.uk**

home in on honey's healing properties

414

Honey has long been recognized for its medicinal properties, but it could be taking on a front-line role in a world of antibiotic-resistant bacteria and superbugs.

A New Zealand research team at Waikato University has been studying the effects of honey from the manuka bush, which has particularly impressive antibacterial properties.

The team has found that honey with a "unique manuka factor" (UMF) works not only on bacteria but also fungi, protozoa, and other infectious organisms. Indeed, while it is being used widely in a variety of medicinal ways at present, its greatest application in the modern world could be to combat resistant superbug strains, such as MRSA (Methicillin-Resistant *Staphylococcus Aureus*), which are an increasing problem in hospitals.

The honey has been used to treat dog bites, leg ulcers, pressure sores, and in post-surgery healing, where it has proved particularly effective for diabetic patients.

Further to its antibacterial properties, the manuka honey also has an anti-inflammatory effect, meaning it can reduce swelling while treating the wound. A cancer specialist has even used the honey to treat wounds and ulcers from radiation therapy.

A company has now taken on board the research and testing and is introducing a hi-tech manuka honey-based dressing for sale around the world. They have managed to create a honey dressing for wounds that is not too sticky or messy to use, yet maintains the effectiveness of using the honey directly.

Of particular note is that, even as modern medical treatment has created its own problems (MRSA due to overuse of antibiotics, immune systems weakened by countless antibacterial products), it has prompted a return to the natural world and the solutions and treatments that have been proven to work for many generations.

→ **www.comvita.com**
→ **www.manukahoney.co.nz**
→ **http://bio.waikato.ac.nz/honey/index.shtml**

learn a language
to stave off mental decline

415

In the past people have promoted chess, gardening, and even ballroom dancing as hobbies that help prevent diseases like Alzheimer's, dementia, and other age-related forms of cognitive decline.

Another activity has been added to the list: fluency in more than one language also helps to stave off mental deterioration. In a study at York University in Toronto, Canada, the researchers found that bilingual older volunteers had faster reaction times than those fluent in only one language when they completed a particular type of spatial response test (called a "Simon Task"). The researchers also found that bilingual older people were less distracted during the test.

While it remains to be established whether learning a language to a level short of becoming fluent also protects against age-related cognitive decline, these findings should provide more impetus for governments to maintain and develop language learning at all stages of education. The benefits may be significant in the long term.

➜ **www.apa.org**

legislate against
genetic discrimination

416

As genetic testing becomes more common and the number of conditions that can be tested for increases, concern about a rise in genetic discrimination increases.

Professor John Sulton of the UK's Human Genetics Commission has called for new legislation to protect against discrimination on the basis of genetic traits. In a world in which DNA can increasingly be tested, the fear is that the information will be used by employers and insurance companies to discriminate.

Genetic testing is available for about two hundred disorders and diseases, and this is likely to rise to over 10,000. Testing of newborn babies is also likely to rise as genetic profiling becomes more available and accurate. This information is open to misuse unless clear legislation is in place banning companies from using results in making employment or insurance decisions.

➜ **www.hgc.gov.uk**

make a bedside journal
for hospital patients

417

People who are hospitalized with a serious illness are often asleep when people visit, due to the need for recuperation and rest. This occasionally means that they can miss a visitor.

One idea to overcome this problem is to simply place a guest book on the table by the patient's bed. If he or she is sleeping when a visitor arrives, the visitor can sign the book and leave a message.

On waking, the patient can enjoy the comments, notes, hopes, wishes, and stories that have been left for them by their visitors while they were sleeping.

create a haven for
patients and wildlife

418

During a two-week stay in Churchill Hospital, Oxford, while awaiting diagnosis of Legionnaire's Disease, Pat Hartridge began to think of ways in which her experience could be improved. A natural solution sprang to mind: birds outside the window would have enlivened her stay, while a bird feeder could have more interestingly replaced the television.

So she came up with a plan for incorporating wildlife areas around hospitals to encourage birds, bees, and butterflies to return, enticed by the judicious use of specific plants, birdhouses, and feeding stations. The idea, above and beyond simply improving the hospital environment, was to encourage patients to record sightings of various species and, in doing so, to create an interest for people outside the daily ward. Ideally, visitors would start to bring birdseed rather than bunches of grapes.

Within two years, Pat Hartridge had created five wildlife gardens at the very hospital she had stayed at previously: Churchill Hospital in Oxford. Countless patients, visitors, and staff members have reaped the benefit of her enterprise. Though some of the garden areas have since had a change of use, that legacy remains as a model for other forward-thinking health institutions to follow.

→ **www.ouwg.org.uk**

learn about illness
in a patient's own words

419

To fill a major gap in healthcare information, a specialist medical team in Oxford came up with the idea of a database of patients' experiences (DIPEx) to be posted on the Internet and eventually to be further disseminated on DVD.

The aim of the UK team is to improve understanding of people's experience of illness, to educate on health issues holistically, and to promote a more balanced encounter between patient and health professional. Patients can use the database as a resource that provides them with some indication of the feelings of others who have experienced similar procedures or ailments. Health professionals, on the other hand, can get an indication of patients' priorities and understand procedures from the other point of view.

The site includes 1,000 pages of accurate medical information and, more uniquely, has over 85 hours of audio and video footage of patients detailing their experiences of conditions ranging from breast cancer to epilepsy, from depression to antenatal screening.

→ **www.dipex.org**

use burnout to kindle life renewal

420

Burnout from a stressed life can be transformed into something new, something wonderful, according to Dr. Dina Glouberman, the alternative travel and image specialist, in her book *The Joy of Burnout*.

To understand how burnout can be transformed, it is important to know what is meant by this catchall term. Glouberman believes it has become part of our natural lifecycle, in the same way as, for example, the midlife crisis. Burnout can recur, as problems that begin in individual areas of our lives can spread and take over. The classic criteria of burnout are:
→ Mental, physical, or emotional exhaustion, which is increasing and remains unchanged by sleeping;
→ A sense of being cut off from oneself and from other people;
→ An increasing inability to function effectively, in the work or home environment.
In addition, symptoms to look out for include extreme exhaustion, physical problems, and illness, and also the less obvious, such as an increase in seeking a means of escape (using alcohol, TV, or computer games), and being increasingly cynical and humorless.

The key to renewing after a burnout, the theory continues, is to recognize that a change is needed: after experiencing burnout, one must not then slip back into the same routine, the same life with the same problems that caused the stress in the first place. It is at this point that the concept of Radical Healing can be introduced. This is an intuitive process, devised by Glouberman, which involves five steps to renew and refresh one's life. These are:
→ Wait. Give up hope. Keep the faith.
→ Give your soul a good home.
→ Build up your "living truthfully muscle."
→ Open up to a soul community.
→ When the way opens, don't leave your joy behind.

These are self-explanatory, and the steps are a way of organizing the movement from a place of burnout and mental exhaustion to a new beginning. With the aid of this program and other techniques (meditative and imagistic, especially), the individual can let the darkness they are struggling with become the light that shows them the way: if they are hope-less, give up hope; if they are humiliated, let go of pride and choose humility… and so on. It is this movement, this turning of negative into positive (or at least a basis for being positive), that underlies the journey from burnout to joy. It is a journey many in the modern world may come to take.

→ **www.imagework.co.uk**

chapter 17

environment
and ecology

use spores on chainsaws
to support sheep and save forests

In forest areas in New Mexico, communities cut fire breaks to contain the wild forest fires that break out in the region. This necessary action involves cutting down trees and, when the cleared wood debris was removed to landfill sites, the decomposition process contributed to global warming.

421

To combat this problem, the ZERI Foundation started a process in which the chainsaws used to fell the trees are lubricated with a liquid containing mushroom spores. These spores mix with the wood debris in the tracks where the trees have been felled to create a rich mulch. This mulch provides a source of food for local sheep, and the alternative feeding grounds (or, more accurately, paths) help give the land around the forests a respite from the flocks. Simply lubricating the chainsaws with the spore-containing liquid not only removes the need to place the wood detritus in landfill, but also helps the local ecosystem to regenerate.

The pastures around the forest benefit from the sheep using the tracks (and the mulch) for feeding because they are given a break and allowed to recover; in times of drought, this can make the difference between the land remaining fertile or becoming desertified. In the long term, this should help ensure the future of the sheep and wool industry upon which many of the locals depend. The ingenuity of the solution is the way that it transforms a seemingly destructive (if necessary) act into one that helps regenerate the forest ecosystem upon which the local community relies for its survival and growth. In this way, internal sustainability can be promoted within local communities as a secure basis for the foundation of future progress and sufficiency.

→ **www.zeri.org**

recycle a can
to ride the bus

422

A school transit program in Chiang Mai in northern Thailand proposed the use of recycled cans, bottles, and newspapers as alternative bus fares. The tram-cum-school buses were introduced to combat the severe traffic in an area of the town where there are six different schools. The bus runs in a circular route, picking up the students from a designated point and then dropping them off in front of each school.

Up to this point, the buses have been free, but the mayor of Chiang Mai plans to introduce the innovative recycled waste fare initiative as a form of payment. The rubbish collected from students will then be sold to recycling firms, with any spare money being given to a free-lunch program in disadvantaged schools in the area.

The mayor, Boonlert Buranupakorn, said that students can bring any used garbage from their houses such as old newspapers, used water bottles, and soft drink cans to pay for the bus. In this way, the mayor hopes to both promote recycling among the younger generation and pay for the new transit system that is getting them to school on time.

unwrap your gift
before leaving the store

423

Products are increasingly packaged and parceled in ever more complicated and wasteful ways. This idea is simply a reworking of the gift-wrapping department in major stores. Instead of a wrapping department, stores could have a product unwrapping department, where a customer could take their purchases and have the wasteful plastic and paper packaging removed and recycled. This could work well in supermarkets and major stores around Christmas time, when packaging is at its peak.

Stores could have a person devoted to unwrapping (or, rather, de-packaging) products. It may prove more cost-effective for them, as much packaging may be able to be reused in store with minor additions. Such a practice happens in Germany, where the onus is on the store to recycle the packaging it uses.

Denis Gaston

make advertisers pay to portray animals

424

Many large corporations use images of animals to promote their products, such as the Esso tiger, the Guinness toucan, the Andrex puppy, and the Penguin biscuit penguin. And we the consumers, feeling some level of affection for these animals, are naturally drawn to these products. Companies profit from the use of these animals, but what does big business give back to the tiger or the toucan? Precious little.

One idea to combat this is to impose a tax on companies that use animals in promotions in this way. All money raised would go to preserving the habitat and ecology of the animal. Prestige may even be added to the use of animals in advertising through such an initiative. If it was known that buying a Penguin helped penguins, it might be an added temptation for customers.

Elliott Cannell

tax trash by the pound to promote recycling

425

People in Ireland will be charged for the amount of rubbish they produce, in an effort to encourage recycling, proposed by the Irish Environment Minister, Martin Cullen.

This pay-by-use system expands a plan introduced to parts of Dublin in 2003, wherein a flat annual fee for rubbish was charged. Under the countrywide initiative, instead of one set fee being paid, people have the opportunity to pay by the amount of waste they produce. People who produce less waste and recycle more will be rewarded by paying less tax.

As the Minister put it, "Those who recycle more will pay less. Those who don't will pay more." The precise charging mechanism will be decided at local level where local circumstances can be considered.

Despite critics' suggestions that this could lead to illegal rubbish dumping by people wishing to avoid paying fees, it has been praised by others for emphasizing the importance of resolving a worldwide issue by putting into action measures to tackle recyclable waste. It also makes a virtue of personal responsibility: those who act in the common good will be better off than those who do not.

→ **www.environ.ie**

have a ball with coral reef repair

426

The destruction of coral reefs around the world is occurring at such a rate that there are estimated to be almost 30,000 square miles of dead reefs around the world, and the number is rising all the time.

A specialized foundation hopes to stop the decline with patented Reef Balls made of eco-friendly concrete and designed to mimic natural reef systems. These balls can be towed behind any size boat, and then sunk to create habitats for fish and other marine species. The Reef Ball Foundation also works with schools and communities on educational projects, as well as with governments and eco-charities around the world. Its aim is to help restore the ecosystems of the oceans, which primarily involves repairing and preserving natural reef systems.

Over 200 projects have been running worldwide, from a Boy Scout program in Florida to a marine turtle sanctuary in Malaysia, and Reef Balls are at the center of the restoration process. Each one measures 3 x 4 feet (90 x 120 cm) and looks rather like a piece of Emmenthal (Swiss) cheese made of stone. Algae or other plant material can be attached to them, or living coral reef can be planted in them to stimulate growth. Gradually, sponges, crab, and shrimp will also be attracted to their replacement habitat. Todd Barber, the chairman of the foundation (and its associated company that makes the balls), intends to sink over one million of the concrete balls into the ocean near the Phillippines where some of the most serious damage to the reefs has occurred. Action on this scale is now necessary, and sinking concrete balls could save the rainforests of the oceans before it is too late.

One interesting addition to the Reef Ball program is Eternal Reefs, Inc., which offers people the chance to contribute cremated remains to a Memorial Reef to help restore deteriorating coral systems. The ashes are simply added into the mixture when the ball is being made. The bereaved are notified of the longitude and latitude of the reef which can be identified by its bronze plaque and accessed by boat on fishing or diving trips. Eternal Reefs' founder Don Brawley said of the idea: "A Memorial Reef becomes an idyllic, eco-friendly resting place, a physical legacy where the remains of one's existence are also part catalyst for a new cycle of life. Instead of having their ashes sprinkled in the sea, people can contribute to regenerating marine life."

→ **www.eternalreefs.com**

motivate international organizations to counter climate change

427

To encourage international organizations to take global warming and climate change more seriously (and act with more urgency), they could be moved to low-lying land in the Netherlands. If organizations such as the United Nations, the World Bank, the International Monetary Foundation, and the US Embassy, were faced with rising sea levels, they might act on this visual encouragement to do something about the problem. Major religious figures could even move there as well, so that they could add their weight to the momentum for change.

Akira Akira

tax plastic bags to combat pollution

428

To cut down the litter and waste problem posed by plastic shopping bags, Ireland introduced a tax of 9p (20 cents) on single-use plastic shopping bags, payable by the shopper, not the shop. The Irish government expects to raise £10 ($20) million annually from the tax, all of which will be put into environmental projects in the country.

In Britain shoppers use eight billion carrier bags a year (134 per person) and plastic bags constitute a third of all plastic waste. They are thought to take between 20 and 1,000 years to degrade in the environment, and hundreds of thousands of birds and other animals are killed by them every year. Landfill sites are filling up rapidly and the other two options are incineration (which is unpopular and polluting) and recycling (but only 0.5 percent of plastic bags are recycled at present). The Irish government hopes that the tax will encourage many more shoppers to buy reusable bags.

Other European countries have taken different approaches, with Belgian supermarkets offering points on loyalty cards for those reusing bags, German stores charging up to 30p (60 cents) for plastic bags, and Dutch bag incineration programs being used to heat hospitals.

Within five months of the tax's introduction in Ireland, use of the bags had fallen by over 90 percent, and over 3 million euros raised.

→ **www.environ.ie**

give a goat a job
as a fire-prevention tool

429

Goats have been used as fire-prevention tools in California, as they are more economical and eco-friendly than traditional methods of human landscaping. The goats were brought in to eat at the undergrowth of flammable grasses and plants in areas of Berkeley and Oakland, which have often been devastated by forest fires. Goats are particularly effective at reducing the risk of fire because they eliminate the grasses and lower branches, which diminishes the chances of a fire spreading upward through foliage to the trees. This movement, called *laddering* by fire experts, can turn a simple fire into an uncontrollable inferno. The goats also have a particular fondness for manzanita, a volatile plant with a low point of ignition.

Residents in the area praised the use of goats for other reasons. One pointed out that they are better than gas-powered vehicles, while others claimed that they bring an air of serenity to the area. They are also cheaper (by $300/£150 an acre) than the equivalent human landscaping would be, and they work all day, every day in contrast to their human counterparts. The demand for their services was such that no less than four companies sprung up in the area to supply goats, with Goats R Us the largest: it has a herd of 4,000 on its books.

The goats are also now diversifying from simple fire fuel eradication to winter brush reduction and the removal of poison oak and star thistle where desired.

Goats have also been used specifically as eco-friendly biocontrols in place of herbicides. Jim Guggenhime started the business Nip it in the Bud with his herd of goats, charging a dollar (50p) per day per goat, and it has proved very successful with those growing organic (and therefore herbicide-free) foods.

→ **www.goatsrus.com**
→ **www.htgv.com**

limit light pollution for better health and spectacular skies

430

The Czech Republic is the only nation to have introduced legislation to combat light pollution. Since June 2002, light polluters can be fined up to £3,000 ($6,000) for various offenses. Lampposts have to be shielded from above with curved glass, and billboard lighting has to face downward from the top, rather than up. The reduction in light pollution over time should help diminish some of the ecological consequences of brightening the night sky with artificial light.

Light pollution at night is thought to impair human production of the hormone melatonin, to increase sight problems, to increase cases of insomnia, and to damage the immune system. Bright lights on towers and skyscrapers also affect migrating birds that rely on the stars to navigate. The birds either flutter about the light until they drop from exhaustion, or they actually hit the object in question.

On a more aesthetic level, excess light denies people the chance to view the night sky properly in real darkness. A survey in the UK found that only 11 percent of the entire country experiences full darkness.

The legislation, the result of a campaign led by the astronomer Jenik Hollan of the Copernicus Observatory, made the Czech Republic the first country to take action on a concerted scale. Catalonia in Spain and Lombardy in Italy have regional initiatives; the Czech law was modeled to an extent on the law in Lombardy which came about after 25,000 people signed a petition demanding action on light pollution. The law defines light pollution as every form of illumination by artificial light which is dispersed outside the areas it is dedicated to, particularly if directed above the level of the horizon. Under the law, Czech citizens and organizations are obligated to take measures to prevent the occurrence of light pollution of the air.

Astronomers in Brno and other Czech cities have since claimed a spectacular improvement in the clarity of the night sky, and the Czech legislation could (and should) provide an example for other nations to copy. The International Dark-Sky Association hopes to encourage other governments around the world to follow suit.

→ **www.astro.cz/darksky**
→ **www.darksky.org**
→ **www.dark-skies.org**

act on local warning
to beat global warming

Few would disagree that urban centers and their outlying sprawl are the individual pistons to the big industrial engine of global warming. Industrial and urban centers appear to not just alter but create their own environments by producing more greenhouse gases than they consume, reducing plant life, and altering terrestrial solar absorption patterns with the construction of roads and buildings. In combination, these three things make cities hotter than they would be otherwise.

The term "heat island" has been coined to describe the effect. Metropolitan regions are typically hotter than their more rural peripheries. In Tucson, Arizona, for example, before 1960 average high temperatures in the month of June hardly ever reached 90°F (32°C), but since 1990, average highs for June have rarely dipped below this temperature.

It is time to reconceptualize the notion of global warming by popularizing a partner term to global warming: *local warming*. As noted, metropolitan areas are hot and getting hotter, at a much faster pace than global warming. The reason should be apparent: cities and indus-

431

trial areas are the individual generators feeding global warming. Global warming is not only a serious problem because of what it is doing to the planet, but also because it is beyond any one community's effective reach.

Local warming, on the other hand, can be affected by city and state ordinance and legislation. Whereas the extent of global warming is up for debate within some deliberative bodies, local warming trends can be significant even at their lowest calculations. Localities can readily determine through their city temperature records the extent of their own local warming problem. While the Kyoto Treaty rests in the hands of global negotiators, local warming is in the hands of the people it affects first. What's more, the specific causes of local warming can be quantified at the local level. Solutions may be spread from early adopters to worldwide implementation, eventually being incorporated into international treaties. Why not? As former Congressional Whip Tip O'Neil put it, "All politics is local."

Scott Stanley

recycle dung
to produce paper

An elephant park in Ayutthaya, Thailand, recycles elephant dung to make paper. Keepers at the park extract the parts of the dung that are fibrous and dry them out to make paper. The remains are used for fertilizer. Not only does the initiative ensure there is no waste of the waste, but sales of the paper raise money to be invested back into the park. The elephants help ensure and protect their environment by doing what comes naturally.

432

The director of the park, Sompast Meepan, calls each elephant a paper factory, and explains that "to produce a higher quality paper, we liquidize the pulp in a blender. [Then] we strain the paper onto a fine sieve and leave it to dry in the sun to create the final product."

The park's resident vet expresses the benefits of the operation more simply: "We call it golden dung."

hang out your laundry
to lessen energy use

Project Laundry List was set up to encourage people to use clotheslines instead of clothes dryers to reduce energy consumption, since 6 to 10 percent of residential energy use in the US is attributable to the dryer. This is equivalent to the amount of energy an average African household uses annually. The project organizes National Hanging Out Day on April 19 every year to promote clotheslines and lobby against communities that ban washing lines for aesthetic reasons.

As well as saving the average household up to $100 (£55) each year and helping reduce

433

the environmental impact of daily living, using a clothesline has other benefits. The act can be therapeutic, giving one a chance to slow down and take in the fresh air. It is also said that clothes last longer. As well as the National Hanging Out Day, the project campaigns against communities that have banned clotheslines: several states introduced so-called Right to Dry legislation. It promotes the project through distributing clothes pegs (clothespins) for people to wear.

→ **www.laundrylist.org**

opt for an oxygen tax
to rescue the rainforests

Rainforests are not only exceedingly biodiverse and a sink for carbon dioxide, they are also the source of much of the oxygen we breathe.

434

In order to provide a real incentive to rainforest host nations to preserve them for long-term human benefit, we need to provide an economic incentive and, by so doing, remove current economic pressures on the forests. It is proposed that the world's nations, via the United Nations, pay an economic rent to rainforest host nations for every square mile of forest left intact. (Satellite imaging could be used to verify the process). In doing so, the forests, far from being viewed as liabilities by the host countries, will become green assets, providing income and foreign exchange.

The introduction of an Oxygen Tax, either as a minute percentage of GDP (gross domestic product), or via a Tobin-type tax on currency speculation, would provide millions of US dollars per annum. This could be paid out as an economic rent/opportunity cost/loss of chance through the UN to rainforest host nations, based on a stipulated amount per square mile of virgin rainforest. Such an economic framework would provide the required incentive to protect rainforests that, from a developing country's short-term economic perspective, are otherwise a liability to preserve in their pristine state. The inescapable reality at present is that destroying forests provides much needed revenue for some of the poorest nations on Earth. An oxygen tax that recognizes the value of those forests, and pays the nations that own such forested areas, can help change the economics of the situation.

Lalu Hanuman

plant trees to boost community and environment

435

Chami Murmu, a young tribal woman in the impoverished district of West Singhbhum of Bihar, India, and her group, Sahyogi Mahila, have provided 1,292 acres (523 hectares) of barren land with forest cover. They planted nearly two million saplings of which 90 percent survived, and this is just the tip of the mammoth task accomplished by the group of mostly uneducated tribal women.

They started off with the remote hamlet of Bhalubasa, consisting of only 70 families. What was once a naked rocky hillock is now a lush green 25-acre (10-hectare) acacia forest. There is a village vigilance committee, responsible for the protection of the forest, which also protects the whole area from cattle, and even patrols the area by night to prevent people from neighboring villages felling its trees. It also enjoys the power to fine anyone caught cutting trees.

The result is that women in the village do not have to trek 6 miles (10 km) to collect firewood. Everyone uses dry leaves and twigs as cooking fuel and no one needs to buy firewood any more. The village committee also oversees equal distribution of timber among the villagers.

A few kilometers down the dirt track, at a village called Panduiti, the Sahyogi Mahila's afforestation program on a 60-acre (24-hectare) barren land has helped check soil erosion. This village, too, has a committee for protection of the forest. The money it has collected so far from fines incurred by people caught cutting trees has been used to provide soft loans for marriages, medical treatment, agriculture, and setting up small businesses.

The committee has also started collective farming in the village. The afforestation program has also spread to over forty other villages in the district, with the group helping the villagers form their own committees and decide to run them.

reduce bovine belching
to combat global warming

436

One of the causes of greenhouse gases and, therefore, of global warming is bovine belching and flatulence. A Canadian power company, TransAlta, is producing a feed supplement for the US's Global Livestock Group that will help cut bovine gas.

The supplement, sprayed on cattle feed and hay, eases digestion and minimizes expulsions of methane gas. Methane is 21 times more powerful a greenhouse gas than carbon dioxide. The United States Environmental Protection Agency has estimated that ruminant livestock produce about 80 million tons of methane annually (equivalent to 1.7 billion tons of carbon dioxide), which accounts for about 22 percent of the global methane emissions from human-related activity. Of this, 75 percent comes from animals on poor feed, mostly in developing countries.

This is an offset project designed in accordance with the proposed guidelines of the Clean Development Mechanism of the Kyoto Protocol. In exchange for funding the project, the firm gained substantial greenhouse gas reductions.

→ **www.transalta.com**

keep it clean with
talking trash

437

Berlin, Germany, decided to take a novel approach to solving its litter problems: providing trash bins that thank people when they put rubbish in them. The bins are solar-powered and can even be programmed to "speak" in other languages. They light up at nighttime, again powered by the internal batteries. The bins are a fun, interactive way of raising awareness about the problem of litter, and therefore encourage tidiness on Berlin's streets. Indeed, people actually want to put their rubbish in the bins to hear them say "Thank you"—or, more accurately, "Danke schön." As Bernd Mueller of Berlin's cleaning service said at the launch, "Every city wants to make itself more attractive to visitors," and the hi-tech bins certainly achieve that.

→ **www.stadtentwicklung.berlin.de/
index_en.shtml**

restore and link wildlife habitats to protect biodiversity

438

The Wildlands Project, founded in 1991, is dedicated to restoring wildlife linkages across America in order to protect endangered species and maintain existing ecosystems.

The idea behind the project is a simple one: parks, wildernesses, and green spaces risk becoming isolated and isolating places. Animals within them cannot roam or escape natural disasters (such as fires and floods), and diversity is limited by the boundaries of the park. Creating biodiversity corridors allows the animals to wander, adapt, and move from place to place so that, as the Project's vision states, "Grizzlies in Chihuahua have an unbroken connection to grizzlies in Alaska [and] wolf populations are restored from Mexico to the Yukon." Further to this ambition, which the Wildlands Project is pursuing across North America (including Canada and Central America), they also hope that it will help the public better understand and reconnect to their habitat and environment.

The vision of the team of scientists and activists who set up the project is steadily unfolding, with work on regional initiatives done alongside work on megacorridors across swaths of North America. The organization, which is in fact small in terms of personnel and funds, achieves its aims through partnerships and lobbying government agencies. By working with a massive range of different environmental organizations, with similar objectives, it has a greater impact than might otherwise be the case.

It is also involved in educating the public on the impact people have on the environment, and why creating the network is important, explaining that small parks and isolated pieces of wilderness are not enough to overcome the effects of urban sprawl and centuries of development. The long-sightedness of those involved is to be applauded, as their efforts will be recognized and enjoyed for a long time to come.

→ **www.twp.org**

prevent soil poverty
with gravel dust

439

The soil remineralization movement recommends that gravel dust, often available free at local quarries or pits, should be added to your garden or field. Why? Because it is rich in minerals and trace elements, and can increase crop yields, stimulate plant growth, increase the level of essential minerals in fruit and vegetables, and help save plants that have become sick.

Some corn crops grown with mineralized soil have been found to have 57 percent more phosphorus, 90 percent more potassium, and 47 percent more calcium than chemically grown crops from the same seed.

Joanna Campe, president of the not-for-profit organization Remineralize the Earth, has said that the ultimate poverty is poverty of soil. The fate of the earth hangs in the balance. The movement believes that remineralization could potentially help avert a new ice age by helping to save dying forests in temperate latitudes. One proponent, Robert Schindele, is even more extreme. He eats gravel dust (two teaspoons a day) and markets it in parts of Europe as a mineral dietary supplement under the name Superbiomin, despite strong opposition from the pharmaceutical industry.

The idea is gaining credence elsewhere, though: the indications of its growing acceptance in the mainstream include various research projects and conferences on the subject sponsored by the US Department of Agriculture.

Eight universities in the US have carried out research into the effects of gravel dust, and there have been similar initiatives in the UK and parts of Europe; the movement is particularly strong in Austria and Germany.

→ **www.remineralize.org**
→ **www.geocities.com/HotSprings/Sauna/
1432/SRInfo.htm**

come on in,
the water's organic

In the town of Biberstein in Switzerland, there is an organic public swimming pool. The water is not chlorinated, there are no brightly colored tiles, and there are definitely no water slides in this pool. Instead, the focus, as it should be, is on clear and clean water and making the experience of swimming enjoyable. As well as banning artificial chemicals, the pool has also had wildlife introduced to it, so that its attractions include dragonflies, snails, and frogs. These additions aside, the water is purer than it has ever been, largely thanks to two new ponds that have improved the purification process. The swimmers of the town are certainly going back to nature—and immersing themselves in it.

440

watch webs
to monitor pollution

The webs of some species of spiders are so effective at trapping airborne particles that they make excellent detectors for pollutants, an eco-toxicologist in New South Wales, Australia, has discovered.

It was found that webs near roads had levels of lead and zinc up to ten times higher than those in caves. The spiders known as cribellates create webs that consist of matted fibers to entangle their prey. This matted structure, as opposed to the more common wheel-like webs, makes the webs especially effective at trapping particles of pollution.

This finding has both negative and positive results. The negative aspect is that the spider population may be in danger in the area, because spiders groom themselves regularly and therefore may be ingesting some of the pollutant material trapped by their webs.

The positive is that the scientist who made the finding, Grant Hose, believes these webs could be used as biosensors to detect and monitor levels of pollution. The low-tech approach would be cheaper than current methods, and also allow scientists to look at readings across a large area, including houses, roads, caves, trees, and so on. They would then be able to pinpoint areas where pollution is high and move in with more sophisticated equipment and techniques.

441

turn out the lights and turn on global awareness

In an effort of coordinated eco-activism, people across the world have been encouraged to hold a blackout on the first day of summer.

The idea serves as a protest, a symbolic act, and a coordinated global power saving, as people turn off their lights and unplug everything from 7:00 pm to 10:00 pm in the evening. As people across the world get involved, the blackout then rolls across the globe.

The blackout originally started among environmentalists as a protest against George W. Bush's energy policies, his rejection of the Kyoto Treaty, and the associated lack of emphasis on alternative fuels, efficiency, and conservation. Not only is it an effective and simple protest—and a money and power-saving exercise—but also simply a nice thing to do. Have a candlelit meal, amble out on an evening walk, or tell ghost stories (and take a break from the television and the radio).

A similar but less political idea is to have an electricity-free day in each season of the year. Rather than people choosing not to use power, the power would be switched off for the whole day (with the exception of hospitals, emergency services, and so on). The first part of this idea is that turning off the electricity for 24 hours would promote family togetherness, as people would have to look for entertainment and amusement away from the television and computers.

442

The second part of the plan is even more ingenious: the electricity companies should still charge for an average day's electricity that day, but the money will then be diverted to funding energy and technology enhancements in developing countries. In this way, the idea will bring families together, save a great deal of energy four times a year, and also help others in greater need overseas.

Kristine Kozicki

work with worms
to transform waste into compost

Breaking down organic waste with worms has been going on for years in back-garden (-yard) compost heaps or small community plots, but now breakthroughs have made the possibility of large-scale vermicomposting of sewage a genuine reality.

An Australian company, Vermitech, has perfected the process whereby manure worms can transform sewage sludge into compost usable on food crops. Each worm is capable of eating its weight in organic waste every day; doing this on a large scale opens up the possibility of dispensing with traditional high-cost sewage treatment methods that usually involve chemical and heat treatment. Worms produce compost that is safe for use on food crops, produces higher yields and less plant disease.

The reasons for the beneficial effects of the vermicompost are not fully understood, though some scientists suspect that the traditional high-heat treatment of sewage kills off many beneficial microbes as well as disease-causing bacteria. Due to the worms digesting the bacteria and making the compost safe without heat treatment, these positive microbes remain, resulting in better yields. These same microbes, it is thought, have also helped reduce plant disease where the worm compost is used and may contain a more complex base of nutri-

443

ents, which may further contribute to its success on farms.

A sewage plant in Australia can process 15,000 tons of sewage a year and cut the costs of a city's sewage management bill by a quarter. This is in addition to the impact that vermicomposting can have on normal organic waste, the everyday waste that is thrown out daily. In the UK, over 20 million tons of waste is thrown in landfills every year, of which almost two-thirds is biodegradable. Imagine if each council had a vermicomposting unit or, better still, if each individual had a worm bin in their garden. A US report into worm composting in 1996 estimated that worm composting could save up to $40 (£20) per ton of waste disposed in the US; almost a quarter of a billion tons of waste are created in the US annually.

Many councils, schools, and community groups have long been aware of this information, but it has never been put into practice on a large enough scale to have a serious impact on the way waste is processed. Only in such places as Toronto, where organic waste is collected from citizens for a vermicomposter, have such plans been put into place.

→ **www.Vermitech.com**
→ **www.WormDigest.org**

support a nobel prize
for sustainable development

While there are Nobel Prizes for the classic sciences, medicine, literature, and peace, no prizes have been added since Economic Science in the 1960s. Considering the major environmental problems we face, a campaign has emerged for a Nobel Prize for Sustainable Development. This would give great publicity to the successful individual or team, and encourage further research.

The initiative is headed by a Dutch MP, a British MEP, a US congressman, and an ex-youth representative to the UN, and is seeking to establish such a prize for research in new fields of technology and the pursuit of new energy resources.

They created a website where people can sign a letter to the Nobel Foundation. The web-based publication claims that by rewarding those who show the leadership to solve these problems, innovations and technological advances will be held up as an example, rather than the usual pessimistic reporting!

→ **www.sustainable-prize.net**

bring peace and protection
to locality with feng shui

We take great care to create comfortable, pleasant living spaces within our homes, but the same cannot always be said of other spaces in the surrounding neighborhood.

One way to improve the local environment is to start with the pavements (or sidewalks). These gray strips of blandness do nothing to make walking along them a more pleasurable experience. Why not use colors such as aqua, olive green, and light blue instead?

According to feng shui principles, aqua gives a feeling of protection and olive green a sense of peace, while light blue fosters tranquility and understanding.

Feng shui principles could be extended beyond colors. Feng shui pavements would be clean, litter-free, gently curving, and plant-lined; whether or not one believes in the concept of chi and its flow, this could be a significant improvement to the pavement status quo.

Sjakie Nabarro

wear thermal underwear
to reduce fuel consumption

446

A systematic campaign to promote the use of thermal underwear in winter climes could vastly reduce the use of mostly fossil-fueled home heating.

An environmental group or organization could team up with a manufacturer of thermal underwear to encourage greater use of the clothing and the corresponding decreased use of home heating by fuel, oil, and coal-fired electricity. There could even be discounts on thermal clothing on joining environmental organizations, and a drive to make thermal clothes fashionable. The campaign could be further extended to include the donation of thermal clothing to the people with the smallest environmental footprint of all: the homeless.

Greg Wright

celebrate earth day like a birthday:
give earth-friendly gifts

447

You give birthday gifts on birthdays. So why not give Earthday gifts on Earth Day? This could help promote the concept of the day, and what it stands for, to a whole new range of people. Gifts would be anything that could help build the relationship with the person receiving the gift, while being considerate of the Earth. All wrapping paper should, of course, be recycled (as can unwanted presents as well).

Earth Day happens on April 22 each year and is intended as a global holiday to celebrate the wonder and joy of living on this planet and to remind us of our reliance on it.

Initially founded to promote environmental awareness, Earth Day is the only event celebrated simultaneously around the globe by people of all faiths, nationalities, and backgrounds. Each year, over half a billion people take part in activities and campaigns on the day. That is a lot of ethical purchasing power to tap into.

Erin Kinstlinger

opt for O2PEC: a coalition of forested nations

448

To provide developing countries with major old-growth forests with the power to change their circumstances, first form an alliance between all such countries. Then they could pressure the international community to recognize them as vital oxygen-producing (and carbon dioxide-absorbing) nations. It could be calculated how much of the world's total forested reserves are within each country in the alliance. The World Bank could then cancel that same percentage of their debt in return for a promise not to sell any more logging concessions. Instead of OPEC (Oil Producing and Exporting Countries), they could be O2PEC (the Oxygen Producing Environmental Coalition).

Marcus Morrell

recycle tires as sandals

449

In the 1990s, Randall Sage of Bothell started using discarded dirt-track racing car tires to make his Big Randall's Racing Sandals. Besides being an effective means of recycling, the shoes are soft and comfortable, because racing tires are a lot softer and more cushioned than conventional driving tires. They also last longer: as Sage himself put it, "If an 800-horsepower engine can't wear out these tires, I want to know what person can."

A dozen sandals can be made from one tire, and each pair is unique because each one features a driver's sipe—the personalized cuts a driver uses to break up a tire's tread for extra grip during sharp turns. Since different drivers use different sipes, the sandals have unique soles.

Tires have also been used to make roof tiles, purses, mouse mats, pencil cases, and even houses (see page 78). The most efficient way to recycle tires, though, is simply to have them retreaded instead of buying new ones. Driving carefully and reusing tires could have a substantial impact on the tire mountains that seem to grow higher and higher with every passing year.

cultivate rooftop gardens
for global cooling

In an effort to fight global warming, rooftops are being given a new green look in forward-thinking cities. By planting rooftop gardens on large structures, cities can use the sun to keep the city cooler instead of letting it heat things up. Hotter temperatures can increase levels of pollution by forcing air conditioning units and electric plants to work harder. Planting lawns, shrubs, and trees (with non-invasive root structures) can provide a reflective barrier for the heat, as well as improve air quality by absorbing carbon dioxide and producing oxygen.

The gardens also have the potential to provide an area for employees to relax at their urban workplace. Imagine taking the lift (elevator) up to the top of the building for lunch in a rooftop garden with birds singing in the trees.

In 2001, a new regulation was introduced in Tokyo that required all new buildings to turn part of their rooftops into garden. Any owners not covering one-fifth of their roof space with plants face substantial fines. Tokyo introduced the measure, also adopted by Germany, because its average annual temperature continues to rise alarmingly.

Chicago is also a notable pioneer in the field, following the lead of its legendary mayor, Richard Daley, who first noted the concept in use in Hamburg, Germany. Chicago City Hall was the first municipal green roof in the US, and Chicago has over 80 municipal and private green roofs. This plan offers incentives to developers who include rooftop gardens in buildings, and has a range of initiatives and programs that are aimed at reducing Chicago's urban heat islands.

450

→ **www.egov.cityofchicago.org**

advocate an alphabetical arboreal avenue

451

Many children and adults living in cities know relatively little (and, in some cases, nothing) about trees. A suitable project to counter this lack of knowledge would be an A to Z Avenue of the most common trees, in a park or garden in the city. The trees would be planted along the avenue in alphabetical order of their common name, though they could be labeled with their Latin names as well.

Thanks to their positioning on the avenue, visitors would find it easier to identify and remember trees (or guess what they might be from what went before and comes after). At the start could be acacia, alder, almond, apple, and ash, while at the other end would be walnut, wellingtonia, whitebeam, willow, and yew. Depending on space and the ground conditions, there could be between 26 trees (an A to Z of native species) and 500 trees (i.e., including more exotic species from around the world). The latter would require a significant space, but would be magnificent.

Ideally, the avenue would lead to a striking building of some kind, one that could perhaps contain a café and multimedia tree study center. Although such a project would take 50 years to reach maturity, it would undoubtedly become a site that many people and organizations would want to visit.

plant a seed, grow a chair

452

Christopher Cattle, a lecturer in furniture design at Buckinghamshire University College, planted three rows of chairs and tables on land in Aberdare, South Wales.

Saplings were planted to grow into furniture shapes along plywood frames, with joints forming where the shoots fused together. This technique was originally used by ancient Greeks and Egyptians. "This is viable and environmentally friendly," said Mr. Cattle. "You don't need nails, screws, or glue. All you need to grow furniture is a seed. Then you sit back for four years for a stool and six years for a chair."

A dining table and three-piece suite could take a little longer.

let the littermovement lead the way

453

Littermovement is a simple idea that started in Finland in 2000, and has since spread to many countries. The idea is for each member of the Littermovement to pick up at least one piece of litter a day, and invites at least one new member to join and do the same. Membership is immediately conferred on invitation.

Tuula-Maria Ahonen

→ **http://koti.welho.com/jpeltora/ littermovement.htm**

spend enus to count environmental costs

454

Just because a consumer has the money for an item, it should not automatically mean they are entitled to it. There is an environmental cost associated with everything and waste should be discouraged. Factoring in environmental cost to every purchase could change the way people use and exploit the planet's natural resources.

For example, a consumer purchasing an item might see a price tag that contained two costs: Kettle $50 + 5 Environmental units (Enus). If spending these Enus on the kettle meant that they had reduced points for car usage, the consumer would be deterred.

The system would also be effective in deciding on which kettle to purchase in the first place, as the number of Enus on a steel kettle would be different from the Enus on a plastic kettle. In this example, the Enus would be based on materials used, their impact on the environment, and the long versus short life of the two items.

Conscious savings on Enus could be made in everyday life. Those driving would use some of their Enu allocation to buy petrol (gas); public transportation would have a lower Enu cost. Businesses would have to take more responsibility for the waste they produce.

A business's Enu expenditure would help determine the Enu amount on the good paid by the consumer, so it would be in the economic interests of businesses to minimize their Enu expenditure.

Bradley Hall

plant orchards to provide education, nutrition, and relaxation

455

In a world increasingly divorced from nature and worried by the industrialization of food production, community orchards are a suitably natural and organic idea. As well as providing fruit for sale or consumption, they can also act as wildlife havens, places to play and relax, or as outdoor village halls for local festivities.

They also generate interest in horticulture, ensuring that skills and knowledge are passed between generations. In these various ways, a community orchard can be a communal asset and a focal point for the village or parish—that is why, in the UK, the Common Ground charity has been promoting them.

The idea for such an orchard is that openness and accessibility should be at the core of its planning: the primary purpose is not intended to be the production of fruit, but the enjoyment of the place itself. Orchards can be owned or leased for the community by a local group, a parish council, or a local authority. Local people are encouraged to take part in gardening and nurturing the trees, and can then share in the harvest or profit from fruit sales. It is often the case that local people eat or cook with the fruit themselves, or distribute it locally, but in years where there is surplus, sales can provide funds to be reinvested in the orchard.

And it should not be thought that orchards are limited to the countryside: Common Ground insist that they can work in housing estates, industrial estates, hospitals, and schools, and backs up this claim with examples from around the country. An old brickworks in Walbottle on the banks of the River Tyne near Newcastle became the site of an orchard that was planted in 1996. Villagers now receive crab apples, Victoria plums, and apples from a couple of trees that self-seeded in the brickworks itself. Schools are also a perfect location: children can improve their horticultural skills on orchards, with the fruit being given to local projects or providing a healthy snack at lunch times.

Although there is little instant gratification, a number of years nurturing and caring could result in great pride in the fruits of a community's labor, in every sense.

→ **www.commonground.org.uk**

enumerate environmental conditions of every nation

456

Currently there exists no scale by which to ascribe a numerical designation to the overall environmental condition of a nation. Numerous disciplines, ranging from geology to economics, use scales formulated to encapsulate, describe, and communicate various natural and social findings and phenomena numerically.

Conversely, the environmental field has had to provide lengthy explanations of environmental research in order to describe the overall condition of a nation's environment. A method is needed whereby the results of environmental research can be read at a glance. Having a State of the Environment Scale would be quite useful in a range of applications: from environmental education campaigns to scientific discussions to environmental lawsuits and even the CIA's world fact book. The UN GEO Project could immediately use the scale to succinctly encapsulate its data on the environmental condition of nations.

The development of a scale as proposed here would best be left to experts in various fields; however, it could work as follows:

Analyze the elements of a nation's environment and assign each a number between zero and ten based upon their condition with zero being the absolute worst and 10 the absolute best. For example, zero percent of national old growth forests left is assigned a zero on the scale, while 100 percent of national old growth forests preserved is assigned a 10 on the scale.

Analyze economic and environmental practices and policies and rank them accordingly. For example, fairly lax enforcement of regulations governing industrial pollution might warrant the assignment of a 3. Meanwhile, the strict enforcement of a law requiring that all new vehicles get at least 30 miles per gallon (12 km per liter) might receive an 8.

When all elements of a nation's environment have been assigned a number, simply add them up and divide by the number of elements to get that nation's score on the State of the Environment Scale. The scale would allow for comparison between countries with similar environments, economies, and policies, and allow for direct comparison between the environmental elements of any country.

Such a scale could factor in existing research (such as that done to measure the ecological footprint of nations), and also provide a one-stop point of comparison for those wishing to take into account all aspects of a country's environmental and ecological activities.

Justin T. O'Conor Sloane

view video games
as educational tools

457

One method organizations can use to reach young people on issues is video games. If they are playable and interesting (and not lecturing), such games can be successful, either online or distributed as CDs.

A game that focuses on environmental issues could challenge a player to balance economic needs with sustainability in a simulated city. This could include, for example, choosing to set up carpooling programs in town. Wrong decisions lead to pollution problems and landscape damage, good ones to a player being fêted as a green pioneer.

Games are often used as campaigning tools, e.g., the United Nations' game "Food Force," which focuses on the World Food Program. Players are challenged to complete missions with guidance from a team of UN characters.

Alpha Lo

→ **www.food-force.com**
→ **www.wilddivine.com**

use coffee grounds
to perk up local gardens

458

In Seattle, home of the Starbucks Corporation, flowers are nourished by a concoction of nitrogen-rich coffee grounds given out by the company to local gardeners. The recycling plan, dubbed "Grounds for Your Garden," has been extended throughout the US and Canada.

Environmentalists have praised the firm for its creation and distribution of the chemical-free fertilizer, while the multinational corporation itself benefits by cutting its rubbish bill significantly, and getting positive publicity.

Enthusiastic gardeners in Seattle are very impressed by this idea. With year-round sunshine and a wet climate, they have the perfect environment to use the coffee grounds. The grounds are particularly beneficial to evergreens and rhododendrons and are also attractive to worms, which turn organic material into compost by eating it and then excreting it. The grounds are also sometimes used as an organic slug repellent.

→ **www.starbucks.com**

visit the green hotel:
a model for eco-tourism

459

The old Chittaranjan Palace in South India, built for Mysore's royal princesses, has been restored as the Green Hotel, a model for sustainable tourism. Wherever possible, the hotel incorporates energy-saving devices such as solar heating and low-energy lighting. The natural control devices include tilapia, mosquito-eating fish in ponds in the hotel grounds. The hotel preserves an historic building and donates all profits to charitable and environmental projects in India.

→ **www.greenhotelindia.com**

go for green miles
on public transportation

460

The Air Miles (or Frequent Flyer) program is a well-known and well-used initiative, particularly by those who use air travel regularly. A more environmentally friendly version might be Green Miles, administered along similar lines: the main difference would be that the vouchers for Green Miles (from purchasing products or tickets on public transportation) could be used only on public transport: to buy tickets for buses, trains, and the underground (subway), and perhaps to buy bicycles as well.

Giving away Green Miles with eco-friendly products would be a place to start, and could help encourage sales of those products. The net could be cast wider than specifically green items to include products such as double glazing or fair-trade food. Beyond this, however, Green Miles could be offered instead of loyalty card points in supermarkets or instead of cashback from credit cards, though there might be products that actively harm the environment (gasoline, for example), which could be excluded.

In offering people vouchers to use on public transportation, the system itself would be promoted, and would help to counterbalance the constantly rising prices of buying tickets for travel. It could also simultaneously encourage people to buy greener or more ethical products, therefore having a dual benefit for society.

Barbara Marion Lockie

buy into woodland burial:
the recycling statement of a lifetime

461

It seems logical that if a person has lived their life in what might loosely be termed a green or eco-friendly manner, then his or her funeral should also reflect this choice. For many years throughout the western world, however, the norm has either been traditional burial or cremation. The former often includes a varnished coffin, glued together, with metal or plastic handles, and takes up space above ground with a headstone. Cremation, although it takes up significantly less space at the end of the process, requires energy to power the cremators and pollutes the atmosphere: a significant percentage of cancer-causing dioxins from household combustion come from cremation and high levels of mercury have been found in the ground around crematoria (from the residue of mercury dental fillings).

All of this makes the case for a truly green option more pressing. Woodland or natural burial is that option: it is burial in which a biodegradable coffin is used and a tree is planted instead of erecting a gravestone. This method opens up new tracts of land for burial, contributes to the environment through the creation of woodland, and results in less ground and air pollution. In the UK, there was one dedicated woodland burial ground in 1993; there are now more than 200. Biodegradable coffins come in many different materials, including bamboo, wicker, untreated pine, cardboard, and even papier-mâché. And the best part of the whole process is that the person's body contributes to the growth of new life in death; as their body degrades, it helps the tree or wildflowers planted above it to grow and prosper. It is, indeed, the ultimate and final recycle.

→ **www.naturaldeath.org.uk**

plant a forest garden
for sustainable modern living

462

We have become increasingly aware of the need for sustainable living: reducing our impact on the environment (our ecological footprint) and increasing our levels of self-sufficiency.

The Forest Garden, a concept devised by the agroforestry expert Robert Hart, could be a crucial tool in enabling modern urban citizens to provide themselves with food, while also increasing the numbers of oxygen-producing plants and trees worldwide.

A forest garden is a miniature reproduction of the natural forest in a small garden. It mirrors the self-sustaining ecosystem of the forest by being arranged in seven stories or layers: the canopy of high trees, the planes of lower trees, the shrubs, the herbaceous herbs and vegetables, the ground plants, and the climbers and root-plants. The plants used are fruit and nut trees, bushes, perennial and self-seeding vegetables, and culinary and medicinal herbs. Once established, the forest garden requires little maintenance (ideal for modern city-dwellers), as it is self-perpetuating, self-fertilizing, self-watering, self-mulching, self-pollinating, self-weed-suppressing and highly resistant to pests and disease.

Hart set up a model garden at his home in Shropshire as a promotional and educational tool for his idea, and forest gardening has since taken off in many other areas in the UK and abroad, particularly with people interested in permaculture.

It is an attractive idea because of the impact it could have on a range of different problems: more fruits and vegetables to combat health and obesity problems, more trees to help restore the Earth's forest cover, produce with less packaging (and no transport), and greener, more attractive urban areas. And thanks to Robert Hart, we know it works.

→ **www.globalideasbank.org/site/store**

chapter 18

international and developing world

use old clothes to catch cholera-causing bacteria

463

Filtering drinking water through old saris (women's clothing made of lightweight cloth) can reduce cases of cholera by half, according to a report in the *Proceedings of the National Academy of Sciences* journal, focusing on remote villages in Bangladesh.

A folded sari cloth was found under laboratory conditions to catch approximately 99 percent of the bacteria that cause cholera. It is thought that the low-tech solution could be used throughout the developing world, particularly in Asia and sub-Saharan Africa.

The clothes do not trap the bacteria, which are small enough to fit through the holes in the fabric, but the plankton the bacteria cling to. The team from the National Science Foundation, who conducted the tests, found that villagers quickly took up the practice of filtering once shown the disease-causing bugs in their water. With many thousands dying from conditions caused by cholera every year, the potential of this idea to save lives is huge.

→ **www.pnas.org**

flag down books on wheels

464

Anywhere Books is a van outfitted with a laptop, laser printer, bookbinding machine, and cutter that travels around Uganda to print free books for children. The van stops at schools and librarians help children to pick out books they would like to print and own. Popular titles include *Alice in Wonderland* and *Peter Rabbit*.

Those involved see print-on-demand as a natural application for the developing world: bringing self-styled digital bookmobiles into these communities can have a huge impact. In the case of Anywhere Books, this includes not only building school libraries and supporting classroom reading, but also creating adult literacy materials in local languages and providing health information. This involvement demonstrates the possibilities in using the technology to target literature and information for particular areas on particular subjects.

→ **www.anywherebooks.org**

count on calls
for a better life

465

A mobile phone project in Bangladesh provides telecommunication services to the rural poor while simultaneously providing women villagers with a sustainable earning opportunity.

The Village Phone program works very simply: the Grameen Bank (the renowned microcredit lending bank; see p. 383) provides a loan to a rural woman villager to enable her to buy a handset and a subscription to a mobile phone service; having been trained how to use it and how to charge for the use of it, she then operates the mobile as a village payphone.

As well as providing a crucial telephone service to rural areas where no such facilities previously existed, the program allows thousands of Bangladeshi women to earn a living, often at more than twice the average annual income.

The telephone service has had a substantial impact in the country, with tens of thousands of village phones in operation, serving a potential 50 million consumers. There are thought to be over 80,000 Grameen phone ladies making a living through the program, resulting in increased respect and financial independence. Indeed, one of the main benefits of the program has been to increase the social standing of the phone ladies, as each has become one of the most important people in the village. With their added financial independence, the women can afford to send their children to school, to build new houses, or to invest in other projects. More recently, the project has been extended to another marginalized group: street beggars.

The economic impact is much greater than merely providing the Bangaladeshi women with the means to earn a wage, though. A single phone call can replace a long trip to the nearest city, allowing more time to be spent on the farm or in the village; thus, telephone access can benefit the whole village economically. Villagers who sell goods in the cities can call beforehand to check prices, preventing possibly wasted journeys, while others can send and receive news from friends and relatives. The access to information that a phone network provides, which much of the world takes for granted, can vastly improve the quality of life for people in the villages. When that is combined with the phenomenon of rural women using new technology to alleviate poverty, this becomes a truly social invention providing people with the means to enact social change in their own lives.

→ **www.GrameenPhone.com**

mobile mobile service is a win-win situation

466

New technology meets old in a program in which rickshaws in India take mobile phones to the people, while helping the poorest members of society. In Rajasthan, Shyam Telelink equipped 200 rickshaws that the drivers pedal in the capital with mobile phones. Rickshaws have a battery, billing machine, and printer. Everyone wins: Shyam gets more traffic on its network, the driver gets a commission, and clients get access.

The drivers are largely employed from the marginalized in society, typically the disabled and women. Suneel Vohra, President of Shyam Telelink, says "Many of these people are below the poverty line. They are dependent on their families for a livelihood and treated very shabbily because of that. Through these mobile payphones, some drivers are now able to support a family of five people."

The company charges employees nothing for the initial set-up costs, despite the 75,000-rupee ($1,715/£857) outlay for the equipment. The drivers are free to work to their own routine, an average of eight hours a day, bringing home around 6,000 to 9,000 rupees ($137 to 205/£68 to 102) per month. Customers now have access to affordable phone calls: currently in India, only seven people out of a hundred have a landline and 23 million people have access to mobile phones out of a population of 1.1 billion.

So what does the future hold for this mobile-mobile venture? Shyam's mission is clear. The way forward is on the hump of a camel. With two camels already in service, fully equipped with wireless computer technology, the company has set its sights on desert expansion. Meanwhile the rickshaw drivers in the cities should have plenty of work as the company explores the possibility of adding Internet facilities to the rickshaws.

→ **www.hellorainbow.com**

televise debates
between national leaders

B efore the conflict in Iraq in 2003, the desperate Iraq government made a remarkable suggestion: that the US and Iraqi presidents conduct a long-distance televised debate. This was, somewhat inevitably, an offer that was turned down, but it demonstrated the possibilities that global communications technology now allow. That is to say, that there need be no excuse for a breakdown of intelligent communication in the prelude to war, as national leaders can continue to debate the issues and put across their point of view.

467

Televised discussions between leaders of nations facing an impending conflict could be one small measure in helping dissolve some of the black and white thinking that leads to prejudice, hostility, and violence. It would also provide an opportunity for the world's citizens to judge each side on the merits of their case and on their actions and words. Whether those in power would want this process to be open and transparent is another matter.

Bill Jordan

cross borders with
humanitarian passports

T o remove some of the nationalistic divides most of us experience, there could be provision for a humanitarian passport that recognizes no boundaries. Anyone in the world could apply for the document voluntarily, and they could also choose to sign up to an associated manifesto (e.g., "I will not act aggressively on behalf of any nation, creed, or race"; "I do not recognize any artificial boundaries set by governments or other ideologies"). While this would initially be more a form of

468

awareness-raising, the passport could be tied into other activities, e.g., international exchange programs.

The idea would be for global society to become truly integrated and for the humanitarian passport to be a formal, recognized document. To facilitate this, there could be ambassadors or heroes chosen to receive the passport, people who have made a telling contribution to society in some way.

Pete Nicholls / Patrick Peltier

pursue a plan for a new world order

469

While some concentrate on small-scale incremental solutions to daily problems, John Bunzl, like others, focuses on the big picture. His Simultaneous Policy is an attempt to replace the global system of competition and free trade with international cooperation—and aims for all nations to implement the necessary measures at the same time.

The theory is simple. The rich are getting richer and the poor poorer. Global competition benefits the few rather than the many, and more and more people are pressing for changes as a result. Tax initiatives, corporation regulation, strict environmental laws, and wealth redistribution are just a handful that spring to mind. But while these might work on a small-scale in a particular country, unilateral agreement is needed across the globe.

The aim of the policy, the transformation of the international economy such that it operates in harmony with the global environment and with the needs of human nature, can only be achieved if it happens at the same time everywhere. This simultaneous implementation eliminates mistrust, fear, and competition.

The main barrier to its implementation is to get all countries to agree. Bunzl proposes the introduction of a preliminary stage, whereby a country can say that it has adopted the policy and is waiting for the rest of the world to join them before implementing it. As more countries adopt, so pressure will build on those who have yet to adopt, until everyone has agreed. Countries will be persuaded to adopt through lobbying, adoption by political parties, and individual pledges.

The policy could be implemented in three stages: stabilization, access, and change. The stabilization stage would include a Tobin tax on currency transactions, dismantling and banning of nuclear weapons, and canceling third world debt. The access stage would include measures to allow access to the boardrooms of major institutions and corporations, with the government holding a percentage of shares in all companies in their country. The change stage could include more ambitious changes, such as taxing corporations to provide funds for the developing world and improving intellectual and property rights legislation.

John Bunzl runs the International Simultaneous Policy Organization, which is the lobbying group he believes is necessary to encourage countries to adopt the policy. Citizens can sign up and adopt the policy online to add their support.

→ **www.simpol.org**

fund low-income entrepreneurs through the trickle up program

The Trickle Up Program, founded by Glen and Mildred Leet in the US, provides people on low incomes with seed money and basic business skills to enable them to work their way out of poverty.

470

The Leets recognized the limits of the trickle down model of international aid, where large sums are given to organizations but rarely make it down to those at the bottom, the people who need it most. Thus Trickle Up began, at first in Dominica, where the couple gave ten entrepreneurs $100 (£50) each to launch microbusinesses.

Since its beginnings in 1979, the Trickle Up Program has helped start or expand over 120,000 businesses, benefiting hundreds of thousands of the world's poorest people. Increasingly, many of those applying for the conditional grants are women and young people, and the program continues to consider those who other aid programs (and, indeed, other microcredit programs) ignore.

The grants are provided if the following six conditions are met:
→ the entrepreneurs have planned the business themselves

→ they are willing to commit 250 hours each to the project in the first three months;
→ at least 20 percent of any profit is reinvested in the venture, or saved;
→ they are responsible for securing local approvals and resources they need;
→ self-growth and profit is anticipated in the future;
→ they report back on their business and results to date.

Trickle Up works with partner organizations in different countries to provide basic business training, and to facilitate the process of reporting back. In this way, they ensure that money is not simply handed over, but that support and accountability are built into the process.

It is a system that has been working for over 25 years, and shows how, in reality rather than rhetoric, the most disenfranchised and disempowered members of society can truly be helped to help themselves: by investing a small amount of money, and allowing them to invest their own energy and creativity.

→ **www.trickleup.org**

steam ahead with the world's largest solar stove

The Brahma Kumaris World Spiritual University in Rajastan, India, is home to what has been dubbed the world's largest solar cooker, as well as several other renewable energy projects. The cooker, at the organization's complex in Shantivan, consists of 84 parabolic concentrators (that look like satellite dishes made of mirror) and produces 7,720 lb (3,500 kg) of steam every day. This concentrated heating of water works out at 6 kilowatts an hour for each square meter of mirrored surface. In turn, this provides enough energy for 35,000 meals each day. With the center receiving hundreds of thousands of visitors and guests every year, the solar cooking system is a hugely cost-effective and environmentally friendly way of feeding them all.

Brahma Kumaris have also developed smaller solar cookers for the hospital and the research center on their grounds on Mount Abu, and have helped outfit the local village of Salgaoun with solar-powered street lighting, solar cooking boxes, and solar lanterns. Their department of renewable energy has also researched and implemented several other energy projects, based on both solar and wind sources. The area is particularly well-suited to experiments and research into renewable energy projects, because Mount Abu is 1,200 feet (366 meters) above sea level and has almost perpetually clear skies. This has allowed them to demonstrate the possibilities of large-scale solar energy production, as with the massive cooking system detailed above.

The university is also renowned for being primarily administered by women, following the teachings of its founder, Brahma Baba. His vision of the future world was one of harmony between the sexes and of a partnership rooted in a foundation of spirituality, which he believed to be the key to trust and respect. What is interesting is the way in which the organization, devoted to aiding individuals in the process of self-growth and personal development, has also devoted much of its time and money to the growth and development of technological solutions to human problems. It may well be its greatest legacy.

→ **www.bkwsu.com**

treat citizenship as a a tradable commodity

472

One radical idea to counter the nationalism and isolationist mentality that sometimes seems prevalent is to let any two people in two different countries voluntarily exchange their citizenships. If such a plan were adopted, citizenships would become a tradable commodity. Poor people from rich countries could trade their citizenship with well-off people from poor countries for a monetary payment. Both parties would freely enter into this trade and therefore benefit from it. Furthermore, the rich country would benefit in that it gains an enterprising new citizen, while the poor country would benefit in that the person who left will presumably continue to support his or her relatives and friends from abroad.

Some retirees from rich countries may prefer to live out their final years in inexpensive and sun-rich countries; they can easily do so by exchanging their citizenships, thereby giving a young person an opportunity in a strong economy.

Axel Boldt

deliver the net to the people— by bus!

473

An initiative to bring rural areas of India online decided on installing computers on buses to quite literally deliver the Net to the people. Known as Post Net, the project was launched by Media Lab Asia, a venture between the Indian government and the Massachusetts Institute of Technology, with the chief aim being to put farmers in touch with agricultural news and weather reports.

Small wireless transceivers were installed on the computer-laden buses, which travel from village to village giving members of rural communities the chance to surf the web and send e-mails.

Using similar methodology, a project in Pakistan used vans to introduce farmers to the Internet, educate them in how to use it, and make them aware of how the technology can be turned to their advantage.

→ **www.medialabasia.org**
→ **www.pakissan.com**

model your city on sustainability

474

The residents of Curitiba, Brazil, may be the happiest in the world. In a poll, over 98 percent of them said they were happy with their city, and over 92 percent happy with their mayor. Yet this is a South American city like many others, which has experienced rapid population growth and has its share of slums, street children, and poverty.

Curitiba is different in that it is innovative and solves problems in the cheapest and most sustainable way possible. In the 1960s, a group of young architects, led by Jaime Lerner, proposed to the mayor a plan for a different kind of city. The mayor asked the citizens what they wanted and turned the process over to the architects; Lerner was made mayor in 1971.

With the economic situation what it was, solutions had to be inexpensive and participatory. One example was the 1.5 million tree seedlings given to neighborhoods to plant and nurture. Another was the diversion of water from the lowlands into new lakes (in the new parks), which solved many of the city's flooding issues. Lerner also hired teenagers to maintain the parks (and added sheep to trim the grass). Streets were pedestrianized and shopping areas revitalized, while street children were adopted by local institutions and retailers, who provide them with food and a small wage in return for doing chores. One street is lined by gardens that the children created and now tend.

The city's transport system is innovative. On five lines out of the city center, triple-decker buses carry 300 passengers at a time in bus lanes. The buses stop at glass tube stations, where passengers pay, enter through one end, and exit from the other. The system works as fast as an underground line, but at an eightieth of the cost, and is completely self-funding.

One way for poor families to buy bus tickets is to bring their rubbish to neighborhood recycling centers, where they can exchange it for tickets (or eggs, milk, and potatoes). This encourages people to recycle and to use public transport and it helps support local farmers.

The final word on this city goes to its mayor and leader for many years, Jaime Lerner, who said: "There is no endeavor more noble than the attempt to achieve a collective dream. When a city accepts as a mandate its quality of life; when it respects the people who live in it; when it respects the environment; when it prepares for future generations, the people share the responsibility for that mandate, and this shared cause is the only way to achieve that collective dream."

→ **www.curitiba.pr.gov.br**

act as an individual to change an ancient city

On a trip to India in 1994, Sue Carpenter spent a week in Jaisalmer, an 800-year-old fortress city of wonderfully carved sandstone buildings. Suffering under the barrage of monsoons and a new drainage system, the building's foundations were being eroded and more than 80 buildings were on the verge of collapse. On her return to England, she wrote an article for the *New Scientist* and appeared on the radio, and was contacted by an architect who had been to Jaisalmer ten years before. They agreed to start a campaign to raise awareness of the threat to the city's heritage, and the Jaisalmer in Jeopardy organization was born.

Following fundraising events in London, the campaign got under way, with the Indian authorities (in the state of Rajasthan) and the Indian National Trust for Art and Cultural Heritage pledging their support. Within two years, Jaisalmer in Jeopardy was a registered charity and had convened the Jaisalmer Heritage Trust to coordinate the funding and administration in India. This was followed in 1997 by the Jaisalmer Conservation Initiative, created to oversee conservation projects in the city. The World Monuments Watch program listed the city as one of its 100 Most Endangered Places and awarded it a substantial grant that went

475

toward the restoration of the Maharani's Palace. Other funds raised went toward a streetscape revitalization project that restored and improved two landmark streets in Jaisalmer to serve as a model for the rest of the city.

The project, which has helped transform one of the world's most beautiful and endangered cities, is living proof of the old axiom that one individual can make a difference.

→ **www.jaisalmer-in-jeopardy.org**

keep traditional medicine alive in India

476

In the past in the northern Indian region of Ladakh, the traditional form of Amchi medicine was widely used, with local doctors providing their skills freely in return for farming chores. This simple system allowed the Amchi doctors to concentrate on treatment, gathering medicinal plants and consulting with patients. The introduction of western medicine, market forces, and social mobility changed this situation dramatically in the late 20th century, with the result that many of the traditional skills were marginalized and began to disappear. Furthermore, the introduction of conventional medicine has not gone as planned: in Ladakh, where isolated communities exist in some of the harshest places on Earth, knowledge is scarce, hospitals are few and far between, and medicines are too expensive.

Laurent Pordié, a French anthropologist and ethnopharmacologist, believed that the reintroduction of Amchi medicine would preserve and revive a valuable tradition, and also improve the healthcare of the people of Ladakh. He set out to educate individuals from Amchi families and to set up banks of drugs accessible to all. The education program began in 1999, with an initial intake of thirteen people; ten of them graduated from the medical school in 2003. Twenty-two health centers have been established across Ladakh, ensuring that almost three-quarters of the population have access to Amchi healthcare provision. The centers are staffed by the older generation of Amchi practitioners, but the new graduates will work in centers near their villages, ultimately replacing their elder colleagues.

Two other innovations have made a difference to the future of Amchi medicine. The first is that each center gathers and produces different medicines from traditional plants to ensure supplies are available. The second is a journal set up by Pordié, which has enabled Amchi practitioners to communicate and stay up-to-date on current findings and developments. This has been followed by an annual seminar, bringing more than a hundred of the doctors together.

The local people have responded with enthusiasm to Pordié's efforts, and his French-based organization is gradually removing itself from the project, so that the Ladakhis themselves own and administer it. Furthermore, as its presence is essential for the cohesiveness and mental well being of their communities, the revival of Amchi medicine could, in the long term, repair and strengthen the very fabric of life in these isolated mountain villages.

→ **www.nomadrsi.org**

enable the poor to work their way out of poverty

Mohammad Yunus established the Grameen Bank in 1977 in Bangladesh, offering loans to the very poorest Bangladeshis. Since these were people barely subsisting, there was no way for them to provide the collateral necessary to make use of conventional credit facilities. Yunus's idea has always been that credit is a human right and he opened up credit facilities to this section of the population to foster micro-entrepreneurship. The philosophy was—and remains—that the poor should be able to work their way out of poverty, what Yunus calls responsible capitalism.

The project has proved a success. Would-be borrowers are formed into groups of their peers and, after training and advice from a bank worker, take collective responsibility for authorizing and approving each other's loans. The loans are given out in a staggered format (two people from five receive the loan, then if they repay successfully after six weeks, the next two and then, after another six weeks, the final member). Though the average loan size is just £35 ($70), this is equivalent to as much as £5,000 in the UK ($10,000 in the US), with the result that thousands of people in Bangladesh have been able to finance their own business projects through Grameen. As a result of this novel microcredit system, the on-time repayment rate on loans has been consistently high (currently running at 98.85 percent).

477

The microcredit movement has grown exponentially, attracting worldwide interest not only from many charities and NGOs, but also from commercial banks and politicians, such as former President Clinton. It has been implemented in different ways in countries from the US to Brazil to India and beyond.

Grameen has diversified into other areas, with efforts such as the Grameen Agricultural Foundation, which owns no land but has agreements with individuals to become a partner (for a portion of the harvest, Grameen provides training, funding, and marketing, for example); Grameen Uddog, which acts as an intermediary for handloom workers; and the innovative Grameen mobile phone initiative (see p. 373).

The initiative that started it all off, microcredit, continues to change people's lives on a scale that was unimaginable at its inception. Grameen Bank is a major achievement of the twentieth century, and there is good cause to believe that the invention of social collateral in combination with peer-group lending is one of the major social inventions of our time.

→ **www.grameen-info.org**

lend books as a novel way to cut crime

478

On the subway in Mexico City, where pickpockets commonly trouble commuters, a novel approach has been designed to try and cut crime.

The city handed out 250,000 free books as part of a plan to distribute seven million books in two years. Trusting that commuters will return them at their journey's end, the project has turned the Metro into a vast underground library, packed with avid readers and booklovers.

"We are convinced that when people read, people change," said Javier Gonzalez Garza, the Metro director, who, while the authorities had been considering other anti-crime measures, decided the Metro should tackle the problem from a cultural angle.

Commuters in Japan, who benefit from lending libraries in stations, say books help foster a sense of community. In Mexico City, as it is mainly the poor who use the Metro, the authorities hope the program will help improve literacy among those who can least afford books.

→ **www.metro.df.gob.mx** (in Spanish)

turn the world upside down to see more clearly

479

It is a cause of irritation to some that the West has an outlook biased toward the northern hemisphere. One idea to counter that is to start a movement called the "upside down society," that would promote the view that the world is actually looked at the wrong way up; in this view, the Antarctic should be at the top of the world on maps and globes.

All people would need to do to join the society would be to register with a website and buy an upside-down map and hang it in their home. The society could sell upside-down globes and clocks with hands that go anti-clockwise, as shadows do in the southern hemisphere. It is amusing , and would help draw attention to the bias of the media, which is US- and Euro-centric. Viewing the world from a different angle literally may help people view it a different way more generally too.

Kerry Brown

→ **www.flourish.org/upsidedownmap**

create a global animal welfare agency on the hoof

480

Many people feel that humanity owes it to our fellow creatures to institutionalize decent treatment of them and to guarantee at the highest possible level of our global society the good care of (and consistent avoidance of cruelty to) the billions of sentient creatures whose lives we control, cause, or permit.

This should include setting standards for the care of animals in international agriculture, commerce, and research; monitoring of international animal care; implementation of sanctions for animal mistreatment; and other relevant activities.

Ideally, these standards should be embraced at the highest possible level, to effectively reduce and prevent as much as possible the horrific mistreatment of animals, which takes many gruesome and unnecessary forms. This global institutionalization of consistent decent and good treatment of animals should be led by the United Nations.

The United Nations system could create a specialized UN agency charged with protecting animal welfare in every relevant arena, internationally and wherever international and national animal-related activities overlap. (The new agency might be aptly named UNAPAW: UN Agency to Provide Animal Welfare).

Critics of economic globalization consistently stress the need for better free-trade rules to protect workers and the environment. An additional set of rules to protect all animals involved in any way in global commerce is needed and should become a third plank in globalization-reform protests and advocacy.

The great humanizing movements are largely considered to include those for human rights, civil rights, women's rights, environmental preservation, and animal rights. Only the latter is not represented by a dedicated United Nations agency: this situation needs to change.

Greg Wright

employ disadvantaged workers to combine capitalism and social purpose

A US company employs Cambodian citizens at a low wage to do monotonous data-entry work: nothing new there, one could argue, with today's prevalence of western exploitation of cheap foreign labor. However, this company only employs the most disadvantaged citizens of the country: those disabled by illness or land mines, slum residents, and prostitutes.

481

Furthermore, the company actively encourages (and pays half the fees for) its employees to get further education, usually in information technology or English language classes. And while Cambodian factory workers making clothes (also bound for the US) earn as little as £8 ($16) for a 48-hour week, the typists earn £3 ($6) more for a 36-hour week. These policies have led some to herald the company as a model for how globalization can work for all: how capitalism and social purpose can be combined.

The company in question, Digital Divide Data (DDD), was started in 2001 by two North American consultants who believed that globalization need not exploit the poor in the developing world, but could be used to help. The company has faced controversy from its first major contract, as opponents of the program highlighted the low wage paid to the workers (much less than US or UK minimum wage).

DDD goes against standard thinking about helping the developing world, and has attracted opposition. It is a capitalist venture using cheaper foreign labor to maintain its margins—nothing new about this in the data-entry world: US insurance claims have been processed in India, and even New York police tickets have been put through in Ghana. Where DDD differs is that it is also a social venture, showing how the most disadvantaged people in the developing world can be helped by the progression in the information economy.

→ **www.digitaldividedata.com**

transform slums with
street committees and small loans

482

Orangi is Karachi's largest slum, long considered a no-go, no-hope area. The Orangi Pilot Project was established in 1980 to fill the gap left by the city's government, which had failed to provide the slum with sanitation. The Orangi Pilot Project took a different approach and organized local people into street committees and loaned them money to buy raw materials to build a sewage system.

The man behind the project was Akhtar Hameed Akhan, a grand old maverick who helped to establish a cooperative movement in Bangladesh when it was East Pakistan. He said "The children were playing in filth. Typhoid, malaria, diarrhea, dysentery, and scabies were rampant. It was clear that the authorities would never be able to build sanitation for the poor. There was only one solution—to find ways for the community to solve the problem itself. It was a difficult decision. But psychologically, it was a revolutionary step."

Thanks to the Orangi Pilot Project, over 72,000 of Orangi's 95,000 houses were connected to covered sewers. The national average at the time was one house in five. The costs were also low: $34 (£17) for each house, on top of the voluntary labor provided by locals. The project also chipped in about $100,000 (£50,000) in research, design, and overhead costs, and the time of its mostly student volunteers, but the total bill for the enterprise—$1.5 million (£750,000)—was met almost entirely by the local community. Residents of individual streets even banded together to elect project managers, and contributed cash and voluntary labor to get their own sewer installed.

The results, achieved at a fraction of the price a government program would have cost, have been remarkable. Sanitation, combined with the OPP's health project, brought the district's infant mortality down from 130 per 1,000 in 1982, to 37 in 1991. Nationally, the 1991 figure was 95 per 1,000. Upkeep costs, to clear blockages and replace broken manhole covers, are still around ten cents (5p) a month. And maintenance work (the bane of most engineering development works) is carried out. Since the people own the project, maintaining the sewage system is also maintenance of their investment and improved health.

As a model for urban development, Orangi is unorthodox, radical, decentralized, and cheap. But most importantly, it is owned by the residents, both financially and psychologically. It is the most novel form of self-service, one that could well succeed in other areas of the world.

buy local water
for smaller footprints

483

It is one of the cruel ironies of modern life that consumers in the western world are prepared to pay millions of pounds for bottled mineral water, while millions of people in the developing world have no access to free, clean water at all (or, more generally, decent sanitary systems).

A project that aims to bridge the gap between those two facts is Belu, a UK-based social enterprise. It sourced a mineral water in the UK, bottled it, and sells it in supermarkets and restaurants; so far, so normal. But the difference is that 100 percent of profits go to fund water filtration and purification projects.

The project also aims to inform via text on its bottles, and encourage people in the UK to buy UK-sourced water, so that it has traveled less far and has had as little treatment as possible. This means the product has a smaller ecological footprint than other bottled waters, consumers are helping to contribute funds to good causes, and the beneficiaries abroad receive funds they need to help them improve things. The first funded projects have been in India, where 1.5 million children die of water-related diseases each year.

→ **www.belu.org**

name a hurricane
to raise research funds

484

The authorities responsible for naming hurricanes (the World Meteorological Organization) could set up a website where anyone who wishes to name a hurricane can make a suggestion and a donation.

People wishing to vote for a particular name could do so by making a donation too. The funds raised would go toward research and aid projects, perhaps distributed by a non-profit

foundation set up for the purpose. The authorities would retain the right to censure certain names, but would otherwise choose the candidate with the most votes at any particular time. The donations would be released when a given name is used, otherwise they would gather interest until that name reached the top of the list and was selected.

Brantgoose Boucher

support self-sufficiency
to re-energize the environment

485

Gaviotas is a self-sufficient village in the savannah grassland of Los Llanos on the eastern plains of Colombia. At the heart of its development was Paoli Lugari, an environmentalist who believed that the pressures of population growth and development would ultimately lead to people having to live in harsh environments. This led him to create Gaviotas, which has proved to be a uniquely successful experiment.

The village of about 200 people is unique because of the myriad features it has designed and introduced to support itself. These include solar motors, prototype windmills, and biogas generators. They use hydroponic nurseries to grow plants and have planted over a million trees to reforest the area (more than the Colombian government's entire forestry program). They don't need to cut the trees down to sell the timber, because they discovered that the sap from the pine forest is twice as productive as anywhere else in the world; they tap the resin using a natural enzyme and add fungus to the roots of the tree, which increases production further, and then they sell the sap for use in turpentine and other products.

Having been designated a model community by the United Nations in 1976, Gaviotas received a monetary grant. When it ran out,

they turned to their ingenuity to survive. They produce and sell windmills and water pumps they have designed, as well as a see-saw which uses child power to pump clean water. The see-saw pump has been fitted in countless playgrounds across Latin America. Schooling is free in the village, as are housing, healthcare, and even food. With everyone earning the same salary, there is no poverty as such, so there is very little crime.

The community has turned their old hospital into a water purification and bottling center, generated power by fueling turbine engines from the pine trees (which are gradually being replaced by native species), and sold its cattle herd to allow diversification of farming to rabbits, chicken, and fish. A new village is planned nearby for the increasing number of workers needed to work collecting resin or producing the village's homegrown products.

The Gaviotas impact is felt far away. In Bogota, over 50,000 apartments heat water with a rooftop solar collector developed in the village. The village also offers a beacon of hope in a country in which political problems and violence often prevent such utopian developments.

→ **www.friendsofgaviotas.org**

bicycle-powered computers turn the wheels of change

486

A project in Laos connected five villages on a wireless network to the Internet with low-wattage, bicycle-powered computers. The Remote Village IT Project, developed by the Jhai Foundation, aimed to provide villagers with the means to get information and skills that would improve their lives.

Getting accurate information about markets in nearby towns improves their chances of selling surplus crops; communicating and coordinating via e-mail with expatriate Lao enables the development of future markets.

The project also provided the ability to perform simple business computer functions, using spreadsheet and word processing software. A rugged computer that can survive in the dust, heat, and monsoon conditions, yet requires very little energy to power it, was specifically designed for the project. Furthermore, the communication center and wireless network were placed under village ownership, meaning that villages can charge users for support costs, thus making the project completely sustainable.

To enable the villagers to use useful computer software, the project developed a Lao-language version of a free Linux-based desktop program and Lao-language versions of office software. Young people in the village were trained up; some became Youth IT Entrepreneurs with the ability to support the elder villagers in using the technology. The wireless network connects the villages and, using antennas situated on rooftops and trees on mountain summits, the village's computers send signals to the bigger village of Phon Hong. From there, the phone lines connect to an Internet service provider.

What is also interesting about the project is the way in which the Jhai Foundation works. It starts by building a relationship with the local villagers; it believes the villagers know themselves what they need to improve their lives. The project is thus a cooperative one, not one imposed by a well-meaning NGO from the West. It is designed to achieve the end benefits requested by local people, not those viewed as desirable for the organization's funders, so the chances of creating a sustainable, replicable solution are higher.

The Foundation was established by Lee Thorn and Bounthanh Phommasathit in 1997: the former was a bomb-loader during the American war in Laos, the latter a Lao refugee from the American bombing. Together, they are helping enact genuine social change through the judicious use of new technology.

→ **www.jhai.org**

leap at the chance
to get villages online

Two computers, a satellite dish, and a set of solar panels have revolutionized life in the village of Robib in Cambodia. As is the case with many small villages in the country, there is no telephone service and no electricity in Robib, and the people are further disconnected by mountains and jungle. Now the village has been transformed, with silk scarves made in the village being sold over the web and profits put into a pig farm. Profits from the farm and the scarves will be used to fund medical care for the village.

The Village Leap project, set up by the American Assistance for Cambodia charity, shows how minimal hardware can have a major

487

impact in developing countries, allowing them to leap out of isolation. As costs of computer equipment fall, the possibilities for improving access to new technologies for poorer countries increase. The only expensive hindrance was the satellite connection, which the charity convinced a company to fund. Any state funding for such projects would have to weigh the pros and cons of spending large amounts of money on new technology. Mit Mien, the chief of Robib, had no doubts, however: "I don't really know what the Internet is or how it works, but it is changing our lives."

→ **www.villageleap.com**

reach out to remote farmers through wireless technology

Yak farmers in remote parts of Nepal (often two days' walk from the nearest village) can now contact friends and family through a wireless Internet network.

The Nepal Wireless Networking project connected seven villages with no means of communication. Farmers can send e-mails with any problems (medicine or food requirements), they can sell products online, and even use video-conferencing technology to talk with each other and the outside world.

The project is led by teacher Mahabir Pun, who was frustrated when he received a dona-

488

tion of computers but could not get them online. There were no phone lines, satellite was too expensive, and the connection from a radio phone was ineffective. A wireless solution was suggested. He set up a Linux server in the nearest big town, Pokhara, which sends signals to a solar-powered relay station. This, in turn, sends the signal to another relay station. The signal is sent from there to wireless access points in the other villages. The final village is Tikot, over 36 miles (58 km) from Pokhara.

→ **www.nepalwireless.net**

ship out self-contained classrooms to provide interactive education

An organization that believes educating women in the developing world is the key to helping them out of poverty, oppression, and injustice is addressing the problem by sending out interactive classrooms in shipping containers.

The portable classrooms, which have so far been sent to Delhi and Assam, India, use the latest interactive technology to provide education for the very poorest communities,

489

technology that is suitable for those who cannot read or write and for those who have no prior experience of technology.

The Starfish Initiative (Thare Machi) plans to send 200 such classrooms into the field, and to develop over 100 interactive lessons. The classrooms contain six DVD workstations giving interactive lessons in the local language.

→ **www.starfish-initiative.org**

treat needy children to their own restaurant

490

A children's-only restaurant was created in the Latin American city of Cuzco because of two travelers whose ambitions changed from being tourists to helping malnourished youngsters.

They decided the restaurant would be a good way to teach children about nutrition and food without simply giving them the money to use elsewhere. Bringing the children together allows them to learn social skills and alleviate feelings of loneliness so common on the streets.

Titus Bovenberg and Jolanda van den Berg set up the free restaurant for children includ-

ing not only healthy foods, but also showers and toilets, a dental and medical check-up center, a school-tutoring program, and hotels. The introduction of a variety of foods steers the kids away from their typical sugary and starchy diet. However, the couple that began the project don't consider it a social project of any kind but more like one big business [with] 300 clients who don't pay. They have built a gym and given the children personalized items such as toothbrushes.

→ **www.ninoshotel.com**

use bean cushions and cardboard boxes to cook

491

A nna Pearce and friends discovered latent creativity while working with Quakers and an organization called Compassion in the poor parts of South Africa.

They created the Wonderbox: two cushions filled with polystyrene beans, used to envelop a cooking pot. A pot of food is brought to a boil, then tucked between the cushions to prevent the heat escaping, and left to continue cooking for two or more hours without using

any more fuel. The Wonderbox was used for other things: to bake bread without an oven and as a cool box for drinks.

The charity that Anna set up, Box-Aid, added the Anahat to their previous creation. The Anahat is a cardboard box solar cooker (lined with foil) that cooks food using only the sun's rays.

→ **www.geocities.com/boxaidinfo**
→ **www.anahat.co.uk**

all rise for the republic of frestonia

492

The Free and Independent Republic of Frestonia was founded on October 27, 1977. The residents of Freston Road, Notting Dale, London W11, threatened with eviction to make way for a factory estate, had a referendum: 95 percent favored independence from Great Britain and 73 percent favored joining the Common Market.

There were 120 residents in Frestonia in about 30 houses on 1 acre (0.4 hectares) of land. Everyone who wanted to take part in the independence initiative became a minister and, in keeping with their ethos of togetherness, there was no prime minister. The Minister of State for Education was, appropriately, a two-year-old, Francesco Bogina-Bramley. The nation's motto on its coat of arms was *Nos sumus una familia*, meaning "We are one family." The motto was more literal than might be thought, as all the residents adopted the surname Bramley (on the grounds that if the council succeeded in evicting them, they would have to re-house them all together).

As a result of this novel and radical move, the media descended on Frestonia from around the world. *The Daily Mail* printed a leader column and a report from our Foreign Correspondent in Frestonia. Japanese television filmed New Zealand television filming nothing much going on in the frankly uneventful communal garden.

The Frestonians were suddenly transformed in the eyes of the authorities from a bunch of squatters, hobos, and drug addicts into an international incident that provided them with the opportunity to show how enlightened they were.

A public inquiry was ordered. The council had their QC, and Nicholas Albery represented Frestonia as the Minister of State for the Environment. He proposed that Frestonia become a mixed-use site for houses and craft workshops: they won the enquiry.

Frestonia was rebuilt to the residents' design with several million pounds of foreign aid from Great Britain, channeled via the Notting Hill Housing Trust to their cooperative. Before his death in 2001, Nicholas Albery (one of the driving forces behind the campaign and the founder of the Global Ideas Bank), wrote:

"I am immensely proud of the development that was built, complete with its overhanging roofs, enclosed communal gardens, and decorated brickwork. Recently, there was a great party in a marquee in the communal garden to mark the 21st anniversary of independence. The spirit is still strong. Frestonia goes to show that with imagination and humor you can run rings round the establishment."

connect education and culture with comics

493

Communicating messages is often a major problem for development workers, as they try to inform people about new farming techniques or teach them new skills. One intriguing option is the use of locally produced comics.

The visual storytelling element of comics can aid communication, particularly when the images are created by local people and thus imbued with local culture and landscape. The organization World Comics India exists to promote this use of comics and to run workshops teaching comic skills to those who can use them most effectively.

Comics are most commonly used for children's stories or for political satire, but as a simple storytelling medium, their potential is much greater. This is particularly the case in countries that have a tradition of storytelling. World Comics India teaches grassroots activists and the people on the ground to use comics to express their ideas and communicate their messages. This has led to wall posters about human rights and AIDS/HIV, as well as educational comic books.

Similar initiatives are taking place in Cuba, Iran, and several African countries although the initial impetus for the movement came from Finland, where comics are very much a part of everyday life.

World Comics Finland, an organization started by Leif Packalén in 1997, not only helped the Indian program start up, but has also collaborated with organizations in Mozambique, Kenya, and Tanzania.

Their mission of promoting comics as a communication medium for social change continues to spread. As people realize that the humor and humanity that characterize comics, when combined with the ability to incorporate local languages and knowledge (less expensively than video or film), is uniquely effective, that process will surely continue.

→ **www.worldcomics.fi**
→ **www.worldcomicsindia.com**

video volunteers to help advance good causes

494

As the price of new technology falls, potential for its use in new areas grows. One initiative uses video to help nongovernmental organizations (NGOs) working to reduce poverty better communicate goals and methods.

The initiative works by sending in volunteer filmmakers to chosen projects for two months to write, shoot, and edit a short film about their work. The films are intended to be shown within and beyond their local communities, as well as on One World TV, an Internet television station. In this way, the Video Volunteers program helps give NGOs, and the people they are helping, a voice to advance their cause.

With the advent of cheaper video cameras and cost-effective computer editing, grassroots organizations can produce short films and videos. These can be used as part of an educative program or for raising awareness in the media and the community. The volunteers also teach the activists to use video to document the progress of their projects in the long term, and to teach them basic editing skills that they will be able to use themselves. They further advise on how to stream video footage, such as personal testimonials, on the web.

A similar organization, Witness, trains partner organizations in video and communications technology, but with a particular focus on human rights. Witness works in over 50 countries, providing cameras and producing films with its partners and training groups to document and record human rights abuses with video. It also broadcasts films from its partner organizations (which range from a gay rights group in El Salvador to an Argentine forensic anthropology team) via its website, broadcasting the work being done and the issues raised.

Witness was started by the musician Peter Gabriel in 1992 in the wake of the Rodney King beating being caught on video (which prompted the Los Angeles riots of that year). If such abuse could be caught at random, what could be achieved if efforts were made to document abuses in a purposeful way? Originally the organization primarily provided cameras, but its work expanded after a successful film in 1996, and it now has 30 in-house productions each year. Its video and broadcast journalism training has had a substantial impact. The webcasts of partner films have attracted large audiences and footage is shown with suggestions for action or how viewers can help.

→ **www.creativevisions.org/videovols.htm**
→ **www.witness.org**

share your skills
with nomadic shepherds

495

In an effort to close the technological divide between the developed world and developing countries, the United Nations Information Technology Services (UNITeS) sends out information technology experts to countries from Benin to Tanzania.

One such operative, Sean Osner, set up a community center in a Bedouin village with ten Intel 486 computers and five Pentium IIIs. And while it might seem that a nomadic shepherd would have no need for the Internet, it can help locals get better education and medical care.

It may help with business, too; as Osner pointed out, "One of the things we designed the community center for was to help the local women find markets in other parts of the world for their products. That would keep those traditions alive in their community."

The UNITeS program, with volunteers coordinated by United Nations Volunteers, aims to play a key role in helping businesses in developing countries exploit the opportunities afforded by the Internet, but it is also aimed at teaching people how to use computers, not just at putting computer systems in place. This should help reduce the shortage of technology-skilled people in such countries, which is often a major hurdle to their involvement in the digital revolution. And the demand is undoubtedly there; in one visit to Zagazig in Egypt, Osner was faced with 4,000 people, all waiting for a chance to use one of four computer terminals. Those who did get the chance learned how to do word processing, send e-mail, search the Internet, and set up their own e-commerce sites.

The program has over 300 volunteers working in over 50 different countries on a large variety of projects, with over 60 percent of the volunteers coming from developing countries.

→ **www.unites.org**

donate skills for disaster relief with professional twinning

496

This idea is intended to provide a means of helping nations rebuild after natural disasters, such as the tsunami that struck southeast Asia.

Professional twinning would work via the Internet, and allow people to be matched internationally with places where their skills are needed. After a disaster afflicts a country, professions lacking at that time (engineers, teachers, accountants, etc) would be posted on the site along with a certain amount of detail. Then people across the globe could volunteer.

The needs in the affected location would be assessed either by existing non-governmental organizations (Oxfam, Red Cross, and so on) or by a new "Professional Twinning" organization in partnership with the location. In the future, employers might even choose to "donate" an employee for a week to a troubled area, rather than simply contributing the money to a general fund. The twinning website, if successful, could be extended to be in use at all times of the year.

Nigel Bradley

prevent mosquito breeding with copper-coated car tires

497

Discarded car tires can be breeding grounds for mosquitoes: the inner cup of the tire can catch small pools which are predator-free. Insecticides cause collateral damage and are expensive—often too expensive for the developing countries where mosquito control is vital. And scientists have found that metallic copper is toxic to soft-bodied invertebrates, including mosquito larvae. Here's an idea that takes all of these facts and brings them together in a potential solution. A small amount of copper could be added to the inside of new tires just after they leave the mold. This could be a thin wire or a puff of metallic copper powder over the entire inside. The copper would adhere to the hot sticky rubber and would not impair the tire utility. When the tire is discarded, the copper will remain. Any water pooling in the tire would reach toxic copper concentrations, which would inhibit mosquito breeding.

William Read

meet your global neighbors online

498

A Netherlands-based online project, Nabuur aims to make the global village a reality by making us all neighbors. It links up communities in developing countries with virtual volunteers ("neighbors") who are willing to offer help with their access to knowledge, solutions, resources, and money.

Nabuur aims to create a mechanism to enable the problems of local communities to be solved on a larger scale around the world than is now possible. The process starts with the community from the developing country creating an online "village" and posting questions or problems. The virtual neighbor can become a neighbor of that village and try to help find a solution, then report back via discussion boards on the site. The local representative of the community discusses the options with the community before deciding which, if any, to implement. The site offers the chance to be a virtual volunteer and contribute by being a neighbor to people you've never met.

→ **www.nabuur.com/modules/news/**

marriage bureau overcomes stigma

499

A s HIV/Aids increases worldwide, ripple effects are felt in other areas of life. One area is the difficulty HIV-positive people experience in finding partners and marrying. This issue raises new problems since, in places like India, being unmarried carries its own stigma. There is a solution, though, at least for those in the state of Gujarat in India: an HIV-positive marriage bureau.

The bureau was launched in 2004 and seven couples were married through its work in the first eight months. It acts like any other dating agency, matching up singles through interests and age, with the sole difference that all of its 600 members are HIV positive. Daxa Patel, of the Gujarat State Network for People Living with HIV/Aids, set up the bureau and is a counselor.

India's number of HIV infections is second only to South Africa, so such projects offer much needed hope and optimism to many in the face of discrimination and other difficulties.

get rolling with
wheels around the world

500

While Merlin Matthews was studying at the London School of Economics, he was nicknamed Dr. Bike, as he fixed bikes and ran cycle repair workshops in exchange for beers on Friday evenings. Mainly due to his burgeoning reputation as a cycle guru, he was approached for advice about the feasibility of starting up a bike factory in Haiti, as people had seen the need for inexpensive, pollution-free, sustainable transport for the masses.

In the process of investigating the possibilities and discovering other organizations working in the same field, Merlin decided that the best use of his abilities would be to work in the UK, setting up a not-for-profit organization to facilitate the collection and shipping of bikes to less developed countries.

Since then, his project Re-Cycle has linked up with various organizations doing similar work (such as ITDP, Bikes Not Bombs, Pedals For Progress, and the International Bicycle Fund) in order to ship bikes across the world and to teach local people the skills of repairing and maintaining bikes to improve their lives in a sustainable manner. Re-Cycle focuses on African nations, as the American organizations listed above have Latin America fairly well covered.

In 2005, Re-Cycle celebrated having shipped over 12,000 bicycles to several countries, among them Sierra Leone, Zambia, Ghana, Liberia, and Nigeria, and their efforts will be assisted in the future by Royal Mail's agreement to donate some 4,000 old bikes from their considerable fleet every year.

→ **www.re-cycle.org**
→ **www.p4p.org**

Cat Diaries

Secret Writings of the
MEOW Society

Betsy Byars
Betsy Duffey
Laurie Myers

Illustrated by Erik Brooks

SCHOLASTIC INC.
New York Toronto London Auckland
Sydney Mexico City New Delhi Hong Kong

Special thanks to Amy Myers for her translation of Chico's story.

ISBN 978-0-545-33988-9

12 11 10 9 8 7 6 5 4 3 2 1   11 12 13 14 15 16/0

Printed in the U.S.A.   40

First Scholastic printing, January 2011

Designed by Véronique Lefèvre Sweet

With esteemed regard
for Sasha Black and Ed Stripe

—*E. B.*

Contents

CHAPTER 1

Full Moon, Empty Streets

It was the third full moon of the year when cats around the world began to disappear. The alleys and streets were quiet. Trash cans stood untouched, lids strangely in place. Dogs sniffed the air anxiously while mice ran freely, unafraid of predators. Music drifted from apartment windows, unaccompanied by feline howls.

The cat population had a meeting to attend. Large and small, old and young, cats headed to an old abandoned theater. When the room was filled, the eyes of the cats focused toward the front, where

a large gray cat with battle scars made his way to the
stage. He spoke.

"I, Ebenezer, call the meeting to order."

"This better be good," called a calico from the back. "I had to plot for three days to get out of the house to come." A Siamese slunk back and forth along the sideline. "And I don't have claws, so I took a big risk getting here." A fat cat yelled, "It rained yesterday. You know how I hate to get my feet wet, but I did it just to get here, even though I heard we might be meeting with dogs."

"Dogs?" a kitten asked, shaking.

"That was just a rumor," Ebenezer said. "There was some discussion about a possible meeting with the WOOF Society, Words of Our Friends. You see, dogs have written diaries too."

"Dogs? Diaries? Our dog can't even clean himself," a cat yelled.

"How many dogs have enough sense to write a diary?" said an alley cat.

"I agree. The dog in my house could no more write a diary than climb a tree."

"Not so fast," Ebenezer said. "I've read some dog diaries. The stories are not bad."

Yowls erupted. Ebenezer waited for the sounds to die down, then spoke. "On to our business."

"Tell us more," called a young cat from the third row. "This is my first meeting."

"As many of you know, for some time now we have been collecting writings by members of our feline community. We call this group MEOW (Memories Expressed in Our Writing)."

Meows of agreement echoed throughout the room. A paw went up.

"Yes, Cisco."

Cisco cleared his throat.

"Hairball," someone yelled from the back. Several cats laughed. Others coughed.

"Order!" called Ebenezer. "Cisco, go ahead."

"What kinds of writings will we hear tonight?"

"There are many different tales."

"Not from the Manx," someone yelled. "They don't have tails."

Everyone laughed, except the Manxes, who hissed.

Ebenezer continued. "Throughout history, cats in their own quiet way have been writing stories— stories of their lives and the lives of others. Tonight, we will hear diaries from a Gypsy cat, a pirate cat, and many more."

"Let's get started," called an Abyssinian.

"We will begin with the diary of a cat named Fuzzy, who learned that it's a delicate balance to keep the best of both worlds. Now, get comfortable."

Some cats curled into balls, others tucked their front paws neatly underneath their bodies. Everyone settled into position and awaited the first reading.

"Fuzzy, please come forward for the reading of the first of the cat diaries."

CHAPTER 2

Fuzzy's Two Worlds

DECEMBER 15

Today my family brought a tree into the house. You heard right, they brought a real tree *in*. This is a special treat for me because I don't go out much. Some cats love *out*. I don't. I love *in*, where it's warm.

When the tree first arrived I sniffed it over and over. I sat underneath the tree while my family hung things on it—fuzzy things, shiny things, round things, things of different shapes and sizes. My favorite is a shiny red ball. It's better than all my cat toys put together.

I plan to sleep under the tree all night and let the rich smell of pine fill my nostrils. Now that I have my own tree, my life is complete. I have the best of both worlds, *in* and *out*.

DECEMBER 16

Today my life is *not* complete. Today I do *not* have the best of both worlds.

This morning I was under the tree letting the smell of pine wash over me, when suddenly I had the most fantastic idea. I decided to *climb* the tree. I have sharp claws. I could do it.

I looked up. My red shiny ball was hanging on one of the top branches, swinging slightly as if to say, "Come on up."

"I'll be right there." I purred.

I tested the tree, first with one paw, then the other. It felt firm, solid. I started up, squeezing past branches, dodging lights. I was halfway up when I stopped to swat at a few items hanging from the outer branches. It was fun!

I continued to climb—past balls, past beads. Then I felt a slight sway. I stopped. It must have been my imagination. I moved slowly to the next branch. Another sway. I paused to give the tree a chance to settle down.

I gazed across the room. The view was fantastic. I could see everything. What a great spot! If I could get a little higher, it would be even better. I could stay there all day, and no one would be able to see me.

I moved carefully to the next branch. Yes indeed, this was perfect.

Wait a minute! Did the tree move again? No. Wait. Yes. It did move. It's moving more. This is not good. Not good at all. I think I'm going dooooooooown.

The tree crashed into the middle of the room, taking me with it. We hit the floor with balls and beads flying everywhere. Then it was quiet. I got up and shook myself off. What do you know? The shiny red ball was right at my feet. I batted it around a few times.

"Fuzzy?" someone yelled from another room.

"Fuzzy!" others cried, hurrying in.

I was beginning to get a bad feeling about this. They weren't happy. Someone picked me up.

"Fuzzy. OUT," someone yelled.

"*Out?*" I meowed. "I love *in*. Wait. Don't put me OOOOOOOOOOOOOOOOOUT."

Slam. The door closed. Quickly I ran to the side window. Sometimes they let me *in* when I'm at that window.

"Here I am," I cried, shivering.

They ignored me.

"Let me IIIIIIIIIIN," I yelled.

They ignored me. They were busy fixing the tree.

"You know you're going to let me in eventually," I whimpered.

Then I noticed they were hanging my red shiny ball back on the tree, on that same high branch where the good view is. Suddenly, I was not worried.

I'm sure they will let me *in*, because they always do. Soon I will be warm. I will be back under my tree smelling the pine. I will climb to that high branch and sit next to my red shiny ball. Once again I will have the best of both worlds, *in* and *out*.

CHAPTER 3

Rama, the Gypsy Cat

Kansas, 1900
Read by Ebenezer

DAY ONE

"Tonight the music is sad," the Gypsy woman said. I was on her lap, purring.

I have two purrs. Purr-one is a public purr. If anybody does something nice for me, I purr-one.

Purr-two is a private purr. It is deeper, warmer, for one person only. My purr-two is only for the Gypsy woman.

The Gypsy woman hummed and stroked my ears, my golden earring. She put the earring there when I was a kitten. She said, "Now you are a Gypsy like me. We Gypsies keep our eyes to the road ahead."

The Gypsy woman lifted my paw and looked at it. "I'll tell your future, Rama. What will tomorrow bring?"

She didn't like what she saw, for she dropped my paw and sighed.

A sudden breeze brought an interesting smell from the forest. I jumped to the ground.

"No, Rama, no!" she called after me. "Not tonight, Rama! Tonight we—" I never heard the rest.

I caught a mouse first thing, then a fat chipmunk. I saved the chipmunk's foot, a gift for the Gypsy woman.

Rain began to fall. I took shelter in a hollow tree. I was full. I was dry. I slept.

DAY TWO

The rain was harder, slanting into the hollow. I moved deeper inside.

By night I was hungry, but it was still raining. I wanted to be in the Gypsy woman's wagon. I wanted to be on her lap. I wanted to purr-two. I ate the chipmunk foot.

DAY THREE

I left the tree and ran to camp. The clearing was empty. The wagons were gone. The Gypsy woman was gone too.

I saw the wagon tracks and started to follow. I ran like the wind. I was hungry, but I didn't stop to hunt. I was thirsty, but I didn't stop to drink.

The wagon tracks stopped at the river. It was not a deep river. Horses and wagons could cross. Cats could not.

I continued to run, hoping to find a way across. At sundown I smelled smoke. Food was cooking.

I thought it was the Gypsy woman. Maybe she had not crossed the river with the others. She was waiting for me!

I ran to the clearing. I stopped. There was one wagon. It was not the Gypsy woman. A man sat by the wagon. He was singing, but it was not a Gypsy song.

"Too-rah-lie-ooooooh," he sang. The song ended. There was a silence.

I sat in the shelter of the trees and watched.

DAY FOUR

Morning came and still no sign of the Gypsy woman's wagon. The man was sleeping on his blanket. His blanket looked comfortable. I had not planned to, but I meowed. The man looked up and saw me. He beckoned me over. I went slowly. He offered me food. I ate.

Then the man lay back down on his blanket. I sat down too and purred my thanks. The man rubbed my ear like the Gypsy woman did, and he saw my golden earring.

He said, "Me darlin' mother, bless her soul, had such earrings back in Ireland."

I answered, "Meiow."

We began to talk. The man said, "Do you think you'd like to be a peddler's cat? If so, then, me darlin', you're welcome to ride along."

I said, "Meiow."

After a while, he pulled me into the crook of his arm and closed his eyes.

I was full. I was warm. I was content.

The man was content too. A human purr-two rumbled inside his chest. I made a decision. My purr-one became deeper, warmer. Now it was a purr-two. The man and I purred ourselves to sleep together.

DAY FIVE

The peddler's wagon pulled out of the clearing. I sat on the seat beside the man. I glanced over my shoulder to the river and then turned my eyes to the road ahead.

CHAPTER 4

Library Cat

There's a large hedge in front of an old redbrick building at the corner of Irwin and Vine streets. In front of that building I was born and lived, but inside that wonderful building I found my life.

One morning a big yellow bus pulled up in front. Children got off and I watched. I felt small and afraid, but my curiosity got the best of me. When they went up the steps and through the door, I followed. I figured out that building was called the library.

The library was an amazing place, warm and quiet. The children's voices hushed as they filed through the rows of books and settled in a most

wonderful place. It was a room filled with sun, a floor covered with pillows of every color, and walls lined with the most amazing things. Books.

I snuggled down beside a girl who began to stroke my back. I purred softly and felt pure contentment. Sun filtered in through the windows, and the children shifted and found comfortable resting spots. A man in a red sweater with a kind face settled in a rocking chair, picked up a book from the top of the stack, and began to read.

In the story, an old man and his wife gave one lonely kitten a home. But then the old man and woman took in more and more cats until they had millions of cats. Finally the cats disappeared, and the one cat was left.

As I listened to the story my heart pounded. I hung on every word and I learned about myself. I

could be loved too. Maybe I could find a home like the kitten in the story. I rolled over beside the girl and slept. This might be the perfect home.

When the children left, I stayed, snuggling down in the colored pillows.

The man in the red sweater said, "Well. What have we here?" He picked me up and looked me over. I purred and rubbed my head on his hand. He rubbed back. I liked the man right away.

"Okay," he said. "Maybe you can stay . . . but just till we find you a home." He made a sign that said FREE KITTEN. He gave me half of a tuna sandwich and a bowl of water.

That afternoon more children came and I hurried to the story nook. I sat by the man's feet and looked up expectantly. He read a story about an incredible journey. A cat and his companions traveled across the country having adventures. I drew closer to the man's feet. I did not want to go on any adventures. But as I listened, I felt my heart pound harder and

I experienced the adventures too. As I listened to their story I learned about myself. I could be brave, if I needed to. I could have adventures, if I wanted to. I purred. Or maybe not.

That night, alone in the dark library, I was afraid. But I grew brave thinking about the story. I wandered through the great rooms. It was dark, but I could find my way easily through the shelves. I explored the library. I sniffed every corner. From one room there were scratching noises, and I hurried back to the pillows and hid. I wasn't ready for that room yet. I was happy to see the man come the next morning. I rubbed around his leg and purred.

That day more children came, and he read a story about the history of Egypt. During a battle the Egyptian soldiers had cats to protect their bows and arrows. Without cats, the rats would come and eat the strings off the bows. The Syrian army did not have cats, so when they went to get their bows for battle, the bows had no strings and the Egyptians won the war. Cats saved the day.

I learned about history and I learned about myself. Cats like me were smart. I learned that I could be smart. I walked taller that day. With my head up and my tail straight, I led the children to the door and saw them out.

"Bye-bye, Library Cat," one boy called to me, and I stood tall.

As I explored that night, I crouched and leaped boldly through the dark rooms. As I thought of the room with the scratching sounds, I thought about

the cats in Egypt who saved the battle and fought the rats. I listened and heard the scratching again, but this time I went inside. The next morning when the man came in I put the mouse at his feet as a gift.

"Aha," he said. "I guess we need a cat around here after all." He took the sign that said FREE KITTEN and threw it away. I purred with happiness. The bus arrived, and as I snuggled down that day in the reading nook with the children, something was new: I belonged here.

I listened to another story, a delightful one about a girl who went down a rabbit hole. In the story was a Cheshire cat who had a huge smile, and the smile became so big that the cat disappeared and only the smile was left.

As I nodded off, I smiled. When I heard the story about the cat, I learned about myself. I was no longer small and scared and unsure of myself.

In front of the library I was born, but inside that wonderful building I found my life. I was loved like the little kitten, and brave like the cat who took the journey. I was smart like the Egyptian cats, and my smile was so wide and my happiness so big, that I felt just like that Cheshire cat.

CHAPTER 5

Whiskers and the Parachute

South Carolina, 1943
Read by Whiskers, a descendant
of the original Whiskers

"**F**ind the cat! Find the cat!"

Anytime Johnny wanted to find me, I didn't want to be found. This time he had two kids to help him; I didn't have a chance. They found me under the sofa and took me to the basement.

"What are you making, Johnny?" one kid asked.

Johnny said a word I had never heard before. The kids looked impressed, so I knew it was something terrible. The word was *parachute*.

Johnny said, "I saw parachutes in a war movie last week."

"What's a parachute?" one boy asked. He didn't know either.

"It's a piece of cloth like this," Johnny explained, "with strings like this. When you jump out of an airplane the cloth fills with air and you float safely to the ground."

"It's too small for us. Who's going to try it out?"

In the silence that followed, six eyes turned to me.

All too soon I was yanked up onto the table and my body was wound in strips of cloth. I struggled hard, but there were six hands now and it was hopeless. I let out meows of protest so high and strange they didn't even sound like my meows.

They hooked the cloth onto the top of the strips. Then, with shouts of excitement, they ran up the basement stairs.

Johnny carried me up more stairs and then up the attic stairs and out onto the roof. It was just Johnny and me up there and, of course, the parachute. The other two kids were standing outside, looking up at us.

At that moment the
mother came out, and
was I glad to see her!
This is the only person
who treats me the way
I like to be treated. I
meowed my "help
me" meow, but it
didn't come out right.

The mother said,
"What's going on
here?"

One of the kids
said, "Johnny made a parachute for
the cat. It's a real neat parachute. You—"

"Where is this parachute?"

The kids pointed and the mother looked up.

I meowed again, and this time I managed to get
out the strongest "help me" of my life.

"Don't—you—dare!" the mother said to Johnny.

Johnny said, "But, Mom, it's perfectly safe. I
promise. I—"

"DON'T—YOU—DARE!"

"Look, Mom," Johnny said. "Will you just take a
look at it?" He held me up and shook out the parachute.

"DON'T—"

She never got to finish.

For at that moment a breeze came up. I felt my fur ruffle where it wasn't under the bindings to the parachute, and the breeze ruffled not only my fur but the cloth, too. Before I knew what had happened— *whoosh!*—the parachute and I were on our way.

"I didn't mean to. Mom, I promise I—"

But the rest of his words were lost to me as the parachute and I rose over the roof.

We sailed over the trees. Then we floated over the barn. We were flying like birds! I could see everything.

Just as I was beginning to take in the view, we started down. This sinking happened over the pond. Johnny had once sent me "out to sea," as he called it, on this pond, so my fear redoubled.

Then the blessed breeze blew again. We flew over the cornfield, over a couple of cows, and touched down in a small bush.

The mother was the first to arrive. She picked me up. "Oh, kitty-witty! Kitty-witty!" I love it when she calls me that. "Oh, my precious kitty-witty."

As she said these comforting words, she managed to undo my bindings and throw the accursed parachute on the ground. She stepped on it as we headed for the house.

I knew what would happen now. Johnny would be sent to his room. The two kids would be sent home. The mother would find a wonderful treat for me, and after I had eaten, she would hold me on her lap and stroke my fur and scratch my ears, all the while saying things like "You're the best kitty-witty in the world. Yes, you are."

I don't recommend parachute rides, but if you ever have to make one, I hope it ends like this.

CHAPTER 6

To Catch a Thief

Read by Chico
Translated by Amalia

Mi nombre es Chico.
My name is Chico.

Soy el gato más pequeño del mundo.
I am the smallest cat in the world.

Soy pequeño. Pero, ¿puedo impedir un crimen?
I am small. But can I stop a crime?

Hay un cotorro que vive en mi casa.
There is a parrot who lives in my house.

Este cotorro solamente puede decir una cosa, "Socorro. Socorro. Policía."
This parrot can only say one thing: "Help. Help. Police."

Lo dijo muchas veces en su juventud, pero nadie lo ha oído desde hace muchos años.
He said it many times in his youth, but no one has heard it in many years.

Todos piensan que se le olvidó cómo hablar.
Everyone thinks he forgot how to speak.

Un día oigo un sonido.
One day I hear a noise.

Soy pequeño. Paso desapercibido al cuarto.
I am small. I slip unnoticed into the room.

Veo a un ladrón robando joyas y dinero.
I see a thief taking jewelry and money.

Corro al cotorro. Él no sabe lo que pasa.
I run to the parrot. He does
not know what is happening.

Hay sólo una cosa que hacer.
There is only one thing to do.

Subo a la jaula.
I climb up to the cage.

*El cotorro encrespa sus plumas. No le gusta que
yo este cerca de su jaula.*
The parrot ruffles his feathers. He does not like
me near his cage.

Subo a la copita que contiene sus semillas especiales.
I climb up to the small cup that holds his special
seeds.

Estas semillas vienen de Bolivia. A él, las semillas son como joyas, sin precio.
These seeds come from Bolivia. His seeds are like
priceless jewels to him.

Consigo pasa, mi pata entre los barrotes y robo unas semillas.

I squeeze my paw through the bars and steal some seeds.

Es más de lo que puede aguantar.
This is more than he can stand.

Al final grita, "Socorro. Socorro. Policía."
At last, he cries, "Help. Help. Police."

Pronto, oigo las sirenas.
Soon I hear sirens.

La policía llega.
The police arrive.

El ladrón es capturado.
The thief is caught.

Soy el gato más pequeño del mundo. Pero, ¿puedo impedir un crimen?
I am the smallest cat in the world. But can I stop a crime?

¡Sí!
Yes!

CHAPTER 7

Miu: The Great Cat of Egypt

Egypt, circa 2000 B.C.
Read by Digger, cat of Sir Henry Boneman

THOU ART THE GREAT CAT, THE AVENGER OF
THE GODS, AND THE JUDGE OF WORDS, AND THE
PRESIDENT OF THE SOVEREIGN CHIEFS AND
THE GOVERNOR OF THE HOLY CIRCLE; THOU
ART INDEED THE GREAT CAT. *(Inscription on
the Royal Tombs at Thebes)*

I am the Great Cat, Miu. To look at me you would
not suspect I am a god. I am small but powerful.
When I walk through the marketplace, the people
bow. My image decorates the temple and is worn
on amulets and earrings. Dreams of the Great Cat

mean a good harvest. Mortals adorn my ears with jewels and gold. They honor me.

There is only one who does not worship me. One who does not bow down in the marketplace. One who drools in the presence of Miu.

It is Abu, the Royal Dog.

I move with the timelessness of the centuries. I scorn mortals who hurry to get here and there. I look down upon the horses and lesser beasts that clomp and run with nervous energy. Chariots stop to allow me to pass. No one gets in my way when I take my regal walk.

There is only one who has the nerve to interrupt my walk. One who comes at me, with yips and barks that make my fur rise. One who makes me lose my composure and even *hisss*!

It is Abu, the Royal Dog.

My fur is perfect, groomed daily, by mortals and by me. A cat, especially the Great Cat, Miu, must be perfect. I lick each paw often to make sure it is free of the dust and dirt from the streets. I keep my whiskers free from drops of milk and honey. I am praised for my cleanliness.

There is only one who does not value the cleanliness of Miu. One who tromps into the palace slinging drool and mud as he shakes his filthy body. One who has the nerve to place a dirt-laden paw on the Great Cat.

It is Abu, the Royal Dog.

The servants bring me offerings, bits of fish and bowls of fresh milk. They place the offerings before me and bow reverently. No one touches the offerings to the Great Cat, Miu. On fear of death no one comes near while the offerings are consumed.

There is only one who dares to interrupt the feast of Miu. Only one irreverent, greedy, clumsy oaf who comes running and sniffing to grab the royal bits of fish and milk.

It is Abu, the Royal Dog.

I maintain my composure at the temple. I stand motionless and dignified, like a statue. I am sur-

rounded by statues of other cat gods who have come before me. We stand tall. We are pictures of perfect composure. No one bothers the Great Cat, Miu. But, as I hold my pose, I hear yipping outside. One statuesque ear bends forward. I pull it back. I will not be disturbed. I stand

taller and make my eyes into small slits. The yapping
continues and my perfectly still tail flips unbidden.
Again it flips and I cannot stop it. The yipping increases
in volume. Involuntarily, the hairs rise on my back.

No one dares to enter the holy space and disturb
the calm, no one except . . . In he comes! I jump up
and lose my pose. My back arches, fur stands in all
directions, and I give out an ungodly growl.

It is Abu, Abu, ABU!!! The Royal Dog!

At night sometimes I prowl. I catch the mice who
invade the granary. After a good hunt I walk home.
The world is bigger at night and sometimes I feel
alone. It is cold in the desert and there are noises. I
hurry past the pyramids and sphinx. When I look

up at the golden moon hanging in the sky and the twinkling of a million stars, I don't feel so much like the Great Cat. I feel very small and I hurry faster.

Then I reach the marketplace. The moon glows, illuminating strange shapes on the streets, and I hurry even faster. I need a friend. I pause outside the royal kennel. All is quiet.

Up I go through the window, for there is one inside who I know can protect me. One who will keep the shadows away. One who is an irreverent, greedy, clumsy oaf, but one who is my friend in the darkness. I tiptoe across the royal cushions and I snuggle up for warmth and protection. *Purrrrrrr*. I sleep safe and warm against his back.

It is Abu, the Royal Dog.

CHAPTER 8

Go-Go Goes Bananas

My name is Go-Go, and you have probably seen me in a book. *Go-Go Goes to the Farm. Go-Go Goes to the Zoo. Go-Go Goes to Camp.*

Only I don't go to any of these places. I stay home with Arthur. I watch him write the books. I watch him draw the pictures.

He will show me a picture and tell me what a good time I had. "Go-Go, look what fun you had at the ice rink. Look at your double axel!

"Go-Go, look what fun you had at your birthday party. See the cake shaped like a bird. You got candy feathers caught in your teeth."

Only I didn't get to skate or eat feathers. I stayed right here in the studio.

Now, at last, I was going somewhere. My books were so popular that Arthur was invited to a school. I was invited too.

The school had a room filled with children and books. I was the star. I heard my name everywhere. "It's Go-Go! Look, it's Go-Go in person!"

We made our way to a small table covered with Go-Go books. Arthur sat and I made myself comfortable on a stack of books.

The children lined up to get books, and Arthur got right to it. He opened the first book and wrote something inside.

"Go-Go's going to autograph my book too," a girl cried. A teacher got her camera ready.

Then a terrible thing happened. Arthur took my leg, pressed my paw first onto a wet black pad and then onto the book beside what he had written. The children clapped excitedly.

"Mine next," a boy cried out.

Now, I am very, very particular about my paws. I lick them clean even when they are clean, and so my horror at this black, wet paw was unbounded.

I leaped from the table, scattering the books in all directions, and ran. There were cries from the children.

"Catch her."

"Go-Go! Come back!"

I paid no attention.

I ran through the room, scrambling between the many legs of the children in line. Children jumped out of the way.

"There goes Go-Go."

"Chase her."

I hurried into another room where children were eating on trays. I leaped over a table. I flew over or ran around everything in my way. Milk boxes and corn dogs hit the floor. A girl in line jumped back, bumping into the other children. Trays were tipping. Lima beans were flying. A blob of mashed potatoes just missed a teacher. I scurried down the lunch line. The children joined the chase.

On I went, down the hall through a door that said PRINCIPAL. I jumped across a desk covered with papers, leaving a trail of black paw prints. The man at the desk yelled, "Stop!" then jumped up and ran after me with the children.

They chased me down a hall into a huge room filled with chairs and a stage with a curtain. All the chairs were filled with even more children. A woman behind a podium was speaking. She was very serious, and when she saw me, her mouth dropped open in surprise. The children cheered and clapped for me. I looked at the curtain and didn't hesitate. Up I went. At the top I settled on a small ledge and gazed out at the children. They were clapping and cheering. It was nice to hear the children cheering for me.

I looked at my paw. It wasn't as bad as I had thought. A lot of the black had come off in my run. The children were calling, "Go-Go, come down." But I ignored them.

It took a lot of licking to get my paw really clean. When I was satisfied at last, I glanced down. I liked it up here. I liked everyone looking at me. It was like I was a king, and the whole school was my kingdom. Arthur was holding out his arms.

The look on his face told me he had learned something about a cat's paws. I backed down the curtain and fell into his arms. The children applauded.

Someone yelled, "Is your next book going to be *Go-Go Goes to School*?"

Someone else said, "Go-Go looked happy being up so high. His next book should be *Go-Go Goes into Orbit*."

"How about *Go-Go-Goes to the Moon*?"

Those children ought to be writing my books instead of Arthur.

We went back to the room with the books, and Arthur signed every one. I did not. I sat on a stack of books and let each child pat me.

On the ride home Arthur said, "Actually, I ought to bring you with me more often. You're the star."

That was the nicest compliment he ever paid me. I can't wait to see where we'll go next.

CHAPTER 9

My Adventures

There's a special place by the window in the living room where the sunshine comes in and warms the floor. That's where you will find me, lying in that rectangle of warmth—dozing, stretching, and being thankful for my home. The sunlight feels good on my fur and reminds me of what it was like to be young.

I haven't been young in a long time. My claws are gone. My teeth are old and dull. My ears miss many sounds. My once sleek body is rounded and soft, and as I roll about in the shaft of light I get sleepy and I dream . . .

✦ ✦ ✦

Suddenly, it is night and I am standing in the moonlight, thinking of the beautiful Tabby next door. But wait! There is another suitor present. Behind the hedge, there is a competitor for her affections.

"MMMRRRROOO!" I recognize his howl. It is my enemy, the one-eared black cat from down the street.

"VAVAVOOOOM!" I hear him call a serenade to Tabby.

I answer with my distinctive howl from deep in my soul. "ROOWWWWW!"

He stops his serenade. For a moment I lose track of him. Where is he? Is he sneaking around to ambush me? I hear a trash can fall next door. He is in Tabby's backyard!

"ROOWWWWW!" I call out a warning to him.

"MMMMRRRRROOOO!" He answers back a challenge. I know where he is.

"ROOWWWW!" I leap over the back fence, and we square off.

"MMMMRRRRROOO!"

"ROOWWWW!"

We circle each other in the night. We growl and howl. We tense our bodies and then . . . I leap! Rolling and clutching we battle for beautiful Tabby. I am winning! I am winning!

My one-eared opponent runs for the hedge and disappears.

"ROOWWWW!"

I am victorious!

+ + +

I yawn and stretch, greatly satisfied with the warm remembrance of my victory. The sunlight patch has shifted a little in the afternoon and I roll over into the new position. *Purrrrr.* The sun is bright and I must close my eyes . . .

Suddenly, I am younger, stronger. I run swiftly through the neighborhood, past houses and street-lights. The neighborhood gives way to the forest, and the ground becomes wild with bushes towering over me. I am running and leaping and the wind is blowing my whiskers. I am free! But wait! There's a sound in the distance. A yip and a bark signaling danger. I freeze.

The yip grows closer . . . closer. I see him, the bulldog from the end of the cul-de-sac, drawing closer. His big cat-biting mouth is open and drool-ing, his huge cat-pounding paws are pulling him closer. I stand my ground and watch his charge. I do not blink. Just as he rounds the bend, his teeth snapping with anticipation, I leap. I leap gracefully, hanging in the air for a moment like a cloud, then land with perfection on a branch just out of reach. He snaps and yips and howls with despair. I slowly lick my paws and smile.

The sun on the floor is warm as I stretch my satisfied stretch and extend each paw one by one. My escape was magnificent. I roll gently to the other side and again I close my eyes . . .

Suddenly, I am back in the forest. My predator is gone. I jump nimbly from the branch to the ground and pause to sniff the forest air. I listen with my keen ears to the forest sounds. The wind blows the trees. The water in a nearby brook bubbles. But wait! There is a crackle in the brush over to the right behind the oak tree. A small noise. There it is again. Now a crinkle and a crackle. Only the keenest feline ears would have picked it out. I crouch and wait. My body tenses. I shift from side to side and wait.

Crinkle. Crackle. The noise draws closer. . . .

Crinkle. Crackle. I think it is my old nemesis the chipmunk. Yes! I see him now nosing in the dry leaves. My muscles tighten, but I remain as still as a statue, waiting for the perfect moment. Waiting . . . waiting. . . .

Crinkle. Crackle.
POUNCE!

◆ ◆ ◆

I wake up, startled, but greatly satisfied by my day's activities. The sun is fading now from the floor by the window, and I roll over and with a little difficulty stand up. I blink a few times and smile, remembering my adventures. Then I hear the sound of food dropping into my bowl. Even old ears can make out this pleasant sound. Even old legs can trot toward the kitchen for dinner.

CHAPTER 10

Pirate Cat, Treasure Hunter

The Caribbean, 1717
Read by Tiger

"**Y**o-ho! Yo-ho! A pirate's life for meeeeeeeeee."

Yes indeed, mate. The day I set foot on Captain Blackbeard's ship, I knew a pirate's life was for me.

I don't look much like a pirate. I don't wear an eye patch—both my eyes are quite fine. And I don't have a peg leg. But I'm a pirate nonetheless.

It happened by accident. I was on the docks when a big catch arrived. I found a fishtail and I slipped inside a crate to have a little privacy while I finished it off. The crate was loaded onto a ship and I set sail with Blackbeard.

For as long as I've been with them, Blackbeard and his men have searched for the treasure of a man named Hollingsworth. They want it bad. It's hidden on an island somewhere in the Caribbean and we have sailed to and fro looking for that treasure.

One day Blackbeard yelled, "Gather around, men."

It was seldom Blackbeard called us all together, so I was curious. I jumped onto the railing beside him. He stroked my back as he spoke.

"I've new information that the Hollingsworth treasure is at Gorda Island. We set sail immediately."

With that the men erupted in cheers.

The wind was steady and strong and the sails filled to capacity. We cut through the water with graceful speed.

Several hours later the lookout yelled, "There she stands."

I leaped to the railing and got my first look at Gorda Island. *Gorda* means big, and big it was.

"Where do we drop anchor, Captain?" one of the crew asked.

"North by the caves."

We pulled close and set anchor. The men lowered the rowboats into the beautiful blue waters.

"Bring Coral," Blackbeard called.

He named me Coral because I am orange and white like the coral in the sea, except for a small

patch of black fur on my chin and on my tail. I think I look a little like Blackbeard.

"That cat doesn't like rowboats," One Arm said.

"Coral goes where I go."

One Arm was right. I don't like the rowboats. They are small and tippy. I started for the ladder to hide below deck. But, *whoosh*, One Arm grabbed me up.

"I don't like rowboats," I cried.

"Nice kitty," he said.

"I don't like rowboats."

"Nice kitty."

"I said I don't like rooooooooooooo—"

One Arm tossed me into the rowboat. One Arm does not like kitties.

I sat on the seat next to Blackbeard. The breeze was light and the waves mild as could be. The water was a deeper blue than usual. We glided into a sandy piece of land and the men began searching.

When I stepped into the first damp cave, I smelled mice. I headed in search of my own treasure.

"Where's the cat off to?" One Arm asked.

"She's helping us look," the second mate, Crazy Jack, answered.

The men laughed.

I caught a few mice as I wandered through caves, bigger mice than on our ship. From time to time I heard the men's voices. I was sneaking up on one mouse when I noticed a tiny beam of light streaming from a crevice. I squeezed through and entered a cave that shone like the sun on the brightest of days. As my eyes adjusted I realized that the cave was filled with treasure: gold and jewels and more.

I could hear the men in another cave nearby. "There is no treasure here," Blackbeard was saying.

"Back to the ship," One Arm yelled. "We'll search the south side of Gorda."

"Blackbeard, where ye going?" Crazy Jack asked.

"I'm looking for Coral!"

"Time be a-wastin'," Crazy Jack said. "We should find that treasure. We're close. I can feel it."

"We don't leave without Coral," Blackbeard said.

"Your old black heart has a soft spot for kitty," Crazy Jack mumbled.

"Another word from you and I'll tear you apart, you dark-hearted mate," Blackbeard said.

I was glad Blackbeard wanted to find me. I knew he would like this shiny treasure. I leaped onto the back of a tall jewel-studded throne and called loudly, "Meeeeeeow."

"Silence," Blackbeard yelled. "I hear her."

"Meeeeeeow."

"She's up ahead."

"Aaaargh," said Crazy Jack. "Ye're wastin' time."

"Meeeeeeow."

I heard them squeezing through crevices, getting closer.

"Meeeeeeow."

"This way," One Arm yelled.

They squeezed through the final opening and into the gold-filled room.

"Blow me away!" One Arm said.

"Coral found the treasure," Blackbeard said and laughed his big hearty laugh.

Crazy Jack gave me a little bow. "Well now, I be beggin' your pardon, Miss Kitty."

I stood tall and proud on the back of my jewel-studded throne. Blackbeard scratched my neck.

"Load up, gentlemen," Blackbeard said.

The mates were merry at supper that night.

One Arm yelled, "Here's to the treasure of Gorda!"

"To the treasure of Gorda!" the mates shouted.

Blackbeard lifted his glass. "And to Coral who found it."

"Yo-ho! Yo-ho! A pirate's life for meeeeeeeee."

CHAPTER 11

Georgio's Recipes for Outdoor Cuisine

When I was young I prowled at night with Mama. I ate what she ate. If she ate stale bread from a Dumpster, I did too. If she ate dead raccoon from the road, I did too. Then one night Mama taught me what fine dining was all about, and now I have recipes of my own.

FRESH FISH FILET

Find a nice pond. The water must be still. Lean over and let a small drop of spit fall on the water. At least one fish will be dumb enough to go for it. I always leave the bones for the ants. Ants will eat anything.

ALL-YOU-CAN-EAT EGG BUFFET

If you are lucky enough to see a turtle laying eggs, lie down and wait. When she gets through, uncover the eggs and stuff yourself. Trust me. They won't be nearly as good a week later.

BIRD-TO-GO

Find a bird feeder. Wait in an inconspicuous place. Lazy birds won't go to the trouble of pecking seeds out of the little holes, and will go for those spilled on the ground. You can usually take your pick. Bird-to-Go is strictly a take-out order. If you dine in, the owners of the bird feeder may see you and ruin your perfectly delicious meal.

WHACK-A-MOLEY

Whack a mole before he goes in his hole and you'll have whack-a-moley.

JUNIOR RODENT BURGER

Unless you are very hungry, give rats a pass. Wait for a mouse. Some novice mousers make the mistake of taking the mouse inside, expecting people to praise their hunting skills. Do not do this. People will yell, throw you out, and keep the mouse themselves.

ONE-BITE DELIGHTS (WITH THANKS TO MAMA)

During our prowls one night, Mama and I turned onto a well-lit street. She stiffened. I knew she was on to something. She darted forward. The air was full of flying things.

Then Mama did something I'd never seen before. She jumped in the air, grabbed one, and put it in her mouth.

"Go, Georgio!" Mama said after she landed. She was always a cat of few words.

I went. My first jump got me nothing. But I saw one on the ground. I pounced and ate.

The taste was tangy; the body crisp. It was my first cricket. I loved it. As we made our way home I decided to share my fine dining experience with the world.

You may not be lucky enough to catch crickets at midnight, but you may find one in your own backyard. Pounce and eat. When the tangy tartness floods your being, remember to thank Mama and me.

Bon appétit!

CHAPTER 12

Sarge's One Wish

One night in the barn, we played a game called If I Had One Wish.

The cow wished that people would be able to make sense of her moos. This was not my problem. My meows were very expressive.

The horse wished his tail was long enough to brush flies from his face. This was not my problem. No fly would dare to land on my face.

The rooster atop the barn door wished that dawn would hurry up and get here because he was about to burst with cock-a-doodle-dos. This was my problem.

I wanted morning to hurry up so I could get out of this barn and go back in the house, where I belonged.

For years and years I was family. It started when I was a kitten. I was a gift for Major. Major was a boy in bed with casts on his legs. I understood it was up to me to get Major well, and I did.

Major grew up and was gone a lot. I still slept in his bed while he was away. When he came home, he would put his hand on my head and it was just like old times.

Then last week, Major arrived with a woman and a bundle in his arms. Mom and Dad pressed around, making clucking noises. This bundle was the most interesting thing Major had ever brought home.

I could smell milk, and I was beginning to worry that it was a new cat when I got a glimpse. It was a tiny, tiny person. I knew right away it was a newborn. I knew that Major was the father, and the woman that smelled like milk was the mother.

I didn't get a chance to check out the bundle until everyone was at supper. I went into the bedroom and jumped up on the bed. It was a tiny living creature. I was just smelling its breath when Major rushed into the room.

"I thought I heard you," Major said. He didn't seem mad, but the woman behind him yelled, "Bad, bad cat!"

She grabbed me and flung me into Major's arms. "Get that cat out of here."

"It's just Sarge," Major said.

"Out! Either that cat goes or we do."

"I'll handle this," Dad said. He carried me to the kitchen, opened the door, walked to the barn, put me inside, and closed the door.

I'd often been in the barn to chat with the cow or to chase the rooster, but this was different. The door was shut.

Next day Dad came in to milk the cow, but the door stayed shut. I meowed at him and he said, "Sorry, Sarge. I got my orders." I stayed in the barn.

Then one morning, when I had almost given up hope, the barn door opened. It was Major. He put his hand on my head. "You can come out now. We're leaving. Sorry for the inconvenience."

I watched their car disappear, and then Mom held the door open for me. "Welcome home, Sarge."

As I lapped up my milk in the kitchen, I thought about that one-wish game. Maybe there's something to it. Maybe people will make sense of the cow's moos. Maybe the horse's tail will grow longer and the rooster's nights shorter. Or maybe not.

All I know is I got my one wish. I am back in the house, where I belong. I am family again.

CHAPTER 13

Meow! Till Next Year!

The cats were up and meowing with excitement. Some were leaping into the air.

"More diaries," they cried. "More! More!"

Ebenezer held up his paws for silence. "Of course there will be more, but not tonight."

"Awww," the calico cried. "I don't have to be home until morning."

"Me neither," cried another cat.

Ebenezer lifted his paws again. "Order! We have a special guest."

Suddenly a hush fell over the crowd as an old cat stood and made her way to the stage.

"It's Sage," someone whispered.

"*The* Sage? I didn't even know she was still alive."

More whispers were heard.

"She's a legend."

"I heard she was on her fifth life."

"I heard she was on a ship called *Titanic*."

Ebenezer helped her to the podium.

"My good friend Ebenezer, may I say a word to our friends?"

Ebenezer bowed. "It would be an honor."

"Story!" a voice called from the back. "Story!" another requested.

"My dear friends, I'm not here to tell my story tonight, although in a way my story has been told." She gestured to all the cats in the crowd.

"Stories from our ancestors about wisdom in ancient Egypt, bravery from the pirate cat in the Caribbean, and adventure from the Gypsy cat are really stories about all of us."

Meows of agreement arose.

"We've seen ourselves in the dreams and weaknesses and humorous looks presented by thoughtful friends."

More meows of agreement.

meow

mmmeow!
meow
MEOW

"Who hasn't had encounters with dogs?"— she paused until the cries of agreement lessened—"or who hasn't experienced doubt about the strangeness of the human world, like Christmas trees and babies?" Murmurs filled the room.

"When we hear the stories of others it reminds us of our own story. We celebrate our catness in tales of hunting and adventure and romance."

A few cats coughed in the back, then silence.

"Never forget our motto, MEOW, Memories Expressed in Our Writing. *Our writing,* my friends, those are the important words—our writing as members of MEOW. It is up to us not only to write our own diaries, but to encourage others to write as well. You might be surprised to learn there are cats who haven't even heard of a diary. It is up to us to teach them and to become better writers ourselves. I don't think I am being overly optimistic here when I say, not only can we become better writers, we can become the best writers in the history of the world."

There was a rustle of pride and agreement.

"And may I say one more thing, Ebenezer?"

"Yes," the audience cried, not waiting for Ebenezer.

"As I sat here this evening I had a vision. A year from now you will be back. You will bring more diaries and friends with diaries. And there will be cats from all over the world. But most of all, there will be stories, wonderful stories. If I had one wish like Sarge, it would be that I will be here with you to hear them. Thank you."

As Sage left the podium there was a stillness in the room. Then, from the back, from one lone kitten came the sound of a contented rumble, a purr. The rumble grew as the cats settled into a peaceful satisfaction. The rumble carried out into the night air. The alleys and streets once quiet were filled with the sound of contentment. Dogs stopped in their places, ears cocked, puzzled by the sound. Mice looked up in fear and scurried for cover, unsure of the strangeness of the sound.

When the purring died down and Sage was gone, Ebenezer turned to the crowd. "That is an appropriate ending to our meeting. We will adjourn with the reciting of our motto. And this time we will recite it with new meaning. All together now."

"MEOW! MEOW! MEOW!"

The cats looked at one another with new understanding and commitment.

Some cats left, others gathered in small groups to discuss the diaries. On through the night, stories were told, diaries were planned, and at last goodbyes were said. As the cats disappeared into the night their tails were high. Their pride swelled. They were going to be the best writers in the world.